RESEARCHING SOCIAL GERONTOLOGY

Concepts, Methods and Issues

edited by

Sheila M. Peace

SAGE Publications
London • Newbury Park • New Delhi
in association with the British Society of Gerontology

Editorial arrangement © British Society of Gerontology 1990
General Introduction and Introductions to Parts One, Two and Three
© Sheila Peace 1990
Chapter 1 © Bill Bytheway 1990
Chapter 2 © David Wilkin 1990
Chapter 3 © Hazel Qureshi 1990
Chapter 4 © Beverley Hughes 1990
Chapter 5 © Graham Fennell 1990
Chapter 6 © David Challis and Robin Darton 1990
Chapter 7 © Eileen Fairhurst 1990
Chapter 8 © Leonie Kellaher, Sheila Peace and Dianne Willcocks
        1990
Chapter 9 © Michael Bury and Anthea Holme 1990
Chapter 10 © Brian Gearing and Tim Dant 1990
Chapter 11 © Alan Butler 1990
Chapter 12 © Margot Jefferys 1990
Chapter 13 © Averil Osborn and Dianne Willcocks 1990

First published 1990

SAGE Publications Ltd
28 Banner Street
London EC1Y 8QE

SAGE Publications Inc
2111 West Hillcrest Drive
Newbury Park, California 91320

SAGE Publications India Pvt Ltd
32, M-Block Market
Greater Kailash – I
New Delhi 110 048

British Library Cataloguing in Publication Data

Peace, Sheila M.
    Researching social gerontology: concepts, methods and issues.
    1. Man. Ageing. Social aspects
    I. Title
    305.26

    ISBN 0–8039–8284–4
    ISBN 0–8039–8285–2 pbk
    9780803982857
Library of Congress catalog card number 90–061929

Filmset by Mayhew Typesetting, Bristol, Great Britain

Contents

Acknowledgements

Looking back on my notes it comes as no surprise that the original ideas for this text began in late 1986 when I was asked by the executive committee of the British Society of Gerontology to explore its potential. Many members of the Society joined me in early discussions, suggesting themes and authors. Many have stayed the course and have become contributors. I want to thank them for their patience in what has seemed at times a rather long process.

I would also like to thank Anthea Tinker and members of the BSG Publications Committee for its guidance at various stages and for helping me to sustain interest in the project.

Greatest thanks go to Leonie Kellaher and Dianne Willcocks, my former colleagues at CESSA (the Centre for Environmental and Social Studies in Ageing) for their friendship and support, and especially to Maureen Fedarb, who has retyped papers and dealt with my own scribblings with patience and good humour. Finally, I must also mention and thank husband Steve and Tom, whose birth during this time made progress slower but infinitely more enjoyable.

Notes on Contributors

Michael Bury, who has research interests in chronic illness, disability and ageing, is Senior Lecturer in Sociology, and Director of the MSc programme in Medical Sociology, Department of Social Policy and Social Science, Royal Holloway and Bedford New College (RHBNC), University of London. Previous publications include, with R. Anderson (eds) *Living with Chronic Illness*, Unwin Hyman, 1988.

Alan Butler is currently a Senior Lecturer in Mental Health Social Work and Deputy Head of the Department of Psychiatry at the University of Leeds. Trained as a social worker and psychotherapist, he has written three books on mental health. He spent four years evaluating sheltered housing's contribution to the well-being of older people and some six months on a Churchill Travelling Scholarship in the United States, examining alarm technology. He has recently completed an MA in the Philosophy of Health Care at the University of Wales.

Bill Bytheway is Senior Research Fellow at the University College of Swansea. He is also a member of the Centre for Gerontology at Swansea and has been involved in the British Society of Gerontology since it was launched in 1973. He is co-editor of *Ageing and the Welfare Experience* (1988).

David Challis is Reader in Social Work and Social Care and Assistant Director of the Personal Social Services Research Unit, University of Kent. Previously he worked in social services departments in Lancashire and Salford. Recent research includes studies of the organisation of social services departments and evaluation of case-management approaches to the care of the elderly in health and social care.

Tim Dant is a Research Fellow in the Department of Health and Social Welfare at the Open University. He is a sociologist with interests in theories of ageing, the development of community care and the social process of discourse. He is currently writing a book on 'Knowledge, Ideology, Discourse'.

Robin Darton is a Research Fellow at the Personal Social Services Research Unit, University of Kent. A statistician, who is currently working on the evaluation of the Darlington Community Care Project for Elderly People with David Challis. He has also been involved in two major surveys of residential and nursing homes, the most recent in collaboration with Ken Wright at the University of York.

Eileen Fairhurst is a Senior Lecturer in Sociology at Manchester Polytechnic where she lectures on social ageing on a number of courses and on research methods at undergraduate and postgraduate levels. Her current research interests are in early retirement and a study of a new sheltered housing development.

Graham Fennell is Head of the Department of Sociology and Social Administration at the Roehampton Institute. His first research project was with elderly people in Eskilstune in Sweden in 1965 and he has since carried out studies in the United Kingdom using a wide variety of research methods.

x   RESEARCHING SOCIAL GERONTOLOGY

These include survey studies of housing for elderly people, observational work in day centres, depth interviews concerning social interaction in grouped settings and large-scale statistical analyses of demographic trends in sheltered housing. He was formerly Lecturer in Sociology at the University of East Anglia and took a special interest in research methods teaching. His most recent book, co-authored with Chris Phillipson and Helen Evers is *The Sociology of Old Age* (1988).

Brian Gearing is a Senior Lecturer in the Department of Health and Social Welfare at the Open University. Previously he held social work and research posts in local authority social services departments. At the Open University, he has contributed to several courses on ageing for health and social service workers and has carried out research which emphasises older people's own perceptions of their needs.

Anthea Holme is a Research Officer at Royal Holloway and Bedford New College and has been engaged in social research for many years. Her previous publications include, with Simon Yudkin, *Working Mothers and their Children*, Michael Joseph, 1963, and *Housing and Young Families in East London*, Routledge and Kegan Paul, 1985.

Beverley Hughes qualified as a probation officer (CQSW) in 1974. After several years in practice, she completed two major DHSS-funded research projects, one concerned with the quality of life in residential care for older people. Now a lecturer in social work at Manchester University, she has written on various aspects of gerontology, including residential care, health services, quality of life, social work and older women. She has a particular interest in the application of critical gerontology to social work policy and practice.

Margot Jefferys is Emeritus Professor of Medical Sociology, University of London. She is the editor of *Growing Old in the 20th Century*, Routledge, 1989, and was formerly Chair of the Centre for Policy on Ageing, 1980–8, and Director of the Social Research Unit, Bedford College, 1965–82.

Leonie Kellaher is Director of the Centre for Environmental and Social Studies in Ageing (CESSA) at the Polytechnic of North London where she has worked as a researcher since 1977. Work in CESSA has focused on the many facets of residential living for older people and her current focus is on the regulatory mechanism which influences these. She is a social anthropologist with an interest in multi-method research, especially in examining the minutiae of residential life in relation to symbols of place, domicile and institution.

Averil Osborn is the Senior Assistant Director of Age Concern Scotland where her time is spread between policy work, heading up the development team, and management. She has a particular interest in the utilisation of research, deriving from her present role and previous posts in social services and health services research, and from library and information user research.

Sheila Peace joined the Open University as a Lecturer in the Department of Health and Social Welfare in January 1990. Prior to this appointment she was Senior Research Officer, and a founder member of CESSA at the Polytechnic of North London. Since 1975 she has been involved in a wide range of research with older people particularly in the area of residential care. She has worked for MIND (National Association for Mental Health) and the International Federation on Ageing in Washington, DC. A social geographer by discipline, she has written widely on many gerontological issues including environment and ageing, mental health in old age and issues concerning older women. She has taught research methods and statistics as well as social gerontology and has been Secretary of the Social Research Association and an executive member of the British Society of Gerontology.

Hazel Qureshi is Research Fellow in the Hester Adrian Research Centre, University of Manchester. Her main research interests are in family care and the interface between formal and informal services. She is co-author of *The Caring Relationship: Elderly People and their Families* with Alan Walker, Macmillan, 1989, and *Helpers in Case Managed Community Care* with David Challis and Bleddyn Davies, Gower, 1989.

David Wilkin is a sociologist who has conducted research on the care of mentally handicapped children, residential and community care for elderly people, and the provision of primary health care. He has written extensively on services for elderly people and methods of measuring health and disability. He is currently Associate Director of the Centre for Primary Care Research at the University of Manchester.

Dianne Willcocks is Dean of Environmental and Social Studies at the Polytechnic of North London and a member of CESSA. She has particular research interests in residential care services and in quality assurance over a range of services for elderly consumers. She is a sociologist with a particular concern for making research work effectively in the public policy arena. She is co-author of *Private Lives in Public Places* with Sheila Peace and Leonie Kellaher, Tavistock Publications, 1987. She is also Chair of Islington Age Concern.

Introduction

Researching Social Gerontology: Concepts, Methods and Issues

The idea of putting together a collection of papers concerning the research process in social gerontology came from the membership of the British Society of Gerontology (BSG) as early as 1986. At that time, developmental work was beginning on a textbook in the field (Bond and Coleman, 1990), and a volume looking at the research process seemed the obvious companion. It seems fitting that this volume, like the textbook, should be written by members of the BSG who have all played their part in developing this area of study through their on-going commitment to research. The Society itself was established in 1973 to provide a multidisciplinary forum for researchers in the field of ageing and its aims are to encourage the 'research and study of human ageing and later life, and the application of this knowledge to the improvement of the quality of life'.

While the Society has a membership whose interests include medicine, biology and the social sciences, this text focuses on research in social gerontology and its authors are all social scientists. The publication of these two volumes now reflects the fact that gerontology has matured sufficiently as an area of study to allow this pause for reflection. As editor, such reflection has led me to grapple with some basic issues about the development of research in social gerontology. Whilst not wishing to pre-empt the more detailed discussions of authors later in this volume, it seems important at the outset to highlight the range of disciplines from which those who can be called social gerontologists may be drawn. These include sociology, psychology, anthropology, geography, social policy and social administration and, in terms of professional training, social work, nursing and clinical psychology. These various fields have their own traditions in the development of research methodology and research debates. It is not my intention to review these here, only to alert the reader to the value of this eclecticism within social gerontology, especially where multi-disciplinary teams of researchers have been able to draw upon a range of quantitative and qualitative methods in exploring particular issues concerning the ageing process and old age. Indeed the attraction of this multidisciplinary approach may be one of the factors to have led some of those involved to stray outside the confines of their original discipline.

The aim of this text therefore is to explore developments in British social gerontology which will give the reader a sense, not only of current thinking in terms of conceptual and methodological development, but also of the context in which such research is being carried out. Consequently our aim is to appeal to a wide audience of researchers, policy makers and practitioners, as well as those with a general interest in understanding how we research the ageing process and, in particular, later life.

So what progress has been made to date? Gilbert Smith in his article in *Ageing and Society*, June 1989, paraphrases Johnson (1976) in outlining three fundamental areas to be tackled by gerontologists. These can be summarised as follows, first, the development of sound theory; second, the redefinition of the subject's core problem with less attention being paid to the needs and problems characteristic of very old people and more attention being paid to the process of ageing. And third, that social gerontologists need to listen more carefully to the clients or users of services (Smith, 1989: 105). As the Bond and Coleman text shows, there has been progress and movement in each of these areas and of course they are, inevitably, interrelated.

In reviewing the progress made within research perhaps it makes sense to focus our attention first of all on the second of these areas. The awareness of an ageing population during the latter half of the twentieth century gave rise to concern amongst policy makers as to how society should cope with the challenge, or some would say 'burden' that this creates. Throughout the 1960s, 1970s and on into the 1980s this problem-oriented approach was reflected in the funding of policy research which concerned the needs and circumstances of older people and how they should be cared for (for example Harris, 1968; Hunt, 1978). Here the concern to describe how older people were living was often met by the use of large-scale social surveys focusing on specific aspects of daily life (see also Abrams, M. 1978a, 1980). The large body of research concerning the circumstances of old people living in special residential and institutional settings was also indicative of this trend (Allen, 1982; Butler et al., 1983; Booth, 1985; Fennell, 1986; Willcocks et al., 1987). Indeed, as Margot Jefferys outlines in her chapter on the funding of research in social gerontology, many research units/centres developed programmes of work in these areas especially to meet the demand for special information.

The fact that the population aged 85 years and over will continue to increase as a proportion of the population as a whole on into the twenty-first century (HMSO, 1989a), has, in recent years, focused attention on issues surrounding support for very old people. Consequently, a great deal of commissioned research work, funded through central and local government as well as charitable trusts, continues to focus on the needs of very old people; how they are supported in later life, and more especially the evaluation of services designed to meet their needs (for example Challis and Davies, 1986). At a time when there is a general decline in monies for research within the social sciences, support for applied social research concerned with the lives of individual older people, and the social institutions which affect people in later life, continues. This support is evident not just in the areas of health and social care but also with regard to broader economic policy, where questions have been raised concerning intergenerational transfers of income and wealth, trends in retirement and the participation of older people in the work force, and the future of pension schemes.

Within policy-related research the survey method has remained central in terms of methodology although evaluative studies of old people living in special housing or institutional settings have allowed researchers to develop techniques in participant and non-participant observation (Godlove et al., 1982; Willcocks et al., 1987), and attempts have been made to develop multi-method approaches to research designs (Smith and Cantley, 1985). In terms of evaluative research a range of methods have been adopted (see Goldberg and Connelly, 1982, for a review of evaluative research in the 1970s and early 1980s) and advances have been made in the development of frameworks for evaluation such as the production of welfare model (see Challis and Darton, Chapter 6). It is noticeable that many of the developments in evaluative research have arisen out of research concerning programmes for older people.

However, while much policy-related research has encouraged a narrow focus on the pathologies of old age, there has been a move amongst those with interests in social gerontology to shift the focus towards normal and non-pathological aspects of old age. Even though there were early sociological studies, both large and small in scale, which focused on the 'ordinary lives' of old people (Townsend, 1957; Tunstall, 1966; Shanas et al., 1968), it was not until the 1980s that the importance of this approach was really recognised. Fundamental to this change have been developments in both theory building and research methodology. During the 1950s the predominance of functionalist perspectives in gerontology, particularly amongst American scholars (disengagement theory and role and activity theory) encouraged the view of old age as a social problem. This perspective was challenged during the 1960s and 1970s (see Fennell et al., 1988) and in Britain we should highlight the contribution made by those theorists who have taken a critical perspective in exploring the social construction of old age and the political economy of ageing (Townsend, 1981, 1986; Phillipson, 1982; Phillipson and Walker, 1986; Walker, 1981, 1986b). Also important has been the emergence of the biographical approach where attempts to contextualise the ageing process have focused on life histories and the charting of careers across the lifespan (Johnson, 1976; Coleman, 1986; di Gregorio, 1987). It is arguable that these two strands of work have had, and continue to make, an impact not only on the questions asked by research but also on how research is carried out (see

Hughes, Chapter 4, and Gearing and Dant, Chapter 10). Such developments have alerted our attention to the heterogeneity of the ageing population and to the impact of social divisions based on class, gender, race and disability on individual experiences of ageing. This diversity has been recognised by researchers who have begun to focus on the lives of older women (Evers, 1985; Peace, 1986; Fennell et al., 1988) and older people from minority ethnic groups (Bhalla and Blakemore, 1981; Barker, 1984; Blakemore, 1985; Fennell et al., 1988).

A complementary development to have taken place during the 1980s is the expansion of the field of study to encompass the ageing process, taking a broader life course perspective. This has come from a number of directions. There are, for example, those psychologists and sociologists whose interests traditionally have not been in the area of old age, but who have been drawn to it by a desire to understand changes in roles and relationships across the life course – for example, the caring role (Finch and Groves, 1983; Ungerson, 1983; Arber and Gilbert, 1989); patterns of marriage and divorce (Clark, 1987); trends in employment (Morris, 1987). This development was reflected in the 1986 Annual Conference of the British Sociological Association entitled 'Sociology of the Life Cycle' which has been reported in a series of publications (see Bryman et al., 1987; Allatt et al., 1987; Bytheway et al., 1989). It was also recognised by the Economic and Social Research Council (ESRC) in their initiative on ageing in 1989, which in its initial publicity material gave the following definition of ageing: 'Ageing refers to all age-groups, not only to the elderly, to all our social and economic institutions and not only to the individual' (ESRC, 1989). Statements like this throw the range of issues for study by social gerontologists wide open and encourage into the field those whose work up until this time has not encompassed old age.

So in reviewing the position of research within social gerontology to date we can see a number of important trends: the recognition of diversity within the ageing population; the focus on 'normal' or non-pathological ageing; the expansion of the subject area to encompass a life course perspective, and developments in theory and methodology. And all of these developments are beginning to make an impact on other aspects of study. Links are being made between emergent theoretical positions and how we define and measure many of the key variables commonly used within research which has a life course or later-life perspective. This trend breaks new ground and demonstrates the inductive/deductive relationship between conceptual development and theory building. In this connection, the increasingly multidisciplinary approach to the study of ageing appears to be a strength, and for research concerning later life much may be learnt from those who have confined their research so far to other areas of the life course. Part One of this book concentrates on some of these developments in conceptual thinking emerging from social gerontology.

There is a continuing demand for information concerning the needs and circumstances of old people, especially towards the end of their lives. In this area of predominantly policy-oriented research, we can see a growing concern to develop ways of allowing old people to speak for themselves through the research process – particularly in the evaluation of services developed for older people (see Booth, 1983; Willcocks, 1984). This means adopting methodologies appropriate to the research task and being aware of the unequal power relationships which can be created by virtue of the way a particular methodology is used. These issues have been widely discussed within feminist research texts (see Oakley in Roberts, 1981) and there are parallels to be drawn between the experiential approach adopted by feminist researchers working in other areas and those researchers developing the biographical approach within social gerontology. In the absence of longitudinal studies of the ageing process, how we tap individual experiences retrospectively becomes crucial. Some of these issues are explored in Part Two of this book, which is devoted to methodological approaches.

Finally, as a true multidisciplinary field of study social gerontology demonstrates clearly the need for researchers to have a knowledge of a wide range of research skills and to know when particular approaches or methodologies may be more or less appropriate and effective. Obviously, given the constraints of research funding and commissioning, researchers may not always be in a position to dictate or control all aspects of their work. However, I would argue that we now have a body of research of sufficient calibre to begin to demonstrate which methods, or combinations of methods, are most effective in particular circumstances. That they may prove unacceptable to funding bodies or too costly is a different matter.

The aim of this book then, is to try and explore some of these emerging issues and to set these developments within the context of trends in social gerontological research in the 1990s. To do this the book is divided into three parts: concepts and measurement, methodological approaches, and issues, each with a short introduction. In this way we hope to highlight some of the areas where social gerontologists have a contribution to make to the social research literature. The field of social gerontology is expanding, and many of those who have been involved in research are now at the forefront of developments in teaching at both undergraduate and postgraduate levels. These teaching initiatives will of course generate new research opportunities and it is hoped that students of these new courses as well as experienced researchers, teachers, practitioners, policy makers and those with a more general interest in the ageing process will find that this book contains much that is both interesting and stimulating, and in addition has practical application.

Sheila M. Peace

PART ONE

CONCEPTS AND MEASUREMENT

Introduction

Robert Burgess in his introduction to *Key Variables in Social Investigation* states 'there are still a number of gaps in the social science research literature, as despite developments in substantive sub-fields of sociology, researchers have still not bridged the gap between theory and research, and between theoretical debates and empirical practice' (1986: 2). This collection of essays, published in 1986, built upon earlier developments in conceptual thinking (Stacey, 1969; Gittus, 1972) and offered new perspectives on a number of key variables such as age, gender, race and ethnicity, social class and education, as well as introducing debates about variables which were yet uncharted such as leisure, politics and voluntary associations. It is our intention in Part One to extend this discussion by considering four complex 'variables' or 'concepts' central to much research in social gerontology: age, dependency, social support and quality of life. Experience in this field has reached a stage where we are able to reflect on the process where-by such complex concepts are translated into variables which are then transformed into measurement through the creation of indicators. The authors of Chapters 1–4 question the oversimplification of this process, where researchers have not fully considered how variables are defined in relation to their research needs, and have failed to make the links between theoretical developments and research methodology.

In Chapter 1, concerning age itself, Bill Bytheway takes a new look at this much used, but often under-utilised and underdeveloped, variable. Unlike the authors of Chapters 2–4, who move from concep-tualisation to measurement, here the author begins with measurement. Age, perhaps the ultimate continuous variable, may appear simple to measure but is shown to be deceptive. Moving from measurement to conceptualisation Bytheway develops earlier debates concerning age as a variable (see Finch, 1986) in his discussion of the relationships between chronological age and definitions of social, biological and psychological age. A central line of argument concerns the dangers for researchers in confusing the process of ageing with the measurement of age within particular types of study. He highlights the advantages and disadvantages of cross-sectional and longitudinal studies.

In 1986 Janet Finch concluded that 'the concept of age needs to be contextualised in wider theoretical debates if its potential is to be fully realised' (1986: 24); here Bytheway considers how we might first operationalise and then interpret social constructions of age within research and points to some of the dangers inherent in compartmentalising what is after all a process through time. He ends with a consideration of the use of age in research within the field of social gerontology.

Chapters 2, 3 and 4 adopt a similar framework in that first the authors discuss the concept of, or 'what we mean by', dependency, social support and quality of life, and then go on to consider a range of issues with regard to measurement. All three authors highlight the fact that all too often measurement is seen as a technical problem and that there is a lack of theoretical underpinning and conceptual development. The dimensions of these complex concepts are explored and there are useful reviews of the literature. David Wilkin presents a framework for the classification of dependency in the form of a useful matrix which contrasts the 'needs for which the individual is dependent on others' with 'the source of dependency'. Hazel Qureshi poses four questions in trying to define social support: What are the elements of social support? From what source? For what purpose? And from whose viewpoint? And Beverley Hughes explores the concept of quality of life within gerontological studies showing how many of the dimensions have been implicit and ill-defined with no debate about definition and measurement. She shows how much of the work to date originates from research into the quality of life of old people in institutional settings. She makes the distinction between quality of life and standards of living, and suggests that quality of life is a multidimensional concept which cannot be defined or measured in a single way which is applicable to all types of research. Definitions of quality of life therefore encompass the definitions of other concepts, some of which are discussed here.

A number of common themes emerge within these chapters. All authors highlight the complexity of concepts that are both constructed and perceived, and the importance of considering both objective and subjective forms of measurement. In particular dependency and social support are considered within the framework of social relationships. Also raised are the importance of other intervening variables within definitions. Whereas gender is given special attention within definitions of social support, the complex interrelationships of class, race, gender and age are also discussed with regard to social support and quality of life.

In moving on to consider measurement the authors adopt a variety of approaches. Wilkin reviews a range of issues of particular importance to a discussion of dependency: How do we measure severity? Whose perspective are we measuring? Are we measuring performance or capacity and confusing disability with dependency? Qureshi discusses how indicators of social support have been developed and used within macro- and micro-level studies, and points to their advantages and disadvantages. She gives a number of examples of methods of measurement. For Hughes the task is more complex. She outlines a model of quality of life as a framework for the development of measurement. Taking as the underlying theoretical basis for her model the critical approach within social gerontology concerned with the social construction of old age, she outlines a network which is complex and multi-faceted. She then looks at a sub-system of her model – social integration – as an example of the difficulties encountered when faced with decisions about measurement.

Finally, as with the earlier discussion of age, all authors end with a call for empirical research that will increase our understanding of these complex concepts and how they interrelate, with researchers paying far more attention to clarifying those dimensions which are the real focus of their study and making sure that these are embodied in their measurement.

1

Age

BILL BYTHEWAY

THE MEASUREMENT OF AGE

Empirical research in gerontology hangs upon the effective measurement of age. Somewhere along the line the question 'How old are you?' and/or its twin 'When were you born?' have to be asked and answered. This chapter begins with these two questions.

The researcher or a records clerk has to ask the ageing person these two questions. It is not possible to employ a measuring instrument. Nor is it possible to count the equivalent of rings in the trunk of a tree. It is possible, however, in looking at someone who is answering the question, to construct a good estimate of their age. For example, if they look about 50, then they definitely will not be 30 (or less) or 70 (or more). It is difficult, however, to know the actual limits of certainty. The important point is that looking at the person who is asked the question constitutes a check upon the answer given. We expect someone who answers 50 to look 50 and not 30 or 70. The person supplying the answer also knows this, and so the scope for error or deception by a large amount is severely limited. Conversely, of course, some people are conspicuously younger or older in looks than their actual chronological age, and regularly they will have to cope with their answers being received with suspicion.

The individual, however, does have some scope to deceive or to make errors in answering these questions. Many people can have difficulty in remembering their current age or their date of birth. For them age has ceased to be a matter of any importance and they may not take seriously what seem to them to be unnecessary and unimportant questions – concealing age may indeed be the subject of a continuing 'game' that they play. Other people may have specific reasons to deceive in answering the question – it may be necessary to under- or over-state one's age in order to secure some age-specific resource or opportunity: a financial benefit or access to housing, for example. On other occasions relative age may be important – that is, that A is perceived to be younger than B – and again this kind of deception may be carried out in the course of an interview.

Overlooking the possibility of error or deception, age is a variable that can be measured precisely. This makes it in essence a *numerical* measure of the individual in the same way as is height, weight and, for that matter, number of children. What is different, however, about this numerical measure, is (1) that its measurement depends upon the production and storage of accurate records, and (2) that it is continually and consistently changing over time. Both participants in the act of measurement, the interviewer and the interviewee, know that there is a particular number to be had. Interviewees cannot easily claim that they do not understand the question nor, for that matter, that they are unable to provide an answer. For these reasons, age is normally an easy item of information to obtain. The question is typically asked and answered in the space of a few seconds. In most situations there is no problem and on the surface it would seem absurdly unhelpful to suggest that there might be. Consider, however, what it is that is obtained when these questions are answered.

'How old are you?'

This question is normally answered in 'completed years'. This is not because this is convenient for the researcher, but rather because it is the number of the last celebrated birthday – it is the form in which the question is answered in everyday discourse. I am 'x' years old because my last birthday was my xth. We should note the central importance of the day and the year as unitary periods of time. The day – in the context of age – represents the point in time and the year is the standard unit of length. It is of course possible to celebrate the birth to the hour and to measure age in days and, as a consequence, the fiftieth birthday would be age 18,262 (give or take the odd day due to leap years). For reasons that are not always clear, however, the tendency in research is to move in the other direction: to measure age less rather than more precisely and in particular in five-year age groups or even broader categories (Nydegger, 1987, for example, refers to 5- and 10-year groups as 'traditional'). As a result the person who celebrated her fiftieth birthday last week is now 'measured' as '50–4' years of age whereas a fortnight previously she was age '45–9'.

'What is your date of birth?'

It is important to recognise that although this question generates equivalent information to the first (and thereby constitutes an important check upon the answers given), it is nevertheless a different question that (1) relates to a past biographical event rather than to a current characteristic, (2) remains the same throughout life and (3) is normally answered in units of days (although only the year of birth may be recorded). If this second question is asked in order to check the answer to the first, then it is necessary to record the full date of birth. Similarly, if it is asked in order to be the sole means of generating a precise answer to the first question, then the full date of the interview is also required. It should be noted, however, that if the only available answer to the second is the year of birth, the calculation of age in complete years is liable to some rounding error.

If it is important that age is accurately measured and that the chances of error or deception are minimised, it may be considered necessary to have recourse to an inspection of the birth certificate. More practically, the enquiry may capitalise on the fact that other, more readily available, records – passports, insurance, etc. – previously required an inspection of the birth certificate. It should be noted that this method of measurement is again generating a quite distinct variable with its own peculiar characteristics – there is the chance, for example, that the certificate that is available for inspection relates to some other person or indeed is a forgery. More generally, what is being measured is not the age of the person so much as the content of the certificate. Whilst the researcher may have every confidence that this provides a more accurate if indirect measure of the person's age, it is important that the method of measurement is critically examined and in due course precisely specified.

DIFFERENT CONCEPTS OF AGE

So far this chapter has considered the measurement of chronological age. In the past, however, gerontologists have tended to be rather dismissive of this 'measure' of age (Neugarten, 1968; Shock, 1980; Schaie, 1986; Harris, 1987). It is sometimes suggested that it is not itself a measure of anything of any consequence. This view is frequently expressed by an observation of the kind: 'some people are old at 50, while others still young at 80'. When one reflects, however, upon the importance of comparative age in respect to significant dated events ranging from marriage to wars (in particular note the findings of Elder, 1974, regarding the consequences of the Depression), and also upon the significance that is popularly ascribed to chronological age (Neugarten et al., 1965) then this suggestion is patently absurd.

What the dismissal of chronological age would appear to represent is the presumption that there is no inner 'clock' within the individual's metabolism that determines either the timing of key age 'events' or the temporal rate of specific kinds of change. It follows from this presumption that we each age individually in different ways according to different meters and at different rates. This being so, we should not be surprised if disciplines within the multidisciplinary endeavour of gerontology should wish to identify and study their own 'brand' of age: biological, physiological, psychological, social or whatever (Costa and McCrae, 1980).

Now this may be an effective and pragmatic approach in developing empirical gerontology, and therefore we should hesitate before criticising such concepts. It is better, perhaps, to examine what in theory each should represent in order to be classed as a form of age. The following argument can apply to any discipline but considers social age as a typical example.

A narrow scientific line of argument would run as follows: the social age of an individual must be something that can be measured at a point in time. Whether it is through questioning or the inspection of records, social researchers must be able to agree upon a procedure which places a numerical value or category upon an individual's social age. A second requirement is that the conception of social age and the operational procedures whereby it is measured, should be such that there is a monotonic relationship between time and an individual's social age. As time goes by, the individual's social age should never decrease (see Shock, 1987).

It follows from this that the discipline of social research should be able to construct some form of measurement of a concept which it is able to identify as 'social age'. It may be that the measure itself is little different operationally from many other social measures – it uses standard social research methodology – but social researchers are able to refer to it as a form of age, social age, for two reasons. The first is that it represents a social research approach to the study of age, a means of collaborating with other disciplines in the joint endeavour to study age. The second is that it is constructed in such a way that the social age of the individual (at least in some idealised or averaged sense), does indeed increase or pass from stage to stage as time goes by, whereas other social measures of the individual may fluctuate up and down.

A very simple example of this can be given in relation to education, employment and retirement. As part of a broader attempt to measure social age, it might be decided to score infants yet to enter school as 1, schoolchildren as 2, students who have gone straight to college (and so on) from school as 3, persons who have left full-time education but who have not yet had full-time paid employment as 4, those in full-time paid employment as 5, and those who consider themselves retired with no future intention to take up paid employment as 6. This could be refined in various ways, but as such it provides a basis for social researchers participating in a multidisciplinary approach to the study of age, and it is formulated in such a way that with time the ageing individual progresses along the scale from 1 to 6.

These two reasons have one important consequence. In that different measures of the age of an individual will vary in a way that is not fully predictable, then the interpretation of the patterns revealed by the different methods of measuring age will become crucial in the attempt to assess the contribution of these different kinds of ageing to the overall process. What, for example, do we make of the finding that the rate of change in the psychological age of a particular group is less than that in their biological age? The discussion that follows this kind of finding has to refer both to the different conceptualisations of such forms of age and to the implications of the methods of measurement. It may be that the outcome of such lines of enquiry is an unsatisfactory stalemate, as competing claims for the 'real' explanation of ageing remain unresolved.

THE PROCESS AND THE VARIABLE

The concept of population dominates much social science (for example, see United Nations, 1956). Indeed it is central to the theoretical basis of statistical inference wherein samples are drawn from specified populations. When applied to people, the most familiar notion is that of 'the population of the nation'. The discipline of demography is largely founded on the analysis of national population statistics and at the heart of these are the statistics that are generated by national censuses. To put it crudely, much social science is about sets of people – populations – who are living *at a point in time*, are 'resident' within a geographical area, and in theory could be assembled in massed ranks within a national football stadium.

As soon as we think of this assembly and of the challenge of studying the variation to be found within it, then it is obvious that age will be a key variable. After all it will be popularly perceived (not least by members of the population itself) to be a means of discrimination, through the unambiguous and visible physical signs of age (and thereby be a basis for ageism; Butler, 1969). Perhaps we should be cautious about presuming that this will necessarily be obvious for *all* populations, but it remains an everyday practice of the current populations of the UK and other industrialised nations.

Thus it is important to recognise that age is a fundamental *variable* in the analysis of populations (Pressat, 1970: 18). It stands alongside gender, ethnicity, religion, social class, education, income, area of residence, type of house, number of children and so on, as a 'dimension' upon which people vary. Age indeed is the classic example of a continuous numerical variable. Not only can we establish that two particular people are of different ages, we can identify who is the elder, we can measure the difference in ages (on the same scale as the measurement of age itself) and, if need be, we can determine the proportional difference. If A is 40 and B is 20, for example, then it can be said that A is the elder, A is 20 years older, and A is twice as old as B ('I was as old as you are now when you were born . . .'). Because it is so readily available and so effective in discriminating between people in a seemingly relevant way, there is a continuing danger that researchers will be 'carried away' by these 'attractive' aspects to the study of age. Conversely, it is all too easy to 'control' for age thereby obliterating the effects of age upon the subject of enquiry.

What is being compared are the ages of people within a population *at a point in time*. As a result, the fact that one year later the survivors will all be one year *older* is beside the point. The analysis centres upon differences within a population of 'static' individuals – between their various characteristics at the one point in time.

The analysis, however, has to draw upon an interpretation of the significance and meaning of each variable and, with respect to age, this is frequently based implicitly upon the assumption that the older persons in the population are representative of later life and the younger persons of earlier life; more precisely, that those persons in the population who are of x years of age are representative of the (x + 1)th year of life. This is open to some doubt, however, given differential mortality rates between groups – see Frost (1939) for a classic exposé of this fallacy.

Now it is possible to argue that the assumption that age differences represent changes in the age process holds a certain legitimacy in so far as the analysis is of the meaning of the age variable in that population at that point in time. When, for example, there is a change in retirement policies, it is reasonable to analyse the age-specific effects of this by drawing upon certain assumptions about change at the individual level. It seems reasonable to assume that the differential effects of the change upon people of different ages will reflect the differential effect of the change upon people as they grow older. If, for example, the changes make it easier for men to retire at the age of 60, and a subsequent survey shows that more men aged 60–4 than previously are now retired, then it would seem reasonably safe to presume that more men have indeed retired at the age of 60 as a consequence of the change in retirement policies.

Researchers, however, should be constantly on their guard for such inferences and these should always be qualified by a phrase such as 'it would seem reasonably safe to presume that . . .'. In general, the interpretation of associations with age in cross-sectional data should draw primarily upon the known differences between people of different ages within the sampled population, rather than upon the apparent effects of the ageing process.

This approach to the interpretation of cross-sectional data, however, should not be confused with the study of the ageing process itself (Riley et al., 1972). The ideal empirical context for this is, of course, the lifelong longitudinal cohort study. The unit of study in a cohort, the subject of research, is not the individual within a population at a point in time; rather it is the individual within a cohort over the entire lifespan or a significant portion of it (Ryder, 1965). The difference in the subjects of cross-sectional and longitudinal research is that between 'the point in life' and 'the life' itself, or between a day in the life and the life lived.

The study of the ageing process is a formidable challenge (see Bengston et al., 1985). Without the aid of adequate lifespan cohort studies, it is necessary to identify distinctive segments of the life course. The fundamental problem in planning such research is the specification of the chosen segment. It is one thing to draw and obtain access to a sample from a clearly defined point-in-time population; it is quite another to obtain access to representative segments of lives as lived whereby valid generalised conclusions can be drawn (Allan and Bytheway, 1973; Bytheway, 1977; Atkinson et al., 1983). It is necessary to select an appropriate event which, occurring within a specified period of time and within a specified geographical area, admits the ageing individual into the cohort of the longitudinal study. Although this event is frequently the individual's birth or any of a specified range of birthdays – thereby directly relating the structure of the cohort to chronological age – it need not be so for it to contribute to the study of the ageing process.

SOCIAL CONSTRUCTIONS

In thinking in terms of, for example, social age, we are of course engaged in the business of constructing a distinctive perspective upon age. Although we may try to ensure that it represents a certain kind of truth, we are continually faced with the problem of specifying satisfactorily its operationalisation, and subsequently with interpreting our findings. Given this, we can hardly deny that we are engaged in activities which are constructional; we are formulating methods of measuring things that are themselves intangible but which we believe to have a certain existence or meaningfulness.

For this reason it is crucial that we who are engaged in researching age should critically examine both our own beliefs about the significance of age, and the changing context wherein we attempt to undertake our research. On the one hand we may all too easily engage in seemingly harmless jokes about age, possibly at our own expense, which both reflects an unrecognised fear of the process and adds authority to the apparent truths that underlie the jokes. On the other hand, research is organised in a way that can seriously distort the knowledge which is generated – typically it is funded on a short-term basis early in the careers of those who come to lecture on the topic.

We then have to relate what we learn from our sophisticated research to the perceptions, ideas and experiences of the wider public. We may, for example, believe that our aim should be to expose popular myths and stereotypes which we believe to be invalid (Butler, 1969). We may think that the most important change that gerontologists should be seeking to accomplish is a change in cultural attitudes, because in that way it may be possible to change the actual experience of ageing for the better. It follows, then, that we should be studying these ideas about age and ageing as much as we should be studying age and ageing themselves.

Gerontologists therefore need a critical appreciation of the consequences of age constructions such as middle age, retirement, pensionable age, senility and, most important of all perhaps, old age. They also need to consider the significance of birthdays, of chronological age itself, and of the use and interpretation of such categories as '50 to 59 year olds' and 'those aged 65 or over'. There is a serious danger that gerontologists will unwittingly construct an alternative set of ideas and constructions regarding later life which are neither more valid than the more popular, nor any the less dangerous in respect of the consequences of such 'knowledge'. It is easy to detect certain fashions in such reactions and it is interesting to note how often these centre upon terminology. A good example is the tendency over the last decade or so to distinguish between 'the young old' and 'the old old'. The attempt to dispute one stereotype results in the promotion of two new stereotypes.

More generally, we should be wary of institutionalising 'as fact' any conceptualisation of life as a series of stages. It is sad to observe how the longest-lasting 'lesson' of many detailed and critical studies of the ageing process is the series of stages upon which it was structured (e.g. Erikson, 1959; Schaie, 1977). Rather than perceive such constructions as 'gerontological truths', there is so much more to be gained from the questions: What was there about the historical and cultural context within which the study was undertaken which is reflected in this outcome? What can be deduced from the intellectual careers of such researchers to explain this particular construction of the course of life?

Of all the conceivable stages of life, old age is the most crucial in gerontology. This is partly because old age, and more specifically organised services for 'elderly people' have come to dominate empirical gerontology today. It is also because it is the end of life, and the last stage of life in particular, that determines the broader perspective of the life that is lived. The empirical weakness of the stage construction is perhaps most apparent in studies oriented to the life cycle (see Bryman et al., 1987: 2) since this implies a reversion to the original state. The construction of life as a cycle wherein the individual inevitably returns to a state of 'childishness' has many dangerous consequences for the ageing individual.

If old age is to be tolerated as a useful construction which helps ageing individuals to comprehend and control their passage through life, then this is reflected most satisfactorily, perhaps, in work on life histories. In this area of research, students of age and older people have been extremely productive in constructing a radically different perspective upon life and old age. The interaction has led to a stimulating struggle to understand how things have changed and how older people have managed to get by, to respond to challenges and to cope with crises. Not only is much learnt from this approach to the study of age, but many older people – positively and actively engaged

in it – have gained much which, in turn, has led to a sense of fulfil-
ment at the end of their long lives. This said, however, we should be
extremely wary about the inferences that are drawn from such studies
regarding the ageing process. Not only is a retrospective account
inevitably selective, intentionally and otherwise, for many different
reasons, but inevitably it is the account of someone who has survived
and who has yet more of the ageing process to survive. The review of
one's life which is invariably involved in any kind of biographical
enquiry can never satisfactorily provide an account of the ageing
experience.

Gerontologists are dangerously inclined to live a double life (Smith,
1989) in which they simultaneously deplore ageism and build their
'careers' upon the study of 'elderly people'. This problem afflicts
anyone who is concerned about the 'special needs' of particular
groups of people (e.g. Purkiss and Hodson, 1983). Research that
pragmatically takes for granted the 'existence' and equivalence of old
age and elderly people should be matched by research that critically
examines the ways in which such conceptual constructions are maintained and deployed (Bytheway, 1987). It is not good enough to debate
half-heartedly the question of how to define old age or elderly people
– what age should be the cut-off and so on – since all such definitions
are intrinsically ageist. Nevertheless the researcher with little choice is
faced with the unseemly task of using the questions at the start of this
chapter in order to identify a population defined by chronological age.

THE USE OF AGE IN RESEARCH

The researcher who is planning an empirical enquiry has to consider
a number of crucial questions regarding the concept of age:

Why is age being measured? What use will be made of it? Is it to
control or limit the scope of the study in order to draw more clearly
defined conclusions about other issues, or is it to be the primary
subject of the researcher's analysis and attention? Are we studying the
intrinsic characteristics and consequences of life at different ages or are
we studying the use that is made of the measurement of age? Is age
itself (however conceptualised and measured) a nuisance that is
frustrating other ambitions? Are we solely interested in the circumstances, characteristics and ageing of 'elderly people' or do our
interests extend over the whole life course? To what extent is the
gerontologist's expertise centred upon the meaning of age?

Behind these questions lies the basic issue of what it is that we
purport to study. It is easy to say that we are studying the ageing
process, but all too often what is claimed to be such a study is
predominantly an age-controlled study of a population, or an age-
restricted study of a social institution or of a form of social action. Thus
chronological age is sometimes measured in order to control its effects,

so that other, more subtle, phenomena can be studied, typified variously by standardised mortality ratios and residential care. It is knowledge that mortality, admission to residential care, or whatever, is so closely associated with age that obliges the researcher to control for its effects, in order that other aspects of the 'age-specific' phenomenon can be studied. (Note, however, the dangers inherent in this process, well exemplified by Alderson, 1975.)

If, however, the study of the ageing process is our primary objective, then we are measuring age in order to study how certain phenomena come to be associated with age in the first place. The answer to this question frequently lies in the study of change over time. Through the examination of the processes, origins and consequences of change in an individual's circumstances and condition, and in particular the changes that are directly consequent upon age, we are able to contribute to the study of the ageing process.

CONCLUSION

It could be argued that chronological age, for all its weakness as a means of explanation, is basic to the measurement of age and thereby the study of ageing. It is, after all, widely used as a means of social regulation throughout ordinary life – from the cradle to the grave. This has major consequences that are not just institutional or social – they can directly affect the psychological and biological condition of the ageing individual.

It is also easy to overlook the intimate relationship between age and time. Sometimes it would seem that the only thing they share – as if by some kind of accident – is a scale of measurement, but the scale itself is of less importance than the sequential ordering of events and circumstances. When change is studied through the 'traditional' strategy of 'before and after' data collection, it is important that the gerontologist recognises that 'after' the subjects are older than they were 'before', and that the change being studied may be part of the accumulation of experience that contributes much to the social element in the ageing process. Similarly, the questions that might be asked of an interviewee can variously relate to the past, the present and the future – indeed the English language helpfully provides different tenses to distinguish such perspectives upon time.

Time, however, constrains the researcher as well as the ageing individual. The former attempts to manage a tight research schedule and the latter the life course. How do we as researchers make effective use of our time in our study of the effects of time on others and how do we cope with the constraints upon us? Unless we fully appreciate the dangers implicit in this ironic question, gerontology will continue to draw upon a distorting body of empirical knowledge.

2

Dependency

DAVID WILKIN

The provision of care services for dependent groups in the population is a dominant theme in health and welfare policies in all advanced industrialised nations. In the United Kingdom successive governments have sought solutions to the problem of providing adequate and appropriate care for those elderly people unable to manage alone. This concern has stemmed partly from a 'humanitarian' desire to meet their needs, but increasingly from a fear of the 'burden' which dependency imposes on the rest of society (McIntyre, 1977). Social researchers have inevitably found themselves drawn into the process of policy formulation, both directly and as providers of information through surveys of elderly people. As a consequence we have seen the development of a plethora of research instruments designed to measure dependency and a continuous stream of publications describing the levels of dependency of older people in every conceivable setting.

The social researcher engaged in policy research cannot adopt a politically neutral standpoint. Researchers conducting studies of the dependency and needs of elderly people have often failed to recognise this, treating the concept of dependency and its measurement as essentially technical problems. What is measured, how it is measured and the interpretations placed on results will depend on the underlying theoretical and conceptual framework adopted. For everyone planning surveys of elderly people in which dependency is a central issue, or even a background variable, it is important to understand the problems of definition and classification and to select a measurement instrument suitable for the particular purpose. This chapter begins with a discussion of the meaning of dependency and its different dimensions, before going on to examine some of the most important methodological problems encountered in the measurement of dependency. The final selection offers some advice on how to select a measure for a particular purpose.

THE CONCEPT OF DEPENDENCY

Definitions

It seems self-evident that anyone thinking of measuring anything should be quite clear about what it is they want to measure and what use the measurement will be. We do not give a second thought to the problem when using a thermometer to measure temperature, or a speedometer to tell us whether we are exceeding the speed limit. But in the social world concepts and measures are more problematic. When a politician requests information about the needs of elderly people, or a service planner wants to know how many hospital beds to provide, it may not be at all clear what should be measured or which of a variety of tools should be used for the job. Whoever is charged with the task of obtaining the information will need to establish precisely what information is required. In order to do this it will usually be necessary to look at the uses to which it will be put. The information necessary to estimate the demand for a physiotherapy service will not, for example, be the same as that required to estimate the need for home helps.

The concerns of those responsible for the provision of services for elderly people tend to focus more on dependency than on disability or handicap. This focus on dependency arises from a concern with the perceived human and financial costs to the rest of society of supporting an increasing proportion of old people whose disabilities mean that they have to be cared for by families and/or by health and social services. Although the concept of dependency overlaps with disability and handicap it is by no means synonymous with either. Thus, for example, people suffering from impaired vision may be disabled, but even if they suffer a limitation of function, there is not necessarily any dependency. Similarly it is possible to be handicapped without being dependent and possible to be dependent without being handicapped. An individual who has lost a leg is certainly handicapped but may, by restricting the range of activities undertaken, be completely independent. On the other hand, young children are clearly dependent but not necessarily handicapped.

It is necessary to place some broad restraints on the concept of dependency. In common with others who have addressed the conceptual problem, I exclude at the outset the biological dependencies (for example the need for oxygen, water, food, heat and so on) except in so far as the meeting of these needs involves other people. Indeed it is the social nature of dependency that might be regarded as the one fundamental feature of any definition. Van den Heuvel (1976), in one of the most comprehensive attempts at a conceptual analysis, notes that 'dependency always has reference to a social relationship'. Unlike disability, it cannot be conceived as an attribute of the individual irrespective of his or her relations with significant others. Although we can say that a person has a disability, it would be meaningless to say that a person has a dependency. Even the characteristic of dependency as a 'state of being' contains an implicit recognition of others. Thus 'A is dependent' implies 'A is dependent on B'. To the extent that instruments are concerned to measure dependency as opposed to disability, they must recognise this reference to a social relationship.

By comparison with the importance of social relationships, it is difficult to identify other components of a definition which might be universally accepted. The use of the term in research concerned with illness and disability has usually been associated with some form of practical helplessness, but dependencies for help with practical tasks do not necessarily reflect helplessness. Thus it is possible to rely on someone to cook and clean without being helpless. Indeed the gender-based division of labour which still prevails in our society makes this quite normal for half the population.

Related to helplessness is the notion of powerlessness. Walker (1983) asserts that dependency rests on the exercise of power, in that a dependency relationship is a power relationship between a person with a disability and others. This emphasis on power is also seen in attempts to define its opposite. Thus Johnson (1983) and Paillat (1976) both introduce the notion of autonomy as the converse of dependency. But to what extent is powerlessness or loss of autonomy a necessary feature of dependency? Is it possible to exercise a choice to become or remain dependent? Goldfarb (1969) points out that in a psychological sense the dependent individual may be exerting control over those who help, and that such strategies may be used more or less consciously as a means of exercising power over others. Qureshi (1986) shows that power relationships established earlier in life continue in old age, so that parents, although dependent, may continue to exercise control over their children.

For the purpose of a general definition, practical helplessness and powerlessness must be excluded because they are too restrictive. The key component is the reference to a social relationship. Among a variety of definitions provided by the Oxford dictionary, 'being maintained at another's cost' seems most suitable, but this appears to place too much emphasis on material considerations. Anderson's (1971) definition offers a better general framework: 'A state in which actions by others are a necessary condition for an actor to achieve his or her own goals.' This, however, begs the question of what is 'necessary' and by whose criteria it is considered necessary. My own suggested definition is: 'A state in which an individual is *reliant* upon other(s) for assistance in meeting *recognised needs*.' The key components here are the terms 'reliance' and 'recognised needs'. I believe that 'reliance' removes the problem of whether support is necessary or not. The fact that the individual relies upon others is sufficient in itself. Reference to recognised needs is preferable to Anderson's use of the actor's own goals, because it allows the possibility that needs might be recognised by society or significant others but not by the actor. Thus, for example, the elderly person suffering from senile dementia may have needs which are recognised by others but do not constitute personal goals.

Dimensions of dependency

Clearly dependency has a variety of different dimensions and meanings which are reflected in different usages. There have been two broad approaches to classification. Firstly, it can be classified in terms of the needs for which the individual is dependent on others, and secondly, it can be classified in terms of aetiology (its causes or antecedents).

A number of authors have offered needs-based classifications (Blenkner, 1969; Van den Heuvel, 1976; WHO, 1980). None of these seems entirely satisfactory but the WHO classification of handicaps comes closest to providing a framework. The first six of the categories of need shown in Figure 2.1 match the dimensions of handicap advanced in the International Classification of Impairment, Disabilities and Handicaps, except that I have chosen to refer to activities of daily living rather than physical independence (although the content of the WHO category is very similar to what most researchers would recognise as activities of daily living). In addition to the WHO handicap categories, emotional and environmental needs seem to be additional categories which, although not appropriate to a classification of handicap, are necessary to a comprehensive classification of dependency needs.

The above dimensions of dependency needs should be kept quite separate from the sources of dependency, despite the fact that the overlap in terminologies sometimes makes for confusion. Thus, for example, a locomotor disability *may* result in a dependence for help with mobility, but the disability and the dependency are not the same thing. Listed in Figure 2.1 are five potential sources of dependency. Life-cycle dependency refers to real or socially defined periods of relative helplessness in an individual at certain times during the lifespan. These dependencies tend to be predictable in occurrence, timing and approximate duration. Childhood is the most obvious example, but dependency in old age is commonly regarded as an example of life-cycle dependency, and it is important to note that it is socially and culturally defined as well as physiologically determined. Crisis dependency is characterised by its unpredictability and will include bereavement, divorce, war, unemployment, and so on. Dependency resulting from disablement is likely to be the most common form among elderly people. It is often the category of dependency in which those responsible for the formulation of policy are implicitly interested. However, it is essential to recognise that there are other potential sources of dependency among elderly people. Neurotic dependency, sometimes characterised as the 'dependent personality', is well recognised in the psychological literature (Goldfarb, 1969). It is generated by particular personality types who believe themselves to be weak and in need of help. Finally, socially or

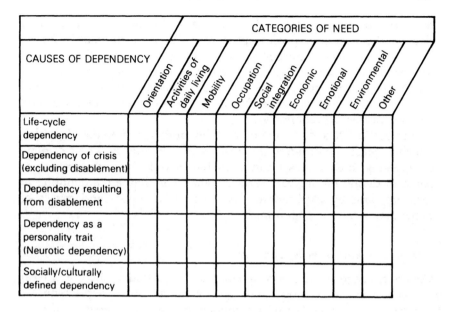

Figure 2.1 *Classification matrix*

culturally defined dependencies are those prescribed, encouraged or permitted behaviours which have their roots in the values and norms of societies, rather than in any characteristics of the individual or the environment. The dependency of men on women for domestic labour and women on men for economic support provide obvious examples. In any individual, dependency will result from a variety of different sources acting in conjunction, and it will therefore often be difficult to establish which plays a more important part.

Figure 2.1 presents the categories of need and causes of dependency in the form of a matrix. This helps to define the area of interest in any particular survey. It should also alert researchers to the dangers of ignoring the complex nature of the dependency situations which they are investigating. It is clear that many of the most commonly used dependency measures address only a few of the possible cells. In research on old people all measures deal with activities of daily living and mobility. Orientation is sometimes included, but is by no means universal, and the other categories of need for help are usually ignored. This leads to considerable problems, so that when interviewing carers of confused old people it is not uncommon to find that the most severe problems for the carer lie in areas such as safety and occupation which the dependency measure does not address.

The causes of dependency are rarely directly addressed in measures. Implicit in their use for elderly people is an assumption that the principal concern is with dependency arising from disablement. But this is rarely made explicit, and interviewers commonly face the problem of how to rate elderly men who have never in their lives cooked or cleaned the house, but who apparently suffer no disability. Should they be rated dependent because they do not undertake the tasks, or independent because they are presumably physically and mentally capable of fending for themselves? Such measures are 'gender blind' or, in a more general sense, blind to the importance of social and cultural causes of dependency.

This section has done no more than outline a framework within which to place the different dimensions of dependency. The discipline of applying such a classification system should help researchers to begin to define more clearly exactly what it is they are attempting to measure, and by implication which aspects of needs and causes of dependency they are ignoring.

Reciprocity and interdependence

Common usage of the term dependency implies that there is a clear distinction between people who are dependent and people who are independent. Dependence and independence are treated as if they were dichotomous, but the fallacy of such a view is rapidly apparent if we ask: 'Whose lifestyle would remain unchanged if those who support them withdrew?' (Johnson, 1983). Dependency should be seen as a condition which occurs in all individuals throughout life. It is not, however, necessarily perceived as dependency by the individual or by society. Where dependency occurs as a component of a reciprocal role relationship it is perceived as a state of interdependence. Where an individual is defined (by self and/or others) as having nothing of value to exchange, any claim made on others is evidence of dependency. This dependency of non-reciprocal roles is not a particular type of dependency as Clark (1969) suggests. Rather, the nature and extent of reciprocity is an additional dimension to all categories which is important because of the way it affects perceptions and valuations of dependency.

The rules governing reciprocity are complex. Only certain goods and services are acceptable currencies, and what is acceptable may vary for different individuals and in different social groups. It has been repeatedly observed in anthropological studies that the elderly in non-industrialised societies are seen as arbiters of disputes and guardians of cultural values. In this way they have 'something of value' to trade in situations where they become dependent economically and/or physically. In our own society the elderly are seen as having nothing of value to trade, but Clark (1969) points out that such a definition is largely cultural and essentially arbitrary.

Reciprocity also has a temporal dimension which further complicates the rules applying in any particular situation. Goods or services rendered in the past do not necessarily entitle the individual to goods and services now or in the future. Thus the provision of care for children does not entitle parents to expect complete care in their old age. However, it is clear that such a rule does not apply universally, even within our own society. The complex rules governing reciprocity are relative to particular cultures and even sub-cultures. Qureshi (1986) is one of the few researchers to have explored in some depth the dynamics of reciprocity in relation to dependent elderly people. She illustrates the complexity of relationships between dependant and carer, and the need to situate the caring relationship in a wider context which includes affect and power.

MEASUREMENT ISSUES

Severity

All instruments for measuring dependency make some attempt to grade severity, rather than simply attempting to classify individuals as dependent or independent. They imply a continuum from complete independence to complete dependence, although it is interesting to note that it is dependence not independence which is measured. In doing so they use a notion of severity based on deviation from some real or imagined norm. However, severity might be measured in a variety of ways.

Severity might be seen as being to do with the nature of the help required by the dependent person. Ungerson (1983) has argued that some personal care tasks are associated with strong taboos, and are therefore only very unwillingly undertaken. Thus more personal tasks (for example, bathing, toileting and changing an incontinent person) might be seen as representing more severe dependency than less personal care (for example cooking, housework, conversation). But severity might also be considered a function of the amount of physical effort required, so that lifting someone into the bath may represent more severe dependency than toileting. Alternatively, severity might reflect the frequency and timing of the provision of help. In some cases (bathing, housework) the help required may be regular and relatively infrequent, in other cases it will be regular and frequent (toileting, cooking), and in others it will be irregular and frequent (incontinence). Lastly, it might be felt that the time at which help is required has a bearing on dependency, so that night-time toileting is of a different order of severity than daytime toileting.

The time scale over which dependency states arise and continue in existence might be considered as a further dimension of severity. Short interval dependencies (as in acute illness) have a very different significance from those occurring over long and indefinite periods of time. Perceptions of severity will be very much influenced by previous history and expectations for the future. Thus the interpretation placed upon isolated instances of incontinence will be very different for a young child and an elderly person. In situations of long-term dependency it is possible to think in terms of a dependency career, and the individual's position on such a career path may be as important as the actual needs and behaviour manifest at a particular point in time. The nature of measurement instruments and the ways in which they are applied mean that these complexities of time scale are usually ignored. The measures are usually applied at a point in time, or at best refer to a brief period, and they make no provision for respondents to situate their responses in the context of a history and an anticipated future.

In practice, most measures rely on a, usually implicit, model of severity which amalgamates all of the different dimensions, without attempting to resolve potential conflicts between them. The result, as those who have used these measures in the field will know, is that the instrument commonly distorts the experience of respondents. Their perceptions of severity are situated in a different context from those of the researcher.

Whose perspective?

So far, in discussing severity, I have omitted to mention from whose perspective we are concerned to measure severity. If we accept that dependency is first and foremost an interactive concept, then the evaluation of severity may be very different from the perspectives of dependant and carer. Not only will perceptions of the significance of different behaviours differ, but even apparently straightforward descriptions of reality may differ.

Even measures which supposedly rely upon simple descriptions of behaviour introduce elements of judgement which systematically affect overall estimations of severity. Differences are likely to be even more pronounced where the researcher is concerned with perceptions of the significance of different behaviours. Thus dependant and carer are likely to have very different perceptions of the importance of requiring help with bathing and housework. The dependent person may find help with bathing much more problematic than help with housework, because of the invasion of privacy entailed in the former. The carer, on the other hand, might regard the provision of help with housework as more problematic because of the frequency of help and amount of time required.

Wenger (1985) compared dependency measured through self-assessment with a measure based on interviewers' assessments. She showed that self-assessed dependency was related to whether or not the elderly person was living alone and drew the conclusion that what was being measured was the availability of help rather than 'true' dependency. However, such a conclusion implies that only certain categories of dependency are legitimate. The differences between self-assessment and interviewer assessment arise from the application of different criteria rather than reflecting superior validity. They are measuring different things.

Performance versus capacity

A basic problem in formulating the items and questions to be used in a measure of dependency is whether simply to describe what the respondent does and does not do, or to try to assess the individual's capacity to accomplish tasks or activities with or without assistance. The former approach will tend to produce a higher estimate of problems because it will pick up all those things which are done for people, although they might be quite capable of doing them for themselves. I referred earlier to the problem of how to classify men who are looked after by their wives. Measures based on descriptions of actual behaviour have little choice but to classify men in this situation as dependent, regardless of whether they are physically active and mentally alert. Similarly, in institutional settings where certain tasks are routinely performed by staff, all residents or patients will be classified as dependent. Measures of capacity might provide an opportunity to distinguish between those who are unable to perform the task for themselves by virtue of their infirmity, and those who have the task performed for them either as a matter of routine or out of choice. However, such a distinction requires the rater to make difficult value judgements. How much of a mildly disabled elderly man's dependence on his wife for cooking is due to his disability and how much to the fact that he has never cooked a meal in his life? Who is to say whether someone who has never cooked is able to prepare a meal? In these circumstances, questions become hypothetical. The same is often true in residential homes and hospital wards, where the rater will have to guess whether respondents could take a bath alone if they were allowed to, or climb a flight of stairs if they existed.

A more serious criticism of measures of capacity, however, is that they are confusing disability with dependency. Regardless of the reasons, the man who relies on his wife to cook and clean is dependent on her. Whether or not his dependency might be reduced through a change in attitudes, the provision of aids or medical treatment is immaterial to a description of existing patterns of dependency. It may be desirable to examine the scope for reductions in dependency, but this should be seen as a separate issue.

Selecting an instrument

There is a wide variety of instruments available for measuring dependency in elderly people. One of the problems in this field is a tendency for researchers to reinvent the wheel by devising their own measures, either because they are unaware of existing measures or because these do not quite meet the needs of a particular piece of research. The advantages of employing an existing measure rather than developing a new one are considerable. Firstly, its reliability and validity are likely to have been tested in a variety of situations. Secondly, it will be possible to compare your own data with that obtained in a variety of other studies. Lastly, and perhaps most importantly, a great deal of time and effort will be saved through not having to undertake development and testing. Most researchers will not have the resources necessary to undertake the detailed development and testing of a new measurement instrument. Without such work the results of a dependency survey are likely to be of extremely limited value.

It is beyond the scope of this chapter to provide even a summary of the most commonly used measures of dependency. However, there are a number of sources to which the user can turn. *Assessing the Elderly: A Practical Guide to Measurement* (Kane and Kane, 1981) is an excellent guide to a wide range of measures covering not only dependency, but also impairment, disability and handicap. Most of the measures described and reviewed were developed in the USA, and anyone considering using them in different countries should take care to ensure that they are appropriate. The same is true to a lesser extent of a more recent WHO guide to multi-dimensional assessment (Fillenbaum, 1984) and a guide to measures of health status (McDowell and Newell, 1987). This latter guide is not confined specifically to measures suitable for use with elderly people, although it includes a number of specialised measures as well as many more generally applicable measures which can be applied to elderly people. Lastly, the *Users' Guide to Measures of Dependency for the Elderly* (Wilkin and Thompson, 1989) focuses specifically on instruments whose stated purpose is to measure dependency in elderly people. It provides critical reviews of the most widely used British measures and includes copies of most of the actual questionnaires. With such a good collection of guides, there can be no excuse for failing even to consider existing instruments. Where these do not meet the particular needs of the research, it may be possible to modify an instrument by incorporating additional questions whilst retaining the original and thus ensuring comparability.

The previous discussion of the concept of dependency, its classification and measurement issues should be kept in mind when selecting a suitable instrument. There are, however, a number of other important considerations. Figure 2.2 lists six criteria which might be applied to judge the usefulness of a measure. Particular attention should be paid to the issues of validity and reliability which are frequently ignored or misunderstood. Each of the guides mentioned earlier offers a straightforward account of the meaning of these terms and the

1 *What does it measure?*
   Dependency has many facets. Which are covered in this measure, and more
   importantly, which are missing? Do the questions or items ask about behaviour or
   ability and are they consistent throughout? There can be a big difference between
   what someone feels able to do and what they actually do. Do the component parts,
   when combined, constitute a balanced whole, or are some aspects given too much
   weight and others too little?

2 *How does it measure?*
   Measurement requires more than the awarding of numerical values to arbitrary
   categories. Is the basis for scaling adequate? Numerical values should at least
   represent a ranking in terms of the severity of problems. Does the measure require
   that scores on individual items are added together? Is this justified? Regardless of
   scoring, are adequate descriptions provided of the characteristics of people in different
   categories when items on the scale are combined? Can results be broken down
   according to sub-scales based on related items or questions? (e.g. household activity,
   self-care, confusion).

3 *Is it valid and reliable?*
   Does it really measure what it claims to measure and does it give the same results
   consistently? Which, if any, of the different ways of establishing validity and reliability
   have been applied to this measure? Would the results of these tests help to convince a
   sceptic (e.g. politician or manager) that the measure is worth using?

4 *Is it practicable and acceptable?*
   Measures vary considerably in the way in which they are administered and, therefore,
   in cost and acceptability. Do you have, or have access to, the resources (skills, time,
   money) necessary to administer this measure? Will other people (elderly people,
   carers, professionals) be prepared to give their time? Are there any areas of
   questioning that might prove unacceptable to respondents?

5 *Is it suitable for my purpose?*
   Most measures have been developed for specific purposes (e.g. surveys of residential
   homes, sheltered housing, hospital wards; comparisons of people in different settings,
   individual assessment). They may subsequently have been adapted and put to
   different uses. Is this measure appropriate and recommended for the particular use
   you have in mind? Note that evidence on reliability and validity may not cover the uses
   which you have in mind.

6 *How widely has it been used?*
   This will give you some indication of the confidence that others have in the value of
   this measure. It will also determine the amount of data available for comparison.
   Interpretations of results can be made much easier if you can compare your own
   findings with other areas, hospitals, residential homes and so on.

Figure 2.2 *Criteria for assessing the usefulness of a measure*

common methods of establishing them. None of the currently available
measures is likely to be satisfactory against all of the suggested criteria
for any particular use. Each will have its strengths and weaknesses.
What is important is that the intending user should be aware of these
in making a choice. It is always preferable to use a measure of known
strengths and limitations than to embark on a survey using an
unproven instrument.

Lastly, it is worth sounding a note of warning concerning the analysis and interpretation of results. Most dependency measures employ relatively unsophisticated techniques of measurement. Some aim to be uni-dimensional and employ ordinal scaling (that is, scores can be ranked as better or worse) but most are multi-dimensional. In this latter type, responses to each item are ranked, but there is no overall ranking across different items. In either case the user should be careful not to employ statistical analyses which are inappropriate to the levels of measurement. The temptation to add scores together and apply statistical tests is often difficult to resist, but the user should always bear in mind the limitations of the measurement tool. Information from dependency measures can make a valuable contribution to the policy and planning process, but it is not at present very precise and should be viewed in the context of a variety of other considerations.

FUTURE DIRECTIONS IN DEPENDENCY RESEARCH

The needs of those responsible for the formulation of policy and its implementation demand simple measurement instruments which yield results amenable to aggregation and classification. But it should be remembered that these simple instruments may distort an extremely complex reality. They treat the concept of dependency as non-problematic, making arbitrary and often unwarranted assumptions about what is and is not dependency, its meaning for the actors involved and its causes. The fundamental failing of most existing instruments is their treatment of dependency as an individual attribute, rather than as a social relationship in which the behaviour and perceptions of all of the actors contribute to the construction of the situation. The problem is defined in terms of the individual rather than in terms of his or her relationship with the social environment. The error in this approach can be illustrated by imagining a person alone on a desert island. Many dependency measures could be applied, even if with some difficulty, but the result is clearly nonsensical. By definition the person alone on a desert island cannot be dependent upon others. The problem arises because measures attempt to describe only one half of a social relationship. Whilst it is difficult to conceive of a relatively simple instrument which would be capable of capturing the complexities of the whole dependency relationship, it is important to move in this direction.

Whilst the need for dependency surveys will continue, they should not be seen as the sum total of research on dependency. There is enormous scope for research which increases our understanding of the nature of dependency relationships. There is a need to understand how these relationships are constructed, how they are perceived by the different parties to the interaction, which aspects of dependency are particularly problematic, how reciprocity works to achieve a balanced exchange of goods and/or services, how much variation there is from dominant cultural values, norms and expectations, and how elements of the social structure act to create or avoid dependency states. Attention to these and similar questions is at least as important in health care and social policy research as the development and application of measures of dependency. Social researchers have obligations towards the elderly people who constitute the subjects for their research, as well as to the more immediately obvious customers among service providers and politicians. Old people, even those suffering from infirmity, have much to contribute and should not be seen by researchers or by society at large solely in terms of the growing burden of dependency which they place on the rest of society.

NOTE

This chapter draws substantially on two previously published papers:

Wilkin, D. (1987) 'Conceptual problems in dependency research', *Social Science and Medicine*, 24(10): 867–73.

and

Wilkin, D. and Thompson, C. (1989) *Users' Guide to Measures of Dependency for the Elderly*. Social Services Monographs: Research in Practice. University of Sheffield Joint Unit for Social Services Research.

3

Social Support

HAZEL QURESHI

Social support is a portmanteau term which has carried such a wide variety of meanings that at least one recent commentator has been led to argue that the term is 'insufficiently specific to be useful as a research concept' (Barrera, 1986: 414). Certainly, the subject has generated a vast academic literature, most of which has focused on the hypothesised positive effects of such support on mental or physical health, or protection against stress. With a few important exceptions, policy makers and service practitioners have tended to assume that it is established that social support is a 'good thing', and thus they have concentrated on exhortations to produce more of it (DHSS, 1981), or on advocating forms of intervention by statutory workers that would appropriately tap this important resource (Whittaker and Garbarino, 1983).

In everyday discourse the term is usually intuitively understood as help or assistance, or other evidence of caring, provided through a person's social relationships. Although this is usually understood as meaning relationships with family, neighbours or friends, social support is sometimes given a wider interpretation than the term informal support (Abrams, 1978a). Whilst the latter includes only support given by virtue of a personally directed social relationship with a particular individual (a daughter, a mother or a friend, for example), some writers on social support have tended to emphasise that this can be given by a variety of people in a range of professional or quasi-professional roles from clergymen through to barmen to hairdressers (Cowen, 1982), although in these instances it is still stressed that such support is 'naturally occurring' (Collins and Pancoast, 1976), to ensure that it is distinguished from artificially created support as provided by paid workers whose specific role is to provide assistance.

The term as generally used is taken to exclude support from statutory workers, although a few authors (for example Hooyman, 1983) have described such workers as part of an individual's social support network. Support has not always been seen as necessarily involving any kind of caring activity – it has been used (Vaux et al., 1986) to reflect a feeling of security derived from a belief that one is loved and cared for.

The intention of this chapter is to discuss the concept and measurement of social support and not primarily to outline substantive results, or theories about social support. However, the area of social support illustrates, *par excellence*, the observation that theory, or lack of it, is reflected in measurement, and that although a concept may appear to have a clear meaning in everyday language, the process of attempting to construct a method of measuring it reveals a wide range of possible meanings and interpretations which may have quite different relationships to other concepts. It also illustrates that many apparently meaningful questions about social support are posed at too high a level of generality to allow an unequivocal answer. As one begins to explore the concept and how it has been used, it soon becomes necessary to specify more precisely the answers to a range of questions – What elements of social support? From what sources? For what purpose? From whose point of view? – in order to discover what should be the focus of interest for any particular study.

DESCRIPTION OF THE COMPONENTS OF SOCIAL SUPPORT

There is broad general agreement on the various modes or components of social support, the most basic distinction being that between *instrumental*, or practical, support as opposed to *expressive*, or emotional, support. These categories clearly can be, and have been, broken down into a large variety of sub-categories, although much less attention has been given in the academic literature to detailed examination of practical, instrumental support than to emotional support. The influential work of Weiss (1974) produced a typology of requirements for individual well-being which could be met through the provisions of social relationships, and this included practical assistance as one element but distinguished five functions of emotional support: attachment and intimacy, social integration, nurturance, reassurance of worth and guidance. Subsequently many measures of social support have attempted to tap all, or some, of these functions. Of course, in order to devise measurements of the degree to which these functions of social support have been fulfilled, it is necessary to understand which specific behaviours by others will serve these particular functions for an individual, and this link is not necessarily unproblematic. Many categorised lists of behaviours have been produced as bases for the operationalisation of the concept of social support. Cohen and Wills (1985), in a comprehensive review of measures of social support, distinguish esteem support, informational support, social companionship and instrumental support, although they make the point that whilst these elements can be distinguished conceptually, they may not be independent in a particular individual situation. Providing a meal for an elderly person might be instrumental support, or it might be more appropriately viewed as social companionship.

Gottlieb (1985b) categorises modes of social support under the headings: emotionally sustaining behaviours; problem-solving behaviours; indirect personal influence; and environmental action. The total list of 26 informal helping behaviours was derived from a study of low-income single-parent mothers (Gottlieb, 1978), and thus has the virtue of being based on asking individuals to identify behaviours which were helpful rather than simply on the researchers' own assumptions. However, in subsequently using such lists of behaviours as measures of support, the question arises as to whether particular forms of help should always be seen as 'support' if the recipient does not perceive them in that light. An activity which the giver might define as 'advice' may be seen by the recipient as 'interference'. Therefore it would seem *prima facie* important in assessing social support to obtain the recipient's subjective view about whether particular behaviours are in fact experienced as supportive. However, the degree to which people are satisfied with the support they receive can be influenced by many things including their personality (Sarason and Sarason, 1985a; Henderson, 1984), depressive state (Barrera, 1986), or the degree to which help comes from people who are expected to help (Antonucci, 1985). Therefore it has been felt desirable to try to separate subjective measurements of support (that is, opinions about its adequacy, or availability if required) from relatively more objective measures, which are, of course, still based on self-report but which concentrate on the occurrence or non-occurrence of specific acts or behaviours in a given time period. This latter, Tardy (1985) has described as *enacted* support, to be distinguished from *perceived* support.

Several writers have drawn attention to different understandings of the term perceived support. Vaux et al. (1986) distinguish the perceived availability of support if needed (which is seen as an individual's own assessment of their potential support resources should a need for assistance arise) from a more general appraisal by the individual of the extent to which they feel cared for and esteemed by friends and family. In a different vein, Henderson (1984) has argued that perceived availability and adequacy should be distinguished, not least because he and his colleagues have observed that measures of support based on these two different concepts show differing relationships with other variables, such as the likelihood of developing neurotic symptoms in the face of high levels of adversity (Henderson et al., 1980).

Veiel (1985) draws our attention to another dimension which might seem particularly likely to be relevant to elderly people: the distinction between support in a *crisis* and *everyday* support. Within the conceptual framework he outlines, everyday support is conceived as related to social integration and therefore concerned with an individual's general social transactions with a range of contacts. Veiel argues that everyday support and support mobilised in a crisis may well therefore influence mental health in quite different ways, with everyday support having an overall beneficial effect, whilst the effectiveness of crisis support would depend upon the match between the type of support available and the kind required for dealing with the particular crisis. Since the main basis for Veiel's distinction is the presence or absence of a problem focus it seems that there may be room for yet another distinction between *crisis* and *routine problem-focused support*.

Since, given the discussion above, it is likely that the effects of social support will be related to the particular support needs of the group of people under study, we should consider briefly what the support requirements of elderly people are thought to be.

Support needs of elderly people

Rosow (1967) documented in convincing detail the process through which people who survive into old age are likely to suffer a diminution of their social worlds. Increasing mortality reduces the number of contemporary friends and kin such as siblings, as well as increasing the likelihood of being widowed. Increasing morbidity means that the elderly person or their surviving friends and relatives may suffer physical disability which will reduce mobility and therefore contact, especially when combined with lower income. Compulsory retirement means loss of regular contact with work colleagues, although there may be some compensating increase in family contact. Although this may have the consequence that the elderly person's children, if they have any, come to represent an increasing proportion of their social world, such children are likely to have many conflicting demands upon their resources and time (Brody, 1981). This description is not to suggest that these factors – loss of work, bereavement, the death of contemporaries, low income and increasing physical frailty – are the inevitable lot of all, or most, people in old age but rather that the longer a person survives the more likely they are to undergo these experiences, so that, for example, almost half of all people over the age of 75 in the UK are widowed women. In addition there will be specific groups of elderly people with particular needs for support, for example people with mental handicap who have grown old (Hogg et al., 1988), or some elderly people belonging to minority ethnic groups (Bhalla and Blakemore, 1981; Barker, 1984).

Overall this suggests that elderly people may experience a wide range of needs for support, which could vary from needs for practical help or assistance in the event of physical disability (or the loss of a partner with gender-related skills), through to needs for intimacy, comfort, company and security consonant with the personal and social losses which have been sustained. Equally, many elderly people are in a position to offer support to others, both to their contemporaries, and, especially among younger elderly people, to other generations of the family (Brody et al., 1984). The diversity of support giving and receiving in later life draws attention to the failure of many studies focused on social support to consider its possible health-damaging effects (Kessler et al., 1985), that is, both the effects on those who give it, which have been increasingly stressed by feminist writers (Finch and Groves, 1983), and the possible psychologically damaging effects of dependency on the recipient of help (DiMatteo and Hays, 1981).

In a wider sense, this reflects a deficiency of much research on support, which is that it does not set support in the context of the many other functions which relationships may have. Wellman (1981) argues that the concentration on support distorts the content, context and structure of social networks because it prevents the investigation of questions about relationships between social networks and support networks. Specht (1986) argues that much of the social work literature has conflated the separate notions of social support, social network and social exchange to the detriment of theory and practice. The following sections will attempt to illustrate how and why this has come about.

Why is social support important?

The bulk of routine social care for elderly people, both emotional and practical, comes from informal sources. Many influential studies from the 1960s onwards demonstrated the widespread and persistent help which elderly people received from kin, neighbours and friends, but particularly from members of their immediate family (Townsend, 1963; Shanas et al., 1968; Hunt, 1978). More recent studies (Wenger, 1984; Qureshi and Walker, 1989), whilst stressing the independence of many elderly people, confirm the importance of social support from informal sources, although they also suggest that differentiation among different informal sources may be important. Evidence from the USA corroborates this, for example, Seeman and Berkman (1988) argue that elderly people's ties with their children are most strongly related to instrumental support, whilst ties with close friends and relatives are more strongly related to emotional support.

Some writers have seen few problems, in theory, in combining assistance from informal sources with that from formal or bureaucratic structures. It has been argued (Litwak and Szelenyi, 1969; Litwak, 1985) that their roles are essentially complementary and the balance required depends on, for example, the amount of professional expertise, as opposed to the amount of personal knowledge of the individual, that is required for a particular task. However, others have stressed the apparently conflicting principles on which the two systems of care are based (Abrams, 1978, 1984), and argued not only that their integration poses difficulties for informal carers in accepting shared care (Parker, 1981) but also that their interaction may be positively destructive (Abrams, P. 1980), with informal care being displaced by formal care despite a preference among recipients for the qualitatively superior benefits of informal help. In truth, at a policy level, the formal services, far from being bent on displacement, have seemed only too anxious to see informal assistance displacing formal help (DHSS, 1981: 3). In the context of the projected increases in the numbers of dependent elderly people, and the likely failure of public funding to keep pace with growing need, the knowledge that informal network members are providing substantial support has been translated into a perception that informal networks might be tapped to provide alternatives to state care. Thus, we find textbooks on social support arguing: 'In a time of scarce economic resources, it becomes imperative to formulate strategies to mobilise informal support systems for older people' (Hooyman, 1983: 133). The argument made by Abrams, among others, that support from informal sources is experienced as qualitatively superior adds a moral gloss to the public expenditure arguments. However, such expectations seem to ignore the process by which people seek help when it is needed.

There are many descriptions of the help-seeking process which suggest that elderly people see informal help as the first choice and will therefore seek statutory help only if they feel the required resources are not available, without undue cost, within their informal network (Cantor, 1979; Gottlieb, 1985a). Even the alternative model, of rationally based help seeking from the most appropriate source (Dono et al., 1977) does not suggest that there are unused resources within the informal sector which are easily tapped as alternatives to help from bureaucratic sources. Exhaustive investigation of help received in relation to available informal helpers in one UK city found few potentially available but uninvolved family members (Qureshi and Walker, 1989), and endorses the view expressed by Bulmer (1987: 221) that there can be only a very limited expectation of effective care on an informal basis by non-kin. It seems likely therefore that careful investigation of the informal networks of those seeking statutory help is as likely to uncover additional needs as additional resources.

Social support and health

It has been argued that one reason for the emphasis on the importance of social support is that it has been seen as a substitute for statutory care, and yet, in curious contrast to this, the emphasis in the great bulk of empirical studies of social support reported in the literature has been upon the affective or emotional support which it is assumed people obtain uniquely from their social relationships and which has been thought to be protective against physical or mental ill health or even death. This focus of interest in social support has its history in the work of Cassel, an epidemiologist, and Caplan, a community psychiatrist. In investigating the health consequences of urban life, Cassel (1976) wished to understand why some individuals suffered ill effects as a consequence of poor environmental conditions whilst others seemed to escape this consequence. As one aspect of his findings he advanced the view that the primary groups of some individuals were able to provide social supports which were health protective. Caplan (1974) attempted to delineate more precisely what kind of support this was, and to classify different support systems. Although he outlined the helping functions which support from primary groups might serve he did not consider the dynamics of support systems: how they are initiated, or develop, or change. Nor did he analyse them specifically as systems, despite his use of that label. Gottlieb complains, 'by coining the term support system, Caplan invented a social aggregate that does not exist in the natural environment. People do not participate in social orbits which communicate exclusively positive feedback' (Gottlieb, 1985b: 9). This neglect of the complex nature of social ties and informal systems carried through into much of the later work on social support.

Stress, social support and health

The vast majority of literature on social support, particularly in North America, has concentrated on various hypotheses concerning the relationships between stressful life events, social support and some kind of health-related outcome measure such as depressive symptoms, physical illness or mortality. The two most frequently posited forms of the relationship are that support itself has beneficial effects upon well-being irrespective of stress, and secondly that this effect occurs only, or primarily, for persons under stress (the so-called 'buffering' model). Useful reviews of the literature are Broadhead et al. (1983) and, for the buffering hypothesis only, Alloway and Bebbington (1987). Henderson (1984) indicates that the two forms of relationship mentioned oversimplify the possibilities. It may be that social support has a therapeutic effect after the onset of disorder as well as, or instead of, preventing disorder. Alternatively, it could be that rather than the presence of social support being protective, its absence is directly pathogenic. Equally important from the point of view of social gerontology, the effects may vary for different demographic groups, so that effects demonstrated for young mothers may not be applicable to elderly people.

All who have surveyed this debate have been led to comment on the vast variety of measures employed to reflect social support, ranging from one item in a questionnaire to intensive interviews lasting several hours. Disputes still continue as to which elements of social support, under what conditions, produce what effects for whom. The concern of many of the studies to investigate the effects of potential stressors has led to a widespread use of various life-event check lists. This gives rise to possible problems of confusion with measures of social support since many threatening life events such as divorce or bereavement themselves reflect changes in a person's social network and likely support resources (Starker, 1986). Those cross-sectional studies which do show associations in the expected direction suffer from the difficulty of inferring causality and it is argued that where baseline data become available, previously observed correlations are invariably weakened (Broadhead et al., 1983: 523), and may sometimes disappear entirely. As Depue and Monroe (1985) point out, even where one has longitudinal measures, individuals are not randomly assigned to, for example, high-stress, low-support conditions; other variables such as personality or social competence (Sarason and Sarason, 1985a) or a tendency to be dissatisfied (Henderson, 1984) are likely to affect both one's capacity for building and maintaining social support and the likelihood of developing depressive symptoms. Barrera (1986) reminds us that a crisis is likely to increase the amount of support mobilised (enacted support), but that depression may cause a person to evaluate more negatively the support they receive. Thus it is conceivable that a measure of enacted support might show an increase, at the same time as a measure of perceived adequacy showed a decrease, and an undifferentiated global functional measure might consequently suggest no change.

MEASUREMENT OF SOCIAL SUPPORT

One approach to the measurement of social support has been to use *broad indicators* of the presence of social ties, such as marital status or membership of voluntary associations, which may give an idea of quantity and range of contacts. It has been suggested that this approach is linked most closely to the concept of social support as integration or participation in society (Gottlieb, 1981) or to social embeddedness (Barrera, 1986). Of course, such broad-brush measures might encompass aspects of social support such as intimacy and con-fiding indirectly by, for example, using existence of a spouse as a measure. The rationale for such measures is that they give an indica-tion at least of potential support resources, although it has been argued that there is evidence to suggest that there may not be a high degree of association between the number of a person's ties and the functional support they receive (Cohen and Wills, 1985: 315). Never-theless, these crude measures have been demonstrated to be associated with health outcomes. Berkman and Syme (1979), in a large-scale epidemiological study (involving over 6000 people) showed that age and sex-specific mortality rates over a nine-year period were related to a Social Network Index (based on marital status, contact with family and friends, church and other group affiliations) in such a way as to show a consistent pattern of increased mortality rates associated with progressively lower rates of social connection. The effects were found to be greater for women than for men (Berkman, 1984).

Blazer (1982) studied mortality risk specifically among people aged 65 or older during a 30-month period. The social support measure included numbers of roles and attachments available; frequency of interaction with friends and relatives and perception of social support. Impaired perceived support appeared to show the greatest effects on mortality, followed by numbers of attachments. Blazer notes that his measure of perceived support is a subjective appraisal of adequacy rather than an objective characteristic of the person's social network. Perceived support has usually been shown to be more closely associated with outcome, but this leads us directly to the problem of intervening variables such as personality or mental state. Blazer (1983) also found that persons initially showing depressive symptoms had more support at follow-up, which might be a consequence of network mobilisation, or, if the improvement was in perceived support, a consequence of some improvement in their condition.

These *macro-level studies* provide little enlightenment as to how social support operates, and which aspects of it exactly are health protective, or in what degree. Certainly such detailed understanding is essential to those who wish to engage in the planning of interventions. The *micro level* of approach to measurement (Gottlieb, 1985b) reflects a belief that social support essentially stems from the quality of social ties, and therefore concentrates on the quality of particular relationships in terms of intimacy and attachment, rather than the quantity of connections to people and organisations that a person may have. At an early stage, Lowenthal and Haven (1968) demonstrated that good health and high morale among a sample of elderly people were associated with the presence or absence of a confidant, and that this was more important than the sheer number of social contacts. Brown and his associates have developed a complex model of the factors governing the onset of depression in mothers of young children, involving the identification of vulnerability factors in the lives of the individuals, and provoking agents in the form of various life events. They stress the importance of the quality of the marital relationship for those who are married, and of confiding relationships (not just people to whom one feels close) for single parents (Brown and Harris, 1984). Building on this work, Murphy (1982) has indicated the importance of confiding relationships in the prevention and remediation of depression among elderly people.

The Social Support measure developed by Brown uses an intensive interview lasting three to five hours and involving hundreds of interviewer ratings – Self Evaluation and Social Support Schedule (O'Connor and Brown, 1984) – but Henderson and his colleagues (Henderson et al., 1980), using the Interview Schedule for Social Interaction (ISSI), have been unable to find a protective effect for the onset of psychiatric symptoms under high adversity except for those support indices which reflect perceived adequacy. This latter association, they argue, may well be linked to personality factors (Henderson, 1984). Brown and Bifulco (1985) criticise the Availability Index constructed from the ISSI for placing insufficient emphasis on confiding, and suggest in general that the operational measure of attachment used by Henderson is inadequate, pointing out that the majority of studies using their methods have replicated their results. This debate is clearly not yet resolved, but Henderson (1984) and other commentators (Broadhead et al., 1983) have argued that properly evaluated intervention studies, which attempt to improve individuals' support and measure the effects, would be an important way forward.

Examples of measurement methods

North American studies of social support have been less likely to use interview-based measures, and more likely to use questionnaires designed for self-completion. One exception, the ASSIS (Arizona Social Support Interview Schedule) assesses perceived availability of support, but is unusual in also asking about negative interactions with members of the informal network (Barrera, 1981). The same author also designed the Inventory of Socially Supportive Behaviours, a 40-item instrument which focuses on the occurrence of support behaviours in the previous four weeks (that is, enacted support) under the general headings of tangible assistance, intimate interaction, guidance, feedback and positive social interaction. Cohen et al. (1985) offer the Interpersonal Support Evaluation List, another 40-item scale covering tangible support, appraisal support, self-esteem support and belonging support, asking not about enacted support but about perceived availability of these potential social resources if needed. Sarason et al. (1983) used the Social Support Questionnaire to assess both perceived availability, and degree of satisfaction with availability, of a range of potential coping resources.

As a last example, Vaux et al. (1986) have made the distinction between support resources (availability), supporting behaviours (enacted support) and appraisals (beliefs that one is cared for and respected), and have designed instruments to measure these. The scales for assessing availability as opposed to enacted support differ only by a change of wording from 'who would help . . .' to 'who has helped . . .' with a range of 45 items covering emotional and practical support. The SSA (Social Support Appraisals) Scale is a 23-item scale where the person has to indicate their degree of agreement or disagreement with items such as 'I am loved dearly by my family' or 'My friends look out for me'. The first two of Vaux's scales do distinguish whether the source of help is from family or friends but few of these global functional measures enable one to say anything specific about the sources of support nor about the structure of people's systems of supporters. Even such a basic feature as the number of people involved in helping may not be derivable from a scale which merely asks, 'Has (or would) anyone help . . .'. Reviews of many instruments designed to measure social support (including most of those mentioned in this chapter) can be found in Orth-Gomer and Unden (1987) and O'Reilly (1988). The former article assesses the contents, applicability, psychometric properties, generalisability and predictive capacity of 16 instruments (which rely on self-completion) designed to measure social support in population surveys and concludes that instruments which satisfy all requirements thought to be desirable could not be identified. The latter paper extends this type of analysis by examining the conceptual basis and the reliability and validity of 24 measures of social support and nine measures of social networks.

There are literally hundreds of studies of social support and its relationship to stress, and it cannot be said that the results are unequivocal. Some commentators have laid this apparent incoherence of results at the door of the vast variety of measures of social support. Cohen and Wills (1985) made a heroic, and partially successful, attempt to try to integrate and reconcile some of the conflicting results by suggesting that it was the integration/participation conception that was related to general well-being and would be expected to show direct effects, whilst emotional support, especially perceived support, would provide a buffering effect in the presence of high levels of adversity.

Perhaps the best hope for integrating ideas about quality and quantity, whilst not conflating social support with informal network, lies in various forms of network analysis.

Social networks

Bulmer (1987, Chapter 4) describes the genesis and development of network analysis from its early use in social anthropology through to a variety of current applications in sociology, psychology and other fields. Network analysis borrows from mathematical graph theory in representing a network as a set of points which may or may not be connected to each other by lines. A number of terms are then available to describe various structures which may emerge. For example, the degree to which each point is connected to every other point is generally termed density. If the network is centred on a particular person and maps their informal ties, then a language becomes available to describe features of structure of the network as a whole. Apart from size and density (connectedness), knowledge about the characteristics of people, or the links between them, can give rise to other aggregate concepts such as homogeneity (the extent to which network members are similar), clustering (the existence of connected groups within the network), geographical density (the proportion who live within a particular distance), composition (proportions of network members who have a particular link – for example, the proportion who provide practical support, or intimacy, or are kin) (Wellman, 1981; Pilisuk and Parks, 1985).

Network analysis has been criticised for emphasising form at the expense of content (Bulmer, 1985), but writers with a clear conception of network have been less likely to make unjustified assumptions about the congruence between support networks and informal networks, because they have seen the analytic power to be gained by treating support as a variable which may or may not occur (Wellman, 1981). As Bulmer (1987) points out, many studies in social welfare have used the word network in a loose metaphorical sense, with measurement if made at all typically consisting in asking for a list of significant others, perhaps with information about the content of each dyadic tie, whereas true network analysis requires information about connections between all members. Specht (1986) argues that density of networks is a significant additional dimension in influencing the likelihood that individuals will be able to achieve particular goals, and echoes Wellman's caution against normative idealisation of close-knit dense networks, given that a number of studies have suggested that such networks may inhibit individuals who need, or wish, to change their lifestyle, or may prevent people who might benefit from help from statutory services from seeking such assistance (Hirsch, 1981; Wilcox, 1981; Granovetter, 1973). Specht suggests that network density may be an important asset for people in life stages when they are highly likely to be dependent on others for support, but again the utility of different types of network seems likely to depend on what the dependent person wishes to achieve. One key dimension which may influence individual differences is gender.

Gender differences

Sarason and Sarason (1985a) report some preliminary results from a study of the relationships between personality and social support, which interestingly suggest that there may be gender differences in these relationships. With regard to gender differences in general, Vaux (1985) argues that the literature suggests that as compared to male peers, women have better social support resources and are superior in both providing and receiving support though they may be less satisfied with the support they receive. A range of studies have indicated that women have more close friends than men and emphasise intimacy and disclosure in their friendships.

Kessler et al. (1985) argue from a review of the literature that, across the life cycle, women establish small intimate friendship networks whilst men have larger networks in terms of numbers, but close relationships with a smaller number of people, usually, it is argued, only members of their immediate nuclear family. Kessler and his colleagues go on to say that men's smaller circle of concern may have the consequence that they are more devastated than women by the loss of their spouse. Widowhood has been shown to have far greater effects on the physical health of men than of women (Parkes et al., 1969; Berkman, 1984). Cohen and Wills (1985) argue that several studies suggest that different components of support may be effective stress buffers for men and for women. Support from a confidant seems to be more important for women, whilst Henderson et al. (1980) found measures related to acquaintanceship and friendship to be significant for men but not for women. Of course, in any investigation of gender differences in support, or support requirements, it is important not to attribute to gender differences the effects of real differences in circumstances. For example, the demographic structure of the elderly population is such that among those aged 75 or more most women are widowed whilst a majority of men are married.

Implications for practice

This chapter has echoed the criticisms, voiced by many authors, of the unrealistic belief that informal networks contain untapped resources which professionals can release (Allan, 1983). An alternative suggestion – that professionals should uncover natural helpers in the community and train them to improve their caring skills – has been dismissed as 'professional imperialism' by Gottlieb (1985b), who argues that we know far too little about which aspects of social support actually do help people to impose a particular method of approach in situations where it may not be effective or appropriate. Gottlieb (1985a) does advocate holding workshops for practitioners, in which consideration of their own networks and their functions may later enable them to engage in more informed and sensitive intervention in the networks of their clients. The work of Murphy (1982) on the importance of confidants for elderly people, and the findings that elderly people's satisfaction with their social support may not be strongly related to the size of their networks (Vaux, 1985), together suggest that practitioners should pay attention to the need to attempt to increase contact with specific people, as much as attempting to increase a person's range of contacts by introducing new people. If it is borne in mind that the members of an elderly person's network are embedded in networks of their own, which may well be making conflicting demands, it should be clear that it might be possible to release desired forms of help for an elderly person by offering assistance to other people in the network.

DEVELOPING THEORY AND RESEARCH

There seems to be less need to develop a comprehensive, once and for all, definition of social support, than for investigators to be clear about which particular aspects of such support are the focus of their interest, and to be sure that these are embodied in the measures used in such a way as to avoid confusion with other relevant concepts, and to enable different aspects to be measured independently. The wider perspective advocated by Wellman (1981; Wellman and Hiscott, 1985) which considers social networks and the processes by which they may or may not be supportive, and the kinds of activities or goals that particular types of networks will or will not support, would seem to be more fruitful as a basis for research than a narrow focus on support networks. We understand very little about the dynamics of support systems and, as Broadhead et al. (1983) have also argued, the role of social support as a dependent variable has been neglected. What are the factors which influence who does, and who does not, get social support? The influence of personality, norms, and structural factors in the wider society all require further investigation. Although some progress has been made (Vaux, 1985; Bulmer, 1987), there is scope for a range of comparative and descriptive studies investigating how social networks and social support vary among different ethnic groups, age groups, across social classes and within and between other population groups. Additionally, there is clearly room for more work on measuring the costs of social support as well as its benefits.

NOTE

The author would like to thank Margaret Flynn, Christina Knussen and Alan Tennant for their instrumental support in the form of access to numbers of articles on social support collected by them.

4

Quality of Life

BEVERLEY HUGHES

The concept of quality of life has played a central role in the evolution of social gerontology. It can be argued that concern about the quality of life of older people generated the questions within research, policy and practice which have led to the emergence of social gerontology as a discipline. And yet, perhaps because the concept was part of the birth process, its definition has become more complex and confused as the infant has grown and developed.

Over the past 20 years or so, a growing body of evidence has been gathered on both sides of the Atlantic about the experiences and circumstances of old people living in various settings (for example Townsend, 1957, 1962; Shanas, 1962; Tunstall, 1966; Tobin and Lieberman, 1976; Lawton, 1980; Evans et al., 1981; Tinker, 1984; Binstock and Shanas, 1985; Willcocks et al., 1987). In America the evidence was used to develop theoretical perspectives about what constitutes and characterises successful ageing. The most powerful theory to emerge in the early 1960s was disengagement theory (Cumming and Henry, 1961). Observing the low levels of role activity and social interaction amongst old people, Cumming and Henry argued that gradual disengagement from the mainstream of life was not only functional for society, releasing roles for younger people, but was also what older people themselves wanted. This 'rocking chair' view of old age defined successful ageing as the acceptance and adaptation to a quality of life in which the need for purposeful activity and social interaction was lower than that for younger people. Thus, disengagement theory implicitly justified the definition of quality of life for old people as different in some critical respects from that of the rest of the population.

Developments in Britain took a different path. Research by Townsend (1957) amongst others (Beveridge, 1942; Abel-Smith and Townsend, 1965; Tunstall, 1966; Hunt, 1978), revealed a disturbing picture of the poverty and poor quality of life of old people in the community and led to investigation of the care of old people in institutional settings, particularly local authority residential homes (Townsend, 1962; Crossman, 1962; Meacher, 1972). However, apart from one or two notable exceptions (Townsend, 1957; Tunstall, 1966), the research evidence was not channelled at that point into theoretical development as in America but rather precipitated further investigative research designed to chart in a detailed – and often graphic (Townsend, 1962; Tunstall, 1966) – way the various dimensions of the life experiences of old people and the impact of policy and services upon them (Peace et al., 1979; Evans et al., 1981; Townsend, 1981; Walker, 1981; Phillipson, 1982; Booth, 1985). The concept of quality of life was central to all of these investigations, but in an implicit and ill-defined way. The unifying notion was that the quality of life of old people was often very poor, that society in general and politicians in particular had failed old people and that the job of researchers and academics was, in this beginning era of social gerontology, to expose that failure. Thus, whilst research into the economic and social conditions of old people has been based implicitly on the fundamental importance of quality of life, there has not been an explicit debate amongst researchers and practitioners about how to define and measure the concept in relation to the lives of old people.

More recently, there has emerged within British social gerontology the strands of a coherent critical approach to understanding old age (Phillipson, 1982; Phillipson and Walker, 1986, 1987; Fennell et al., 1988). The critical approach argues that old age is a socially constructed experience and embodies two central principles. Firstly, it argues that the factors and criteria which define a good quality of life for older people are exactly those which apply, in general terms, to people of all ages. In this respect, critical social gerontology has at last provided a theoretical challenge to disengagement theory whose legacy has persisted for so long. Secondly, the critical approach accepts that the experience of old age is determined as much by economic and social factors as by biological or individual characteristics. Both of these principles have important implications for the definition of the concept of quality of life of old people.

In summary, although there has been, over the past 25 years or so, a growing concern within research and policy arenas with the quality of life of old people, neither within the research community nor amongst policy makers has there been a systematic attempt to clarify and define the concept or how it might be measured. Whilst the concept has been fundamental to the development of social gerontology, different studies have used different definitions and different instruments. This is at least in part because quality of life presents important conceptual, definitional and methodological problems for social gerontologists. The remainder of this chapter reflects on each of those different problems before attempting to introduce a possible framework for the operationalisation of the concept.

THE CONCEPT OF QUALITY OF LIFE

The concept of quality of life is multi-dimensional and has no fixed boundary. As with similar concepts of 'need', 'well-being' or even poverty (for example Mack and Lansley, 1985; Wilkin and Hughes, 1987), there is much room for debate not only about the *constituent elements* of the concept, but also about the *standard* for each constituent element below which the quality of life would be said to be unacceptably low.

Constituent elements

Various studies have brought together different combinations of elements to investigate the quality of life of old people in different environmental settings. Over a wide range of research, much of which has focused on the impact on old people of institutional environments, particularly residential homes (in Britain) or nursing homes (in the United States), the broad categories of elements included can be summarised as follows:

- *individual characteristics of old people*: for example functional abilities, physical and mental health, dependency, personal characteristics such as gender, race and class (Hunt, 1978; Abrams, 1978a; Evans et al., 1981; Willcocks et al., 1982a; Booth et al., 1983a, 1983b; Thompson, 1983; Phillipson et al., 1986; Wilkin, 1987).
- *physical environmental factors*: for example facilities and amenities, standard of housing, control over environment, comfort, security, regime in care settings (for example Pincus, 1968, 1970; Lipman and Slater, 1977; Evans et al., 1981; Willcocks et al., 1982a; Lawton, 1983; Willcocks et al., 1987; Hughes and Wilkin, 1987).
- *social environmental factors*: levels of social and recreational activity, family and social networks, contact with organisations (for example Felce and Jenkins, 1978; Felce et al., 1978; Gupta and Marston, 1979; Booth, 1985; Moos and Igra, 1980; Evans et al., 1981; Willcocks et al., 1982a).
- *socio-economic factors*: for example income, nutrition, standard of living, socio-economic status (for example Bonjean et al., 1967; Henretta and Campbell, 1978; Bosanquet, 1978; Townsend, 1981).
- *personal autonomy factors*: ability to make choices, exercise control, negotiate environment (for example Tobin and Lieberman, 1976; Evans et al., 1981; Clough, 1981; Willcocks et al., 1982a).
- *subjective satisfaction*: the quality of life as assessed by the individual old person (Willcocks et al., 1982a; Willcocks, 1984; Kellaher et al., 1985; Wilkin and Hughes, 1987).
- *personality factors*: psychological well-being, morale, life satisfaction, affect, happiness (for example Bradburn, 1969; Bigot, 1974; Morris and Sherwood, 1975; Lawton, 1975; Neugarten et al., 1961; Wilkin and Hughes, 1987).

Standards

For any particular element, there also has to be a decision about the standard at which quality of life will be assessed as poor, acceptable or good. Although it is not difficult, per se, to define in an *a priori* way that, say, below a certain level of income an acceptably good quality of life cannot be achieved, the difficulty lies in the ability for researchers, and people in society generally, to reach a consensus on what that particular level should be. And yet without a degree of consensus, the ability of research to make progress through time, for studies to build upon each other, for findings from different studies to be compared and contrasted, is severely restricted.

The concept of quality of life, however, is more than that of, say, 'standard of living', although standard of living would be one element of the quality of a person's life. 'Quality' cannot be reduced to a series of objectively defined standards, nor can it be encompassed entirely by subjective satisfaction expressed by the individual. On the one hand, it must be grounded in theoretical constructions of ageing, but it also relies upon normative judgements of either the researcher or the researched. It is a multi-dimensional concept which has to be conceptualised as a matrix, or network, of interrelated elements whose integration determines the overall quality of life for a particular individual. The task facing social gerontologists is to define and operationalise that concept in ways which make it a simpler task to assess an individual's quality of life and make comparisons with the lives of others in similar or different settings. There can be no single way of defining and measuring quality of life which is applicable to all types of research. However, the concept offers social gerontology a rich vein for progress not only in knowledge about old people but also in the development of theoretical constructs and research methodology, provided the definitions and methodological problems can be addressed in a systematic way.

DEFINITION OF QUALITY OF LIFE

> On the whole, social scientists have failed to provide consistent and concise definitions of quality of life. The task is indeed problematic, for definitions of life quality are largely a matter of personal or group preferences; different people value different things. (George and Bearon, 1980: 1)

The concept of quality of life has also been used as the basis of research at very different levels: firstly, within theoretical research, largely American, to develop hypotheses about what constitutes successful ageing (for example Cumming and Henry, 1961; Havighurst, 1968); secondly, within applied research, to assess the status and needs of old people (for example Hunt, 1978; Townsend, 1981; Walker, 1981); and thirdly, within policy and practice agencies, to develop, evaluate and improve service delivery (Evans et al., 1981; Tinker, 1984; Booth, 1985; Willcocks et al., 1987), and assess output or outcome of particular service inputs (for example Peace, 1987).

> Quality of life is thus a concept which serves the interests of the basic scientist, the applied research investigator and the service practitioner. It has relevance to both social science theory and social policy. (George and Bearon, 1980: 6)

The particular definition of the concept for any one of these different purposes may vary, or at least, may emphasise to different degrees the various elements within the conceptual network. For example, in research designed to investigate the definition of successful ageing, the researcher might place great emphasis on the subjective assessment by the individual of the quality of her or his life. However, in a study whose aim was to compare the quality of life of individuals in a sample population, heavy reliance on subjective assessment may undermine the comparative design.

The definitional issues which need to be addressed derive in part from the problem of integrating objective and subjective elements and, indeed, of determining which elements ought to be included. However, these particular problems are compounded by two further issues: firstly, the relative lack of a well-established theoretical base about human ageing in a social context, and, secondly, the way in which cultural factors such as race, gender and class mediate definitions of quality. This section examines each of these issues.

Objective and subjective dimensions

'Life quality includes both the *conditions* of life and the *experience* of life' (George and Bearon, 1980: 2; my emphasis). The integration of objective and subjective elements within the boundary of a single – albeit multi-dimensional – concept has been recognised as a fundamental problem in the definition and measurement of quality of life (George and Bearon, 1980). Whilst most researchers have acknowledged these two dimensions, there has been disagreement on their relative importance. In relation to the experiences of people with a mental handicap, for instance, Beswick and Zadik (1986) argue that, quality of life 'is an individual subjective concept'. Thus, its measurement 'should identify individual – even idiosyncratic – needs, the relative subjective importance of those needs and the extent to which a person feels they are being met . . . . It follows that it may be illogical to try and develop meaningful group measures of quality of life' (1986: 1). The work of Havighurst and his colleagues within social gerontology has, to some extent, endorsed this stance with the implicit assumption that quality of life can be wholly or largely defined and measured by life satisfaction indices (Neugarten et al., 1961; Havighurst, 1968).

However, to abandon the application of the concept to group populations entirely on the grounds of the difficulty of integrating its objective and subjective elements would be to deny gerontological research vital evidence of how the elderly population fares in relation to other sections of society and, indeed, how quality of life varies between different groups of old people, across time or across cultural and ethnic factors.

Theoretical dimensions

Whilst the relative importance of objective and subjective elements of 'quality of life' is an issue that cannot be resolved in any absolute way, the difficulty in applying the concept of quality of life to old people is compounded by the absence of an agreed-upon body of theoretical knowledge of human development in old age. The biological, psychological and medical constructs of human ageing have almost exclusively been concerned to chart degenerative, as opposed to adaptive and developmental, progress. Biological and medical theory has tended to confirm a construct of ageing as a time of decline and decay. This is in marked contrast, for example, to the theoretical constructs of childhood and adolescence where patterns of normal development have been charted, resulting in well-established and broadly agreed definitions and milestones of normal development, within a broad range. The establishment of theoretical bases of this kind are important to provide an infrastructure upon which can be – and have been – developed ideas about the conditions of life which are either essential or preferable to maximise a child's potential for normal development.

Thus, whilst children themselves and their immediate carers will have important views on the quality of their lives, researchers and social policy makers have felt sufficiently secure to appraise the lives and experiences of children as much in relation to objective criteria, derived from theoretical constructs about child development, as to subjective indicators.

Social gerontologists have had no such theoretical construct of human development in old age apart from those which have focused on the pathology of ageing and which have, in so doing, reinforced the largely negative stereotype of old people which has been part of Western cultures in recent times.

Cultural dimensions

The impact of cultural experience upon quality of life is considerable and researchers must take this dimension into account both in designing research instruments and in interpreting data. Personal characteristics such as class, race and gender are powerful intervening variables which will have a determining effect not only on the conditions of life people experience but also on their expectations and values and thence upon their subjective views of what constitutes 'good' or 'bad' quality of life. Indeed, one can argue that age itself will also be an intervening variable in that people of different ages in the same culture, with different historical experiences of life conditions and social attitudes, will define quality of life differently. Faragher (1978) has emphasised the importance of this issue for the current generations of old people, whose experience of deprivation and hardship during war years, of the development of welfare provision within the punitive ideology of the Poor Law is likely to result in expectations which are much lower than those of people, yet to become old, who have experienced a society with richer and more comfortable conditions of life.

The negative social construct of old age, outlined by Phillipson (1982), has not only obscured the positive aspects of old age, but has also, in its uniform greyness and pessimism, presented a false image of homogeneity amongst the elderly as a social group. Thus, the idea that old age itself is the great leveller, the most powerful determinant of quality of life, has become deeply entrenched in Western ideology and has served to obscure the connection between poor quality of life in old age and the economic and social conditions which affect people throughout their lives. The political and economic factors which cause poverty in old age for some social classes are denied, whilst the condition of old age itself is defined as the problem. Thus, not only does this view fail to acknowledge the evidence of a wide range of quality of life amongst old people (see for example Townsend, 1981), it has also prevented examination of the impact of class, race and gender on quality of life in old age.

Sociologists have continued to chart, with dramatic and powerful evidence, the way in which social class variables influence both the objective and subjective elements of quality of life (Townsend, 1981; Walker, 1981). Indeed the likelihood of ever reaching old age is five times lower for unskilled manual worker males than for professional men in social class 1 (Bosanquet, 1978). In so far as ageing for some individuals may result in disability (and, of course, the incidence of disability amongst old people is itself class-related) then clearly a person with the material and financial resources to compensate for that disability is likely to have, overall, a better quality of life than a disabled person in poor housing with low income and no social support network.

Factors such as gender and race will also influence the material conditions of life adversely, relative to white males, and, indeed, the relatively poorer conditions which women and black people experience throughout life will inevitably be carried into, and be compounded by, old age (Glendenning, 1979; Phillipson, 1981; Peace, 1986; Fennell et al., 1988). However, the social experience of being a woman or a black person, in a society which has particular social attitudes to those groups, will also affect people's self-images, expectations and desires. Their respective definitions of quality of life, and their assessment of what constitutes 'good' quality of life, will be influenced profoundly by these factors.

MEASUREMENT

A model of quality of life

The remainder of this chapter is concerned with developing a possible model of the concept of quality of life. My purpose is not to propose a definitive model but rather to seek to establish some of the principles and theoretical constructs upon which a model could be built and thereby to initiate debate which may catalyse the development of a more systematic approach to quality of life within the research community.

Principles

There are two basic principles which have informed my thinking during this process of developing a model. Firstly, any model or definition has to recognise the multi-dimensional nature of the concept. It has to address the issues of objective and subjective elements. It has to identify a theoretical base and also be sufficiently flexible to accommodate important cultural variables. Secondly, therefore, there can be no single definition which can be applied universally. We are seeking, then, a multi-dimensional model which encompasses all major elements or components in its definition of quality of life. However, through the process of development, the aim should be to identify those key components (and valid ways of measuring them) which are central and universal.

Establishing a theoretical base

The theoretical constructs I propose are those which have been articulated by Phillipson and Walker (1986, 1987), Townsend (1981) and others and which could be brought together under the umbrella of critical social gerontology. The fundamental hypotheses of this theoretical approach could be summarised as follows:

- The social construct of ageing – ageism – reflects social and political values which present old age in a negative stereotypical image.
- Ageism has not only contributed to the *experience* of old age of individual people but has also shaped and determined, to varying degrees, all aspects of social policy towards old people at national and local levels.
- Ageism has therefore been a major influence on quality of life via two routes. Firstly, ageism has influenced the nature of services and conditions of life of old people at the level of policy, and, secondly

it has determined, in part, the expectations and experiences of individual old people.
- The existence of ageism has to be seen as a product of the economic and social system from which it emerges.

Propositions
The acceptance of the tenets of critical social gerontology as a theoretical base allows us to derive a set of propositions which become the foundation of both the definition of quality of life and the development of operational research methods. The main propositions are:

1. Quality of life for old people has to be defined in similar ways to that of younger people. Thus, this proposition rejects the view implicit in disengagement theory, that the nature of the quality of a good life for old people is intrinsically different to that of the rest of the population.
2. Definitions and investigations of quality of life of old people have to accommodate two contradictory positions. On the one hand, it is important to acknowledge that the experience of old age itself, in an ageist society, will run common, shared threads through the lives of many old people. On the other hand, we must reject the view that old age is the great leveller and acknowledge that other factors pertaining to a person's whole-life experience are crucial in determining quality of life in old age. The synthesis, or articulation, of these contradictory positions is a difficult but important task.
3. Definitions and investigations of quality of life have to include both objective and subjective criteria. However, there can be no *a priori* assumption of the relative importance of these two sets of criteria, and, indeed, it has to be accepted that the two dimensions are related, in that the *conditions* of life influence the *experience* of life and therefore expressed satisfaction.

A model of quality of life
The purpose of a model is to portray the concept of quality of life as it emerges from the principles, theoretical bases and propositions already identified. The definition of quality of life must comprise a multiplicity of factors in some relationship to one another. The model which best fits the proposed relationship, I believe, is that of a network – an interacting system of factors which together define and assess quality of life. The factors, however, are not random, but could usefully be linked, within the overall network, into sub-systems. Figure 4.1 illustrates the model.

Figure 4.1 illustrates the view that quality of life is comprised of a range of constituent elements, each of which is a sub-system of related factors, and all of which are related directly or indirectly to one another through the network. It would be a futile and spurious exercise, I would argue, to reduce the assessment of quality of life to a

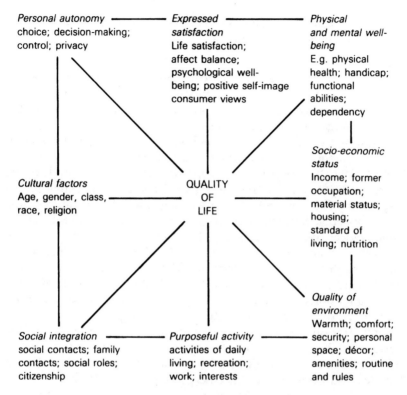

Personal autonomy ——————— Expressed ——————— Physical
choice; decision-making;   satisfaction   and mental well-
control; privacy   Life satisfaction;   being
                                affect balance;   E.g. physical
                                psychological well-   health; handicap;
                                being; positive self-image   functional
                                consumer views   abilities;
                                                        dependency

                                                        Socio-economic
                                                        status
Cultural factors   QUALITY   Income; former
Age, gender, class, ———————   OF   ———————   occupation;
race, religion   LIFE   material status;
                                                        housing;
                                                        standard of
                                                        living; nutrition

                                                        Quality of
                                                        environment
Social integration ——————— Purposeful activity ——————— Warmth; comfort;
social contacts; family   activities of daily   security; personal
contacts; social roles;   living; recreation;   space; décor;
citizenship   work; interests   amenities; routine
                                                        and rules

Figure 4.1 *A conceptual model of quality of life*

single indicator by summating the sub-systems in one way or another. Rather, in using the model, researchers need to investigate and report on the sub-systems themselves, building up information and developing methodology, and attempting to identify a set of key indices which appear, over large samples, to explain most of the variance observed. Other studies could usefully investigate connections and relationships between the different sub-systems. For example, a study investigating cultural factors, social integration and expressed satisfaction would yield important information about a number of objective and subjective dimensions of quality of life, as well as progress in establishing sound methodology for the collection of information on social networks, support networks, social roles as well as attitudes.

This approach involves resisting the temptation to reduce the complexity and multi-faceted nature of this concept to a single factor analysis, and requires a qualitative *approach* to research, although not an exclusively qualitative methodology for investigation of every single element. The approach inevitably involves researchers themselves in making qualitative (i.e. value) judgements not only in answering difficult methodological problems, but also in interpreting data. It is important that researchers do not shrink from this task but that such judgements are made explicit so that their usefulness in developing theory can be evaluated by others.

Methodology

The definitional questions and the operationalisation problems are not, of course, resolved by producing a model. This is rather a first step in generating a more consistent and systematic approach to quality of life across the range of empirical studies.

The next steps would be concerned with clarifying the elements of each sub-system and developing more standardised methods of collecting data. It is beyond the scope of this chapter to evaluate all existing methods and identify new methodological directions for all sub-systems of factors which are encompassed by quality of life. Indeed, this book contains chapters which examine in some detail the methodological issues pertaining to some of these factors (see Chapters 1, 2 and 3). As a further aid the section 'Constituent Elements' of this chapter has summarised some of the most important research studies which have developed instruments to assess the various dimensions of quality of life, although most of these have been concerned with old people in institutional settings.

My intention in this section is to explore the *process* by which the researcher might seek to translate any one of the sub-systems into a number of operational indices, and to illustrate the methodological difficulties and decisions which emerge along the way.

Taking the sub-system, Social Integration, as an example, the process begins by identifying those factors which together could describe a person's degree of social integration. Let us suppose that *social integration* comprises a person's *social networks*, *social roles* and *social rights and responsibilities*, as in Figure 4.2.

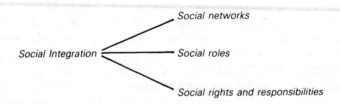

Social networks

Social Integration

Social roles

Social rights and responsibilities

Figure 4.2 *Operationalising the model: stage one*

The formulation of such a definition even at this stage inevitably involves selection and judgements. The second stage of the process involves translating each of the identified factors into operational indices. For example, we may decide to develop the definition of social integration as shown in Figure 4.3.

Finally, the third stage involves deciding how each factor will be measured and it is at this stage that the difficulties of decision-making

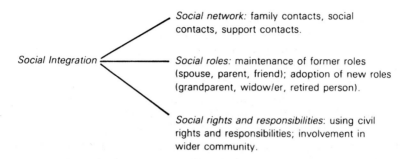

Social Integration

Social network: family contacts, social contacts, support contacts.

Social roles: maintenance of former roles (spouse, parent, friend); adoption of new roles (grandparent, widow/er, retired person).

Social rights and responsibilities: using civil rights and responsibilities; involvement in wider community.

Figure 4.3 *Operationalising the model: stage two*

are brought into especially sharp relief. Consider, for example, how the factors, 'family contacts' and 'social contacts' might be measured. At the simplest level, numbers of contacts is one obvious indicator, but even at this level there are questions as to what constitutes a social contact. Could the weekly call by the milkman for payment or the monthly GP visit be included as part of a person's social network? If a daughter/son calls in three times a week, but stays for only 10 minutes, is that sufficient to be classed as a family contact?

Already, it is clear that issues of *quality*, as well as number, are important in measuring these indices and qualitative judgements have to be made in order to develop research instruments and interpret data. In Chapter 3, on support networks, Hazel Qureshi makes the point that dense, large networks are often considered best by professionals. However, in addressing some of the methodological decisions which face researchers, it is also important to base judgements of what is 'good', 'best' or 'ideal' upon the *meaning* of particular kinds of contact or support for the old people concerned.

Tunstall (1966) made a similar point, over 20 years ago, when he demonstrated that loneliness as experienced by the old person was often the result of desolation (that is, loss) rather than isolation, per se.

In order to address some of the theoretical and methodological problems presented in this and other chapters of this book, researchers need access to the accounts of different groups of old people of their experience of ageing and the aspects of life they value most in old age. In particular, we need the kind of data generated by biographical, life history approaches which illustrate the complex way in which factors are woven together, and the authentic significance of particular issues for particular individuals or groups.

The research tasks

The task of generating more systematic, and ultimately simpler, ways of defining and measuring quality of life begins to look hopelessly daunting when the complexity of the subject is examined in this detailed way. However, there are two tasks which can greatly assist these processes. The first involves the articulation of explicit theoretical principles within which development can be grounded, and it is this task which I have attempted to initiate in this chapter.

The second urgent task lies in empirical research and involves the generation of a much more thorough and comprehensive understanding of the views of both old people and of the wider population about the conditions necessary for a good quality of life in old age.

However, whilst *theoretically* there are important reasons for building upon the views of old people themselves, I have already indicated the *methodological* dangers of relying heavily on the subjective definitions of current generations of old people whose expectations, derived from their own histories, may be very low. Thus, in addition to the kind of studies outlined earlier, there need to be large-scale surveys amongst the whole population which could be used to generate a consensual picture (within broad limits) of what constitutes a good quality of life in old age. Mack and Lansley (1985) have advocated a similar approach to the definition of poverty in terms of a consensual view of need, derived by researchers (thereby involving judgements) but on the basis of both qualitative biographic and quantitative survey methods amongst samples of the population. Thus, they argue for 'a measure of poverty based on the social perceptions of needs' (1985: 37). In a similar way the model of quality of life presented in this chapter has to be articulated within the social perception of the quality of life of old people, derived by researchers from old people themselves and from other groups in society.

PART TWO

METHODOLOGICAL APPROACHES

Introduction

Interesting reviews of both methodological approaches and research design within social gerontology are found in *Old Age in Modern Society* (1987) by Christina Victor and *The Sociology of Old Age* (1988) by Graham Fennell, Chris Phillipson and Helen Evers. Taken together these texts provide the researcher with an overview of the wide variety of research methods commonly used, including small- and large-scale surveys, case studies, participant and direct observation, cross-sectional and longitudinal research, documents of life and secondary analysis of data sets. They also discuss a number of methodological issues: the nature of age differences inherent in our data; how we distinguish between age, cohort and period effects; and the diversity of the older population with regard to concerns over bias, reliability, validity, sampling and response rates.

While much of this ground will be touched on again in Part Two, the aim is not to provide a review of methods used or issues raised but to focus on areas of research methodology which have so far received less attention and which reflect the experiences of research in practice. The six chapters cover defining whom to study and sampling; experimental designs within evaluative research; an experience of ethnography in a geriatric unit; triangulating data or how we analyse and utilise data from multi-method research; the particular issues that arise when researching very old people and finally, how we do biographical research. What these six chapters have in common is that the authors, with the hindsight of experience, have all been able to step back from the basic description of method, technique or issue and offer their own commentary on the problems and pitfalls, advantages and disadvantages they have encountered within a variety of different types of methodological approaches.

In considering just whom to study, Graham Fennell seeks to 'show researchers the variety of routes to samples of elderly people and the merits of different forms of sampling for different types of information yield'. He notes that given the multi-disciplinary nature of social gerontology researchers will be influenced by their own disciplinary background in terms of methods used. However, putting aside such biases, he suggests that three factors should affect whom we study and why: the primary purpose of the research; the availability of resources, not merely financial, and the ease or difficulty of access to our subject. Only when these factors have been considered should decisions be taken on sampling. In the remainder of his chapter Fennell looks in detail at various forms of sampling – non-random and random – using examples from the research literature to explore why researchers have adopted certain strategies and to what effect. He also considers sampling within the bounds of ethnographical studies and the use of key informants. Finally, he reminds us of the value of both secondary analysis of other data sets as a precursor to carrying out 'new' research, and of panel studies for looking at processes over time, enabling us to disentangle the effects of cohort and age differences.

In Chapter 6 David Challis and Robin Darton discuss the use of experimental or quasi-experimental research designs when evaluating social care programmes. They begin with a review of developments in evaluative research and outline the production of welfare approach as developed within the Personal Social Services Research Unit at the University of Kent. Their chapter explores the advantages and disadvantages of the experimental design in relation to other forms of evaluation, and examines the limitations of the approach, both ethical and practical. They conclude with an extremely useful discussion of issues which arise during the implementation of experiments and quasi-experiments, looking at the influence of the choice of design; the relationship between project and research staff; the importance of feedback during the course of the project, and how control groups are maintained.

As outlined earlier, a great deal of research within social gerontology has been concerned with the lives of older people living in special settings, and Chapters 7 and 8 look at approaches to research within institutions. The relationship between the researcher and the researched is a central theme to Eileen Fairhurst's chapter 'Doing Ethnography in a Geriatric Unit'. The author offers a personal record of her own experiences of doing ethnography in one's own society from the setting up of the study, through fieldwork and on to recording and data analysis. Importantly, she explores the ethical dilemmas and consequences of having to confront disturbing and difficult situations during the course of observations on a geriatric unit. Here the researcher is faced with the everyday realities of life for old people in hospital and how the researcher reacts to this reality becomes an important part of the research. Fairhurst's very honest account raises a number of important questions concerning the dual role of ethnographer as both observer and participant in settings within their own society.

Methodological triangulation forms the focus of Chapter 8 where Leonie Kellaher, Dianne Willcocks and I consider how data from a national study of the residential life of old people has been analysed in order to maximise the value of a multi-method approach to data collection. The chapter explores the realities of analysing data from different sources. The complex nature of settings in which some old people live out their days is dependent on the interactions of residents, staff and others, and the environment itself, both physical and social. Here the emphasis is placed on understanding process as well as outcome within a study which demonstrates some of the features of pluralistic evaluation.

Chapter 9 also touches upon the lives of old people within special settings but only by virtue of their advanced age. Michael Bury and Anthea Holme provide a detailed account of the methodological issues raised by a study of people aged 90 years and over. Of particular interest are two areas. First, the painstaking procedures involved in establishing a representative population and sample of very old people in England. Second, the design of the interview used in the study and how it was administered. Here the authors consider how they handled problems of communication with people who were suffering from deafness or some degree of mental frailty. How the interviews were presented to respondents, indeed how they were approached, is discussed as well as the use of proxy interviews or joint interviews in cases where the old person needed a relative or member of staff to act as an interpreter. The meticulous attention to such aspects of methodology allow the authors to state with confidence that 'the ability to interview the very old, allowing for an inevitably higher incidence of severe memory loss, was comparable with that of inter-viewing younger age groups'. Indeed this chapter demonstrates clearly the importance of rigorous planning at each stage of the research process.

In the final chapter of Part Two Brian Gearing and Tim Dant reflect on 'Doing Biographical Research'. It has already been noted (p. 3) that the recognition of the value of older people's own subjective experience has been an important development in gerontological research since the mid-1970s. This chapter provides the reader with a valuable introduction to the origins of the biographical approach, its concepts and applications in terms of reminiscence, assessment and research methodology. The authors use examples from a number of studies with which they have been involved to explore how a bio-graphical interview is undertaken and how such data might be analysed. They raise a number of issues concerning how the approach can be used within applied research, and suggest strategies for its development in gerontological study and practice.

5

Whom to Study? Defining the Problem

GRAHAM FENNELL

Social gerontology is a multi-disciplinary field of study with a particular focus of interest rather than an academic *discipline* like psychology or sociology. As such, it is eclectic in its methods and data collection procedures, not dominated by a particular technique such as the experiment or the social survey. How can we best capture the nature of this gerontological interest? Although answers might be given that it lies in *ageing*, or *older people*, this does not either pinpoint the concern quite accurately enough or encompass the generality found within social gerontology.

While some gerontologists are concerned with ageing, they typically confine their interest to ageing in old age, or ageing from middle age onwards, rather than ageing over the whole life course. Similarly, while many gerontologists study older people, we must guard against so-called 'methodological individualism'; that is, the assumption that we can learn all we need to know by studying individual *people*. Some gerontologists will want to study topics which are more system-based, like the social construction of old age through the media or the impact of social policy; others will be interested in hospitals or residential care homes as social systems; yet others will approach matters from a historical perspective, perhaps examining the emergence of retirement over time. The best way of capturing the focus of social gerontology is to say it is concerned with *late* or *later* life (Gubrium, 1974; Marshall, 1986; Altergott, 1988) – not only people in later life but also the social institutions which particularly affect that period (such as retirement, pensions and welfare policy).

Most researchers are working with modest budgets and are restricted by considerations of time and money in their chosen focus and research method. Going by past form the typical researcher is likely to be a methodological individualist, gaining the information desired from a relatively small number of older people who are also typically located in residential care (Abrams, 1978b). However, we must always remember that the immense volume of research on old people in 'special settings' (Fennell et al., 1988) is partly an indication of the specialness or atypicality of the people in care – or of the situations which lead them into care. We should never, unreflectingly, sample from the nearest conveniently captive group of people for this may introduce biases into our study of which we are unaware: for instance, elderly people in residential care may differ in their marital status, age distribution and kinship networks from a random community sample (Townsend, 1962; Booth, 1985).

Two general formulations of what researchers do are to be found in Galtung (1967) and Bateson (1984). Galtung uses the concept of the *data matrix* to suggest that (whether or not they are consciously aware of it) researchers at the data collection stage set out to fill an empty box. One dimension of this box is given by the number of *units* studied (commonly – but not necessarily – individual people).[1] Another dimension is the amount of information collected in respect of the *variables* under study for each unit. A third dimension might be the resources available for the study, though this obviously affects other dimensions too. Once researchers know the size and shape of their box, they fill it with data: only then can analysis and writing begin. To illustrate types of study which are dimensioned in different ways, we might contrast opinion polls, perhaps carried out by means of computer-assisted telephone interviewing (CATI) – which takes a large number of people, ask them relatively few questions and perhaps report the results within 48 hours – and intensive life history studies, where relatively few individuals are interviewed but data is collected over a rich spectrum of variables and the researcher(s) may spend years analysing, thinking and reporting.

Bateson (1984) sees social research as purposive activity which involves the expenditure of resources. What purpose could this be, which justifies the resource expenditure? In Bateson's view (he is writing about survey analysis) the respondents inhabit a particular social milieu or milieux. They understand it well enough to operate within it, using commonsensical (unsystematised) knowledge. Bateson then posits another set of people (research sponsors, managers, policy-makers, readers) who want to know about these social worlds and employ researchers to penetrate them. Researchers make transparent the opaque commonsense knowledge with which the subjects operate and return with a codified and systematic version of it, making it accessible to those in a different milieu. Gerontology is replete with studies like this which try to convey to others the reality and meaning of older people's lives and activities, as we may deduce from titles such as *Older People and their Social World* (Rose and Peterson, 1965), *The Limbo People, A Study of the Constitution of the Time Universe among the Aged* (Hazan, 1980), *Number Our Days* (Myerhoff, 1978) – described as 'a triumph of continuity and culture among Jewish old people in an urban ghetto' – or *Idle Haven, Community Building Among the Working-Class Retired* (Johnson, 1971).

If researchers have any choice of research style, objective and method, they are bound to be influenced by their disciplinary background. The ideal of academic research – that the scholar, being perfectly acquainted with everything which has gone before, *decides*

what needs next to be done following his or her professional assessment of the state of knowledge and priorities (gently seasoned with a
whiff of personal interest and a nod towards personal capability) – is
somewhat remote from reality. At least three factors other than
personal interest and training affect whom we study and why.

The first is the broad *primary purpose* of the study, for instance
whether it would be regarded as descriptive, evaluative, insight-
generating or hypothesis-testing. Most studies in practice are a mixture
of all these in different proportions but simple description must come
first. Although studies are sometimes disparaged as 'merely descriptive', unless we can accurately describe and report back what we
observe (or unless we have a foundation in others' descriptions, on
which later types of research can be built) there is no basis for
constructing theories or testing hypotheses. For instance, to generate
hypotheses about who goes to day centres for elderly people and why,
we have to have an agreed definition and description of what a day
centre is (for instance, does the definition include social clubs; are
centres designated as 'for the blind' or some other category to be
included or not?). To compare time use and daily activities by older
people in different societies (Altergott, 1988) we have first to be able
to describe what people do with the time at their disposal in one
society. After this it is possible to classify time into various types, such
as 'necessary time' – devoted to eating, sleeping, personal hygiene;
'free time' – which people can allocate to leisure activities; and various
other sorts of time (Andersson, 1988).

An example of an 'insight-generating' type of study is that by Hazan
(1980) where, by spending time with elderly people, the author sought
to explore the feeling of time in old age. As a combined insight-
generating and hypothesis-testing study we might cite Phillipson's
early work on retirement (1978). Here the researcher's orientating
hypotheses were that the retirement experience for men might vary not
only with social class and the ability to 'carry over' life skills from work
to retirement, but also with their social environment. To test his hypotheses, Phillipson contrasted a group of retired architects with three
groups of manual workers in different locations – retired miners in a
former pit village; retired car workers in the 'affluent' suburb of Long-
bridge; and retired unskilled workers in a declining inner-city area.

A second factor influencing the decision as to whom to study is
resource availability. Anyone with experience of fieldwork will know
how expensive and time-consuming it can be, particularly when considering the ratio of unproductive calls to completed interviews. This
is one of the factors which exerts a pressure towards concentrated
locations (such as residential homes, sheltered housing schemes, day
centres) where the fieldworkers can feel fairly assured they will find
someone to study. To spend perhaps half a day travelling backwards
and forwards fruitlessly to an address without achieving an interview

– because the person is out, or unwell, or has unexpected visitors – creates tensions caused by the feeling of unproductivity and puts pressure on the fieldwork budget.

As well as resources in terms of time and money (which translate into how many people can be employed in the research, for how long and over what geographical area) we should remember other resources like special skills. To interview 'ethnic minority elders' (Fennell et al., 1988) may require either the command of a great variety of languages and dialects or the ability to work through interpreters (children sometimes help in this way, which can create dilemmas of its own). The Western model of the private person-to-person interview is a cultural artefact which may not be familiar to the subjects: some interviews will be conducted with a complete household, often with a male acting as speaker. To interview people with particular handicaps (those whose hearing is severely impaired, for instance, or whose concentration or short-term memory is failing) requires skill, experience and patience.

A third factor influencing decisions about whom to study is *ease or difficulty of access*. Certain sorts of institutions – like state psychiatric hospitals – have been regarded as 'closed' and difficult to penetrate, though fruitful work has been done by researchers who have penetrated the interior. Today, 'private' institutions such as private residential homes or private sheltered housing schemes may be more exclusive, more protective, harder for researchers to penetrate than those in the public domain. Certain forms of name list – which might be ideal for use as a sampling frame – may be closed to researchers: lists of people receiving pensions from the state, doctors' patient lists (which identify older patients for purposes of remuneration) and the identification of elderly people as ineligible for jury service on the electoral rolls.

From this it follows that there can be no single prescriptive model of the right sort of research or the right persons to study. Effective research projects need to be self-consciously designed, taking sensible decisions on the basis of the above factors. We may learn more from depth interviews with only a handful of older people carried out by a sensitive and well informed researcher or by simple observation of certain settings at particular times (Godlove et al., 1982), if our aim is an insight-generating study, than from a huge random sample contacted by a large team of interviewers. If, however, our aim is confident generalisation on the basis of which social policy can be formulated then extensive sampling to overcome selective bias is essential and it is to some sampling considerations that we next turn.

TYPES OF SAMPLING

Non-random samples

All researchers take samples, though they are not necessarily random representative ones. Two main types of non-random sample have been used in social gerontology: the first to consider is the quota type, often a sequential one. The defining characteristic of a quota sample is that the researcher decides in advance how many people of what type to study and stops when the required number is obtained. Alexander and Eldon (1979) contrasted 100 consecutive new admissions to residential care with 100 consecutive geriatric hospital admissions and 100 new lettings of sheltered housing tenancies, all in Southampton. Sidell (1986) selected for an intensive study of coping with senile dementia, 30 consecutive referrals to a team of psychogeriatric nurses and 30 to a social work team in adjacent counties.

Another method of quota sampling is to define a time period and examine whatever number of individuals present themselves within it. Isaacs et al. (1972) examined every consecutive admission from home to the Glasgow Royal Infirmary in one year (252 people). Way and Fennell (1985) analysed all the moves in one quarter of a year from sheltered housing to residential care among tenants of a major housing association operating throughout England (exactly 100, as it turned out). Such consecutive quota samples are presumed to be typical, unless there is reason to argue the number is too small or the time period too limited.

The second type of non-random sample, snowball sampling, has to be treated more cautiously. The idea conveyed by the term is that the researcher begins with a small quantity of subjects and asks them for additional contacts, so the potential sample size expands geometrically as it rolls along.

Snowball sampling has been adopted by researchers where they do not have ready access to the population under study and do not mind (indeed may positively wish) their subjects to have similar character-istics. Here, in effect, one begins with a particular elderly person or small group and asks, 'can you pass me on to someone you know – or other people like you who might have common interests?'.

The main risk with this (and it should not be exaggerated) is that the sample has a certain bias. The most notable example is the Kansas City study of disengagement by Cumming and Henry (1961) where the snowball sampling technique took the researchers to an overwhelm-ingly middle-class sample, because, by and large, people draw their friends from within the same social class rather than across class lines. A bias of this sort can distort the findings: 'disengagement' was postulated as a universal response to the ageing process, but perhaps the researchers were misled by contact with a self-recruited sample of middle-class disengagers.

Researchers can compound these problems and have to be open and clear about their criteria of inclusion and exclusion in sampling: it is not that choices *should not* be made, for they are unavoidable. However, the grounds for choosing whom to include and whom to exclude must be explicit and should not be arbitrary. The Kansas City researchers, for instance, excluded non-white and lower-class individuals who turned up in their snowball, on the grounds that they would require 'special interviewing techniques'. This might be true, but what if these excluded individuals were also, typically, not 'disengagers'?

In a highly segregated mass society, the people we know are likely to be similar to ourselves and we typically underestimate the sheer diversity to be found in the world 'out there' because it is socially invisible to us. One advantage of random sampling is that it forces the investigator to penetrate social worlds which would otherwise be closed and invisible.

Random samples

Let us imagine we want to carry out a small-scale descriptive investigation of 'elderly people'. Leaving for a moment the question of the *sampling frame*, i.e. whatever actual list one works from in drawing a sample, the issue of whether to use a *simple* or *stratified* random sample has always to be addressed. A simple random sample will tend to over-represent the 'young' elderly. If our implicit objective is to learn about 'old' age, we may need to stratify to ensure the older age groups are represented in adequate numbers. Similarly, if we want to distinguish the situations of men and women in old age, we may need to take special steps to ensure there are *enough* men to form the basis for generalisation.

One of the great strengths of the random sample survey is that – so long as the researchers overcome any tendency they may have to avoid fieldwork or devolve it to others – they are brought into contact with a wide range of people, whose existence they might otherwise never suspect or be able to imagine. In an early classic of English social gerontology, Sheldon makes this point:

> Perhaps one of the deepest impressions left in my mind after conducting the survey is the fundamental importance of the random sample . . . . It does not make for ease of working: all sorts of inaccessible personalities may be encountered, and it is more time-consuming; but the degree of self-selection imposed by the population on itself in regard to [other methods] inevitably gives anything other than a random sample a considerable bias. (1948: 8)

One of the apparently simplest types of random sample is where researchers are concerned to describe and analyse the distribution of various social forms, activities and patterns among elderly people as a whole. A classic example is Peter Townsend's study of *The Family Life of Old People* (1957); another more recent example is Clare Wenger's *The Supportive Network* (1984). How did they draw their samples?

Townsend was interested in discovering the family patterns and relationships of elderly people and also the distribution of what might be regarded as the obverse of that, social isolation and loneliness. Hence he simply required a representative sample of elderly people: it was not necessary to establish in advance whether or not they had families, since part of the object of the investigation was to establish the distribution of what might be regarded as kinship resources.

Townsend first took one defined geographical area (Bethnal Green), subsequently countering critics who thought this an untypical area by demonstrating the consistency of his findings with those resulting from other samples (1963). He selected nine GPs at random from a list of practices in the borough and asked if he could sample addresses of older people in their records. Since approximately 98 per cent of the population are registered with GPs, this is likely to provide a good sampling frame for many purposes, though it will tend to exclude those in large residential institutions or hospital, people of no fixed abode or those 'on the move' between areas and not yet registered.

Two of the nine doctors refused to cooperate, introducing an unquantifiable – but in Townsend's view – unimportant, bias. Two hundred and sixty-one names of possible respondents were selected. Of these, ten refused to be interviewed, ten were in hospital or ill at home, and thirty-eight had died. This elegant solution to the problem is not, however, open to researchers today, since the Department of Health has ruled that doctors' lists of patients are confidential (though doctors themselves, of course, can use them if they wish to research their own practice).

Where resources nowadays permit, the best way to overcome this problem is the two-stage screening sample. In Stage I, a complete door-to-door census is carried out to screen addresses containing an elderly person or persons; in Stage II, a random sample is drawn from the sampling frame generated by the first-stage screening process. This type of approach was adopted in Wenger's study in North Wales. The researchers first selected eight rural settlement types:

> Ranging from small nucleated towns (under 3,000), including two small seaside resorts with high proportions of retirement migrants, to a highly dispersed sheep-rearing area. The communities, on a wide range of outcome variables, demonstrate a high degree of similarity, the main differences being between incomers and long-term residents . . . . A door-to-door census of occupied households, using rating assessor's lists, was conducted . . . (which) . . . made it possible to collect basic background data on *all the elderly* so that any subsequent sample could be checked for sampling error. (1984: 5)

Among the data gathered at this first stage was information on the preferred language used in the household – nearly three-quarters of the sample in Stage II were interviewed wholly in Welsh.

Another use of the screening sample is where a particular type of second-stage characteristic is required. A good example is Tunstall's *Old and Alone* (1966). In contrast to Townsend's study mentioned earlier, Tunstall wanted to investigate only various types of social isolation, aloneness, being alone or feelings of loneliness: to interview the majority of elderly people (who do not experience these phenomena) would be a waste of resources. Tunstall's sample was selected in the wake of a larger one used for the cross-national study reported in Shanas et al. (1968).

Here, names and addresses of males and females aged 65 and over were drawn at random from the lists of 16 GPs in four contrasted areas of England. Of 20 GPs originally approached, four refused to help (three of them in one area – Harrow). Six hundred and ninety-six names were selected for screening interviews, the number completed (538) being reduced by deafness, illness, non-contacts and refusals. Tunstall selected 217 for reinterview by himself alone and there was further loss due to deafness, illness and refusals: 195 interviews were achieved with people identified at the screening stage of being in 'at risk' categories. These were people who were single, recently widowed, housebound, had low social contact scores or who said they were 'often lonely'. (Some of these categories of course overlap.)

Any sample based on 'community' records will exclude between 2 per cent and 5 per cent of people living in residential and hospital care. In addition we should be aware of the alleged 'systematic exclusion' of up to 20 per cent of elderly people in all social surveys, by reason of direct or proxy refusals or unavailability on account of illness or infirmity. Streib (1983) argues in his review of research that failure to recognise and overcome this omission of frail and housebound elderly people is 'one of the noticeable shortcomings'. He suggests that researchers tend to regard the ill or people who are otherwise difficult to interview as 'out of scope' of their samples and calculate non-response only on the narrower band of 'in-scope' contacts.

Two more approaches to sampling of a somewhat more complex type may briefly be considered. Willcocks et al. (1982a and b) wished to achieve a representative sample of 100 local authority residential care homes and, within them, to select ten residents and four staff members in each home. The procedure is described in detail in methodological appendices to the study. A sampling frame of *homes* was first constructed using three sources – the Department of Health and Social Security database on homes based on RA2 returns; postal questionnaires about each home sent to the local authority; and further information from individual homes. In sampling from this database, the researchers incorporated various stratification criteria. These included size of home, type of local authority, whether or not the premises were purpose-built and the regime in the home.

Having selected their sample of 100 homes, a second sampling frame was constructed by listing all the permanent *residents* in the homes and drawing a systematic random sample from this list. (In a systematic random sample, the first name is selected by a random procedure and subsequent selections drawn at a fixed interval to achieve the target number.)

The requirement in Fennell's study of Anchor sheltered housing (1986) was a sample of tenants which was nationally representative, stratified by variables which might relate to tenant satisfaction – such as scheme size – and clustered for cost-effective use of interviewer time. In this case, the Housing Association supplied a complete list of sheltered housing schemes, identified by region and scheme size. Four size bands of schemes were identified and different sampling fractions used in each band. Within each size band every scheme had an equal probability of being selected, but larger schemes (being rare) were relatively over-sampled, to ensure that at least some examples were selected. Selection of tenancies was varied according to scheme size, so that in the smallest schemes one in two tenants was selected and in the largest, one in five. Where a flat was occupied by two people, interviewers were instructed to interview a husband at one flat, a wife at the next, alternately; or in the case of other pairs, the first-named or second-named person alternately (Field, 1985). Calculating sampling error in these more complex designs requires its own special expertise.

'Anthropological penetration'

Those using the observation or participant observation method of data collection are constrained in their sampling by the limits on what one observer can keep in view and by how possible it is to gain and maintain access. Participant observation has been broadly defined as 'a process in which the observer's presence in a social situation is maintained for the purpose of scientific observation' (Schwartz and Schwartz 1955: 344) and participant observers are recommended to 'find a role' which enables them to do this, though Wax (1972) cautions that such roles do not necessarily exist.

Successful examples include Erving Goffman, who worked as a part-time remedial gymnast in a state mental hospital of the type he later described as a 'total institution' (1961) and Arlie Hochschild, who studied a group of elderly widows (1973). Hochschild had the good fortune to be employed by the Recreation and Parks Department as an 'Assistant Recreation Director' in the block she wished to study and this legitimated her presence. She then hit upon the idea of collecting the widows' biographies for publication in a monthly newsletter, which permitted her to visit everyone and ask them questions which would otherwise be regarded as 'prying'. This role helped overcome one of the problems of participant observation, that access to some respondents may preclude contact with others in the group (Lupton, 1963).

The typical attractiveness of participant observation studies to the reader is the vividness of the descriptive writing to which they can give rise, the feeling that the researcher *really knows* the subjects and the sense of empathy which the report often conveys. Although examples can be found of participant observers who develop a sustained dislike of their subjects (Turnbull, 1973), this is unusual, for lack of rapport generally causes a study to peter out unreported.

Gold (1958) and Junker (1960) draw attention to the fact that observation studies may involve different degrees of 'participation' and 'observation' and that the objectives of the researcher may vary along a continuum from overt to covert. Whilst 'covert' observation clearly poses ethical problems for researchers, there may be subjects – such as physical, emotional or financial abuse of elderly people in relatively 'closed' settings – where other methods of social enquiry will be ineffective, but it is in the public interest for the facts to be brought to light (Robb, 1967).

Use of 'informants'

The use of key informants is perhaps more akin to journalism in Galtung's paradigm than to social research as commonly understood: relatively few people are sampled, but their word is accepted as authoritative. Here the rule of thumb is to stop sampling when the researcher can predict what the next answers will be (Bertaux, 1981). The objective is to understand a phenomenon in such a way that it can be accurately described to others: credibility based on scientific numbers is less important than the researcher being able to sustain the claim that further interviewing would yield little additional information. In random sampling, every individual counts equally but when informants are used, those who are more perspicacious, informative and talkative count more than the unobservant, unreflective and uncommunicative. The researcher's task is to locate the good informants and invest more deeply in them than in others.

Researchers making use of the 'focused' conversational interviewing technique are likely – at least implicitly – to lean in this direction, particularly if they make use of tape-recorded interviews. In writing up their studies the 'quotable quotes' are often drawn from a small handful of favourite interviews and it is from these that the insights are gained. The others in the sample are there to make up the numbers, to illustrate the typicality or untypicality of the informants and (often) because this was the only way the researcher could locate productive interviewees in the first place.

To produce informants other than by random sampling one might use a variant of the snowball technique. The researcher might begin with one or two potentially key informants (the secretary of a relevant committee, club or association, for instance; a local shopkeeper, publican or postmistress; a local councillor, member of the clergy or community worker) and ask, 'Who knows about this topic locally? Who would be willing to talk to me about this? Can you suggest anyone who is a fund of information on this subject?'.

Use of other data sets

It is often the case that the intention to carry out a field study precedes a review of the need for it. For instance, students at many different levels are required to carry out a small project as part of their training, or they themselves may wish to do so, to escape from the library and the classroom and meet some 'ordinary' people operating in the 'real world'. Experienced researchers, too, may wish to carry out a field study or receive a commission to do so. However, this chapter would be incomplete if we failed to point out that information may already exist, so that, in answer to the question, 'Whom to study?', our first thought ought to be, 'Is it necessary to study anyone at all – afresh and at first hand?'.

Increasingly, research materials are being archived (for instance at the ESRC data archive at Essex University) and are available for secondary analysis. Nor should we merely think about studies directly concerned with elderly people. For instance, any random community sample such as *The British Social Attitudes Survey* (Jowell and Airey, 1984; Jowell et al., 1987) will contain elderly respondents. So long as age is a recorded variable, elderly correspondents can be disaggregated for analysis and compared with other age groups. Examples of work involving focused reanalysis of secondary data sets include that of the University of Surrey team using data from the General Household Survey (Arber and Gilbert, 1989) or Mark Abrams' work using the four-volume study produced by the BBC Broadcasting Research Unit entitled *Daily Life in the 1980s* (1985). The potential value of such data sets may be deduced from Abrams' account:

> Using an aided recall technique, respondents were questioned about everything they had done on the preceding day; the 'day' covered 21 hours; and the questions dealt with respondents' activities in each quarter of an hour from 6:00 a.m. to . . . 2:59 a.m. The 'daily life sheet' sought information on 40 possible activities (counting 'sleep' as an activity) . . . (1988: 32)

Following the general principle of parsimony, if results can be obtained from existing data sets, this might seem preferable to commissioning a new field study, with its attendant delays. Imaginative use of secondary sources can throw light quickly on newly identified problems, as for instance 'the growing concern about the housing opportunities open to the increasing number of elderly people with "modest" incomes and/or capital resources' identified by Bull and Poole in their report, *Not Rich: Not Poor* (1989: 1).

An important proviso in making use of existing data sets is to know how the original samples were drawn and with what response. In general population surveys it is not uncommon for response rates to be less satisfactory among elderly people than other age groups. In a somewhat similar exercise in Norway to the BBC study mentioned earlier, the non-response rate was 42 per cent (Andersson, 1988: 101). If data from such a source is compared with other studies with non-response rate closer to the 10–20 per cent range, the researcher must do more work to check for possible biases between respondents and non-respondents.

Panel studies

Researchers are often interested in *processes over time*. We might be generally interested in the ageing process, wonder how later experience of retirement compares with pre-retirement expectations, or speculate about the success or otherwise of retirement migration as the years go by. These are all questions which can be studied at the level of the individual. Taking a different unit for analysis, concern is sometimes expressed that sheltered housing schemes inevitably 'age', creating difficulties for the solo warden; and general processes of population decline and regeneration have interested researchers in the theoretical and practical study of retirement communities and 'ageing in place' (Streib et al., 1985; Warnes, 1987; Fennell and Way, 1989).

Studying such processes suggests the use of panel or longitudinal studies and these may be particularly desirable for disentangling ageing from cohort effects. One type of design takes a 'panel' of respondents and, after an initial interview, contacts them again for repeat interviews at specified time intervals. In studies of ageing, such panels inevitably experience attrition – not only through the physical contraction of the numbers available for subsequent interview but also because people may refuse to cooperate or are lost to the panel through untraceable moves. One variant to cope with these problems is 'panel sampling with replacement', where new individuals are inducted to the panel at each stage, to replenish the numbers lost for whatever reason.

There are some noted panel studies in the United Kingdom, but chiefly in the field of child development (Newson and Newson, 1963, 1968, 1976; Douglas, 1964; Douglas et al., 1968) or follow-up work to determine the success of some form of 'treatment' – such as medical or social work intervention or a custodial sentence (Stimson and Oppenheimer, 1982). Longitudinal studies of ageing, though not unknown in the United Kingdom (Milne, 1985; Taylor and Ford, 1981,

1983) have not reached the development of the Duke or Gothenburg University studies in the United States and Sweden respectively (Palmore, 1981; Svensson, 1984). This may be because longitudinal studies require a planned resource commitment for many decades, unusual in British social science funding and perhaps because there has not hitherto been a sufficiently well-endowed and secure institutional base for such a study. Tentative and preliminary results can be produced periodically, but long-term longitudinal studies require an institutional commitment which is likely to outlive the productive career and indeed perhaps the interest of any researchers involved.

Some processes over time may be studied by access to records: for instance whether admission characteristics on entry to residential care change, particularly with the expansion of private homes, or even whether or not the aggregated proportion in care has changed over the centuries (Wall, 1984). The impact of women's mass induction into the factory work in the Second World War (and with it the exposure to new health hazards, such as smoking at work) is beginning to be discernible 50 years on in annual mortality analyses. However, such record analysis may be highly labour-intensive unless the data is kept in a form which makes it accessible to research enquiry.

CONCLUSION

If we compare the United Kingdom with the United States the 'ageing enterprise' (Estes, 1979) is still at the 'craft' level of production. The subject is not thoroughly institutionalised and is seldom characterised by the big-budget 'number-crunching' of much American work. Despite these resource limitations, the yield of British social gerontology has been surprisingly high and this may be attributable to the craftmanship of the different individuals who have contributed to it and the different disciplinary perspectives and opportunities they have brought to their work. The aim of this chapter has been to illustrate the potential gain from different answers to the question of 'whom should we study?', to show intending researchers the variety of routes to samples of elderly people and the merits of different forms of sampling for different types of information yield.

NOTE

1. 'Units' could be households, day centres, sheltered housing schemes, television programmes, column inches in newspapers, units of time in which observations take place and so forth.

6

Evaluation Research and Experiment in Social Gerontology

DAVID CHALLIS AND ROBIN DARTON

During the 1980s there has been a substantial reconsideration of the services provided to elderly people, accompanied by an increasing concern for the development of evaluative research into care services. Goldberg and Connelly (1982) identify five reasons for the importance of evaluation: public accountability, deployment of resources, effectiveness, cost-effectiveness, and safeguarding against over-enthusiasm for the new. Underlying the first four of these are cost pressures of the scarcity of resources and a concern with the three Es, of Economy, Effectiveness and Efficiency, associated with the work of the Audit Commission (1985). In relation to safeguards against the new, Cochrane (1972) gives examples from medicine of therapies which were introduced without proper evaluation and subsequently found to be ineffective or disadvantageous when subject to experimental evaluation and Gilbert et al. (1977) note that there may be resistance to studies of the effectiveness of treatments once they have become established.

The term 'evaluation' implies using criteria to make a judgement of the efficacy of a service or mode of care. Suchman (1967) has defined evaluation as 'a method for determining the degree to which a planned programme achieves its desired objective. Evaluative research asks about the kinds of change desired, the means by which this change is to be brought about, and the signs according to which such change can be recognised' (quoted in Goldberg and Connelly, 1982: 12). In other words, this requires clarity and specificity about goals or objectives, inputs and outputs (Illsley, 1980). In the natural sciences, the effects of well-defined interventions have been examined in controlled environments to build substantial bodies of scientific knowledge. In medical research the randomised controlled trial, or RCT, in which a random allocation procedure is used to assign experimental subjects to the different treatments under examination, has become a powerful technique for assessing the effectiveness of different treatments. Outside the controlled environment of the laboratory, the measurement of the impact of interventions is complicated by difficulties in defining inputs, outcomes and goals or objectives, and is exacerbated by a lack of basic descriptive information about problems, inputs and postulated outcomes (Goldberg and Connelly, 1982).

Firstly, the definition and separation of inputs is much more difficult outside a fully controlled environment (Goldberg and Connelly, 1982; Illsley, 1980). Secondly, outcomes may be multi-dimensional and require aggregation, taking account of their relative importance (Illsley, 1980), or there may be disagreements about appropriate outputs or no valid measures of outcome (Smith and Cantley, 1985). Thirdly, goals or objectives may be vague or unstated, or there may be ambiguities and confusion in an organisation due to differences in the objectives of different members or groups within it (Bulmer, 1986; Edwards et al., 1975; Smith and Cantley, 1985). Bulmer, Edwards et al., Illsley, and Smith and Cantley argue that rational models do not characterise the policy-making process within organisations, and that means and ends usually cannot be separated in the development and implementation of policies. However, the existence of different interest groups does not obviate the experimental approach (Challis and Davies, 1986; Davies and Challis, 1986). Although the implementation and evaluation of a programme within an organisation presents a range of problems, concentration on these may obscure the potential for evaluating the effects of the programme for individual clients, that is, process evaluation should be distinguished from outcome evaluation (Robertson and Gandy, 1983). The distinction between process and outcome is made clearly by Donabedian (1980), who distinguishes between the amount of resources or facilities available (structure), the way in which resources are used (process) and the effects of their deployment (outcome). In his discussion of needs and outputs, Davies (1977) distinguishes indicators of levels of provision, throughput and the effects of services, which broadly correspond to measures of Donabedian's concepts of structure, process and outcome. An essential aspect of effective evaluation research is the need to ensure that the methodology is sensitive to the inputs and outputs in question.

The definition of evaluation offered by Suchman omits the measurement of costs, as noted by Thomas (1988) and others, reflecting the separate spheres in which much work has been undertaken. Weiss (1972) notes that cost-benefit analysis is often viewed as an alternative to evaluation research, instead of a logical extension to it, and Challis et al. note that

> Evaluative research has conventionally focused almost exclusively on the *outcomes of alternative packages or programmes of care . . .*, to the neglect of the resources that make such care a possibility. At the same time financial appraisal has concerned itself, with equal myopia, with the resources and costs of services without consideration for the effects of such services on clients and their significant others. (1988b: 104)

The production of welfare model, described below, explicitly introduces the costs of inputs into an analysis of the relationship between inputs and outputs. However, in addition to the problems of subject discipline myopia and the need for clarity of evaluative criteria, problems also arise in differences of opinion on the meaning of the term itself (Smith and Cantley, 1988).

Bulmer (1986) distinguishes between descriptive, explanatory and evaluative research, in terms of the aims of the research, and discusses different research methodologies in terms of these three categories. During the 1960s and 1970s there was a substantial growth in the United States in the systematic evaluation of social programmes using social science research methods, which has become known as 'evaluation research' (Bailey, 1987; Bulmer, 1986; Kish, 1987; Rossi and Freeman, 1985; Weiss, 1972). Bulmer and Weiss both note that the ideal design for such evaluative studies is an experiment, although this is rarely realised in practice, and that a wider range of research designs needs to be employed to assess the impact of social programmes. Goldberg and Connelly (1982), Illsley (1980), Smith and Cantley (1985, 1988) and Webb et al. (1966) also recommend a broader approach to the definition of evaluation, using available methodologies to provide triangulating evidence about a research problem. As noted earlier, Goldberg and Connelly emphasise the importance of collecting sound descriptive information about a service as an essential prerequisite for evaluation. Descriptive studies are not restricted to providing basic information, however. Systematic monitoring, in which descriptive information is collected over time, enables service providers to examine whether plans are achieved, and thus move towards an evaluation of the service (Goldberg and Connelly, 1982). For existing services, cross-institutional designs (Sinclair and Clarke, 1981) employ descriptive techniques to compare and evaluate the types of provision within the service under consideration.

This chapter will be concerned mainly with prospective rather than retrospective evaluation, and particularly with experimental and quasi-experimental studies, which we shall refer to as examples of 'experimental evaluations', rather than with systematic monitoring. Experimental evaluations and systematic monitoring are capable of answering different questions, and complement each other.

Experimental and quasi-experimental evaluations involve the special collection of detailed information over a prescribed time period for more than one group of cases specifically identified as in receipt of different types of input. Systematic monitoring, on the other hand, uses data generated routinely as part of the day-to-day operation of an agency or a service. The experimental approach provides the means to tackle questions such as: 'What is the effect of service A upon elderly people and their families compared with service B?'. It can move further to answer an efficiency question such as: 'Which elderly people presenting with which problems are most effectively and efficiently cared for in service A rather than in service B?'. In contrast, monitoring can provide information about the characteristics of the users of a service, the types and levels of care provided to clients with different needs, and the costs of providing care. Such information can be used by individual workers to evaluate their work by examining aims and achievements, by agencies to plan services and to identify areas for further research and development, and for an examination of the extent to which individuals with similar characteristics and needs receive similar services within and between areas (Goldberg, 1981). Examples of the collection of such routine data include psychiatric case registers (Wing and Hailey, 1972), social work monitoring (Goldberg and Warburton, 1979), specifically of services for elderly people (Challis and Chesterman, 1985), and monitoring of the home help service (Gorbach and Sinclair, 1989). In addition, routinely collected monitoring data on large numbers of cases may be linked with specially collected small sample data, to maximise the yield from both data sets (Neill et al., 1988).

Experiments may be used to show whether different types of input have different effects on outcomes, but they do not explain why a particular outcome occurs (Achen, 1986; Goldberg and Connelly, 1982; Sheldon, 1988; Smith and Cantley, 1985; Thomas, 1988). Monitoring provides indicators of organisational process, such as activity or throughput, but is less able to provide measures of the effectiveness of specific interventions (Goldberg and Connelly, 1982). Only limited measures of outcome, such as destinational outcomes, are available in monitoring studies. A process evaluation is a poor basis upon which to draw valid conclusions about the relative merits of different approaches. The comparative study of social work with elderly people in three area offices by Black et al. (1983) provided evidence of different styles and approaches to helping elderly people, but the process data collected provided no basis for comparing the relative effectiveness of these approaches. Similarly, in the Care for Elderly People at Home Project conducted in Gloucester (Dant et al., 1989), process information and indicators of client satisfaction were collected, but only limited comparative information was collected. Experimental evaluations provide information on the impact of an intervention, whereas monitoring provides information on how it is implemented. Thus routinely generated data can provide information on processes and specially collected data can provide information on the outcomes or the effects of services. This is shown in Figure 6.1, which presents a simple model of an experimental evaluation.

As noted earlier, Goldberg (1981) suggested that routinely collected data may be used to identify further areas for research and development. In an ideal model of research an interactive process could be developed between these two methods of data collection. Questions arising from routinely monitored data could be answered through a specific experimental design. The results of the experiment could be used to specify desired norms, and the degree of conformity to these could be monitored as process indicators acting as performance

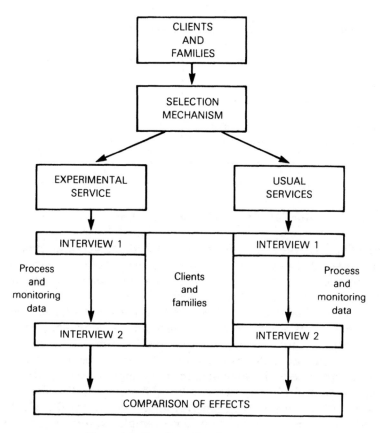

Figure 6.1 *Experimental evaluation*

indicators. The validity of such indicators would depend upon their level of association with desired outcomes, as measured in the experiment. Monitoring could also lead to the specification of further questions, new experimentation and so on.

AN APPROACH TO EVALUATION

As already noted, effective evaluation requires specification and clarity and understanding of the relationship between needs, inputs and costs, characteristics of service users and the effects of services upon them. The production of welfare approach, described by Challis et al. (1988b), Knapp (1984) and Davies and Challis (1986), provides a theoretical framework for analysing the relationship between these categories, and explicitly brings together the issues of cost and effectiveness. This approach provides a model of the relationship between resource inputs with their associated costs, non-resource inputs, intermediate outputs and final outputs, as shown in Figure 6.2. The basic premise of the production of welfare approach is that 'final and

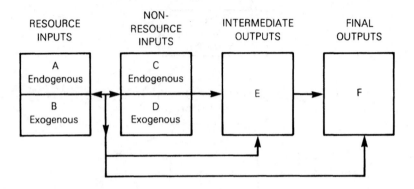

Figure 6.2 *The Production of Welfare Model*

intermediate outputs are determined by the level and modes of combination of the resource and non-resource inputs' (Knapp, 1984: 25). This approach to evaluation underlies the studies of community care for elderly people in Kent, Gateshead and elsewhere (Challis and Davies, 1986; Challis et al., 1988a, 1989; Davies and Challis, 1986).

Resource inputs are the elements which are conventionally costed in the analysis of care services, for example the time of nurses, social workers or medical staff, patients' use of day centres, or the occupation of hospital beds. Endogenous resource inputs (box A), which are under the control of, and alterable by, the service in the short term, are distinguished from exogenous resource inputs (box B), which are beyond the control of the service. For example, in a new community psychogeriatric service, the staff time allocated to different patients, or the amount of day-care support provided, are likely to be under the control of the service, but other resource inputs, such as housing, will be either beyond the control of the service or substantially less influenced by it except in the long term.

Non-resource inputs represent less tangible inputs than resource inputs, although they are frequently the factors of central concern in clinical and psychological evaluations. The distinction between resource inputs and non-resource inputs is between, for example, the amount of care and the style or quality of care, or between the 'what?' and the 'how?'. As with resource inputs, it is useful to distinguish between endogenous non-resource inputs, within the short-term control of the intervention (box C), and exogenous non-resource inputs, beyond the short-term control of the intervention (box D). For example, for a new support service, non-resource inputs under the control of the service might include whether or not particular forms of counselling or psychological support are available as part of the service, or the type and style of such psychological support. Exogenous non-resource inputs might include the initial characteristics of elderly people receiving the new service, for example their levels of disability and factors such as depressed mood or confusional state, and the presence or absence of a social network and levels of family support.

The outputs of an intervention may be subdivided into intermediate outputs and final outputs (Davies and Knapp, 1981), the distinction being between the receipt of services and the effects of services: these are boxes E and F. Intermediate outputs would include the receipt of welfare benefits, day care or home care, or the provision of chiropody services. Final outputs, however, are effects valued in their own right, that is, the effects of services upon clients and their significant others, for example changes in levels of disability of mental state, alterations in mood state, changes in the stress levels of carers and measures of change in family relationships. Thus, final outputs represent the success of an intervention in achieving its care objectives.

Unravelling the nature of the relationships between the components can clarify our understanding of an evaluative study, and provide the possibility of undertaking a cost-effectiveness analysis, in which the costs of obtaining the measured outputs may be determined (Challis et al., 1988b). As noted above, the underlying premise of this approach is that both intermediate outputs and final outputs are determined by the extent and ways in which resource and non-resource inputs are combined. Indeed, much of the complexity which has to be unravelled in understanding the process of care in an intervention results from the interaction of resource and non-resource inputs. Non-resource inputs such as disability, mental state, attitude, personality or other characteristics may be crucial determinants of the uptake of services, but they will also influence the amount of service provided and the extent to which those services are effective in practice.

The model also provides an *aide memoire* for ensuring that relevant data are collected, by specifying the key dimensions influencing the care process and formulating the relationship between inputs and outputs, and provides the basis for the use of multivariate techniques of analysis in tackling fundamental research questions. For example, the model may be used to examine how the costs of the resource inputs employed in providing care for an elderly person vary according to differences in non-resource inputs, such as their symptoms, their level of social support, their family relationships, and their physical health characteristics, and to changes in their welfare, the final output. Thus the model provides the basis for examining one of the key questions facing the development of services for elderly people today: 'For which elderly people, in which circumstances, is which approach to care provision the most cost-effective?'. In the next section, we discuss experimental designs appropriate to teasing out such questions.

82   METHODOLOGICAL APPROACHES

EXPERIMENTAL DESIGNS AND APPROXIMATIONS
TO EXPERIMENTAL DESIGNS

Experiments may be distinguished from other forms of investigation by the degree of control available to the investigator. Bailey (1987) identifies four forms of control: control over the environment in which the experiment is conducted; control over the composition of the groups receiving different treatments; control over the independent variable; and control over the measurement of the dependent variable. The control exerted by the investigator has a direct bearing on their ability to draw conclusions about causality. Three types of evidence are required for a variable X, the independent, predictor or treatment variable, to be judged to be a cause of the effect Y, the dependent or predicted variable (Moser and Kalton, 1971): there must be an association between X and Y; X must precede Y in time; and other variables must be eliminated as causes of the association between X and Y. Experiments provide the investigator with the means of measuring the appropriate variables to confirm their association, in a sequence to establish the temporal priority of the causal variable; and, by being able to determine the composition of the groups receiving different treatments, that is, different values of X, the investigator can eliminate other, disturbing variables as causes of the association. By randomly assigning individuals to different treatment groups, the investigator can ensure that differences between the groups on all other variables result from chance variation only, which permits the use of statistical tests to determine whether differences between the groups could be attributed to chance variations or to the effects of the different treatments (Fisher, 1966). Although randomisation ensures that differences between the groups result from chance fluctuations only, the investigator can design a more efficient experiment, particularly in small-scale studies, by equating the groups of key variables which are related to the dependent variable, rather than leaving the process to chance. The degree of equivalence of groups formed by a random assignment procedure is demonstrated in the field experiment by Goldberg and her colleagues (1970), designed to test the effect of using trained social workers in helping elderly people. In addition, the investigator can refine the technical procedures used in the study to exert greater control on the environment and the measurement of the variables, and can introduce control during the statistical analysis of the data (Cochran, 1983).

Quasi-experiments and observational studies

In many cases a true experiment, involving random assignment of individuals to different treatment groups, with or without the additional control of equating groups on key variables, is not possible. A randomised study may be physically or socially impossible, if the investigator is unable to determine membership of the groups to be compared, economically or politically impossible, or ethically impossible; and even when a randomised study is possible, external events may cause a breakdown in the random procedure (Achen, 1986). In such cases, other types of studies, variously termed observational studies, investigations, correlational studies, quasi-experiments or natural experiments may be employed. In this discussion the term 'quasi-experiment' will be used for studies in which the investigator is able to '. . . introduce something like experimental design . . . even though he lacks the full control over the scheduling of experimental stimuli . . .' (Campbell and Stanley, 1966: 34), and the more general term 'observational study' will be used where the '. . . investigator is restricted to taking selected observations or measurements that seem appropriate for the objectives, either by gathering new data or using those already collected by someone else' (Cochran, 1983: 2). Observational studies should be distinguished from sample surveys which, using Bulmer's (1986) threefold classification, provide data for descriptive or explanatory research, rather than for evaluative research. The term 'observational study' is not used here to refer to studies in which observational methods of data collection are employed, such as those by Evans et al. (1981) and Willcocks et al. (1987), although observational studies may employ observational methods of data collection, for example the study of elderly people in four different care environments by Godlove et al. (1981). When random assignment of individuals to different treatment groups is not possible, the role of control in the design or the analysis assumes much greater importance. However, only a small number of disturbing variables can be controlled, leaving the majority of such variables uncontrolled, with potential biasing effects on the relationship observed between X and Y.

Internal and external validity

A study in which a true measure of the effect of the experimental treatment is obtained has internal validity, and a study for which the results can be generalised to other populations, settings and independent and dependent variables has external validity (Campbell and Stanley, 1966). Discussions of external validity have often concentrated on the representativeness of the sample compared with a target population, and experiments have been contrasted with sample surveys, experiments being stronger on internal validity and sample surveys being stronger on external validity (Moser and Kalton, 1971). Laboratory sciences, including experimental psychology, have not sought generalisability of results through the representativeness of the sample, but have emphasised the importance of the replication of results by independent researchers (Campbell and Stanley, 1966).

Although the exact replication of a study using different subjects may provide further support for the hypothesis, it will demonstrate the internal validity rather than the generalisability of the design since the exact standardisation of experimental conditions will limit the range of conditions to which the results apply, as noted by Fisher (1966).

Although the replication of results is an important scientific principle, few studies in the social sciences are replicated (Bailey, 1987). Bailey notes that this may be due to later researchers trying to improve, rather than just replicate the study; to a shortage of research funding which makes the funding of an initial study very difficult and replications even more so; and to a greater interest by researchers in obtaining new results. However, Reid and Hanrahan (1981) note that the North American social work interventions which they examined in their review of the effectiveness of social work drew on the results of previous experimental tests. In the United Kingdom small-scale research undertaken by small research teams predominates, and is generally undertaken with a specific focus on service issues within social services or social work departments or sponsored by central government (Thomas, 1988), although there has been an expansion in the independent research sector (Bulmer, 1986) and in research institutes based in universities and colleges. The existence of well-established research institutes probably provides more opportunities for replicating studies. For example, the service model developed in the Kent Community Care Study (Challis and Davies, 1986; Davies and Challis, 1986) was evaluated in a retirement area, and has been replicated in Gateshead, an inner-city area (Challis et al., 1988a). The similarity of the results obtained in these two different areas suggests that the service model could be applied more widely in the UK. Some of the key features of the Kent and Gateshead studies have also been replicated in another urban area (Challis et al., 1989), and the approach forms a key element in the government's proposals for community care contained in the White Paper *Caring for People* (HMSO, 1989b).

Using the three criteria, randomisation of treatments for subjects (internal validity), representativeness of the sampling units (generalisability) and realism of the measurements of the independent and dependent variables, Kish (1987) notes that experiments are strong on control through randomisation, sample surveys are strong on representation and observational studies are relatively strong on the realism of measurements. However, Kish notes that the advantages of each type of study are only relative and recommends that each method of data collection should be considered when planning a research study, noting that improvements can be made to the weaker aspects of each method, and that more than one method can be used to tackle a research problem. Several authors recommend the use of available methodologies to provide triangulating evidence about a research problem, as noted earlier. In some cases the different methods can be combined, for example the cross-national study of elderly people in New York and London (Gurland et al., 1983) employed random sampling to obtain samples of elderly people, who were assessed twice, with an interval of one year. An evaluation by Bond and his colleagues of continuing-care accommodation for elderly people provided by the National Health Service illustrates the use of different research methodologies for explanatory and evaluative research, and the role of experiments in providing information on whether different types of input have different effects on outcomes, but not why particular outcomes occur. The evaluation included a randomised controlled trial to compare clinical and social outcomes for patients in experimental nursing homes and conventional hospital wards (Bond et al., 1989), and a multiple-case study to explain how features of the facilities influenced outcomes (Bond and Bond, 1989).

Forms of experimental and quasi-experimental design

In the simplest form of true experiment a sample of individuals is divided into two groups, using some means of random allocation. The experimental group receives the treatment of interest and the control group receives no specific treatment. At the minimum, the dependent variable is measured for the two groups after the experimental group has received the treatment, and the responses of the two groups are compared. This design, termed the 'post-test-only control group design' by Campbell and Stanley (1966) may be represented schematically as follows, modifying Campbell and Stanley's notation:

$$R \quad X \quad Y_E$$
$$R \quad \quad Y_C$$

The symbol 'R' denotes random allocation. An alternative design includes a measure of the dependent variable before the experimental group receives the treatment. The pre-test value can then be used in the statistical analysis, either by comparing changes in levels of the dependent variable for the two groups or, preferably, in an analysis of covariance. This design, the 'pre-test-post-test control group design' (Campbell and Stanley, 1966) or the 'before-after design with control group' (Moser and Kalton, 1971), may be represented schematically as follows:

$$R \quad Y_{E1} \quad X \quad Y_{E2}$$
$$R \quad Y_{C1} \quad X \quad Y_{C2}$$

One of the most well known among the small number of examples of this approach in the UK gerontological literature is the experimental study by Goldberg and her colleagues (1970), which was designed to test the effect of using trained social workers in helping elderly people.

Cases referred to a local authority welfare department were randomly assigned to trained social workers or to untrained welfare assistants. Other examples include randomised controlled trials of regular assessment of elderly people living in the community (Hendriksen et al., 1984), and of health visitors screening and monitoring elderly people in their own homes (Vetter et al., 1984). The evaluation by Bond and his colleagues of continuing-care accommodation for elderly people, discussed earlier, included a randomised controlled trial of clinical and social outcomes for patients in experimental NHS nursing homes compared with conventional continuing-care hospital wards (Bond et al., 1989). In true experiments with random allocation to the experimental and control groups the pre-treatment measurement of the dependent variable Y is not essential, although it may be useful for the investigator to know how successful random allocation has been in equating the two groups. On occasions the pre-treatment measurement may be impossible, for example when introducing entirely new topics in educational research (Campbell and Stanley, 1966), or it may be undesirable if it sensitises the members of the experimental group to the experimental treatment. More complex experimental designs can be built from these two designs, by introducing additional levels or different types of experimental treatment, or by combining the two designs to produce extended designs, for example the four-group design (Solomon, 1949).

The quasi-experimental designs corresponding to the above two designs are the 'post-test-only design with non-equivalent groups' and the 'untreated control group design with pre-test and post-test' (Cook and Campbell, 1979). Cook and Campbell note that the post-test-only design is usually uninterpretable because the lack of a pre-test prevents the investigator from knowing whether there were selection differences between the two groups. However, this design, also termed a 'retrospective' or 'ex post facto' design (Moser and Kalton, 1971) has the advantage of speed, for example in medical studies, when a disease may take a long time to develop, and of economy when the response is a rare event. In such cases the investigator will need to obtain information from the subject or from records, with inevitable problems arising from memory distortions and inaccurate or incomplete records. The information collected can then be used to adjust statistically for differences between the groups in the analysis. The pre-test and post-test design, or 'prospective' study, is more satisfactory than the post-test-only design since the pre-test enables the investigator to compare the characteristics of the two groups before the treatment is applied. This design compares pre-existing groups, but if the investigator can choose which group receives the experimental treatment the design more closely resembles a true experiment than if the groups are self-selected for exposure to the treatment. In the latter case the groups are probably more likely to differ on the pre-test, and attempts to match the groups or to adjust statistically for the differences in the analysis will introduce greater problems of interpretation, as discussed in the following section. The Community Care studies in Kent and Gateshead used quasi-experimental designs, comparing cases referred to an experimental service in one area with similar cases in an adjacent area (Challis and Davies, 1986; Challis et al., 1988a; Davies and Challis, 1986). Other examples of quasi-experimental designs include the Coventry Home Help Project (Latto, 1982), the Hove Intensive Domiciliary Care Project (Dunnachie, 1979), and the studies by Power and his colleagues of the use of volunteers to support elderly people in their own homes (Power and Kelly, 1981) and in residential homes (Power et al., 1983).

SOME LIMITATIONS OF EXPERIMENTAL DESIGNS

True experiments may be ethically impossible or suffer from practical limitations, and, even when true experiments are technically possible, they can suffer from problems of implementation restricting the realism of the measurements of the variables of interest and the generalisability of the results to other populations.

Ethical limitations

Ethical issues arise in all types of study, but in true experiments they relate particularly to the ability of the investigator to select subjects randomly to receive the experimental treatment. Medical experiments present the greatest risks to the well-being of subjects, but other types of study can have negative effects for the participants, such as loss of dignity, increased anxiety, embarrassment, loss of trust in social relations, loss of autonomy and self-determination, and lowered self-esteem (Nachmias and Nachmias, 1982). Nachmias and Nachmias note that for all types of study the principal ethical issues concern obtaining the informed consent of the subjects for their participation and safeguarding their privacy, and that informed consent is essential when individuals are exposed to substantial risks or are asked to forfeit personal rights. The principle that it is unethical to introduce poorly tested procedures is generally accepted (Cartwright, 1986; Gilbert et al., 1977; Hill, 1971), and Gilbert et al. note that poorly designed studies which are either inefficient or too small to have sufficient statistical power may be regarded as unethical, although they do not completely reject the use of controlled unrandomised studies where these are able to demonstrate substantial effects. Similarly, in relation to social programmes, Gilbert et al. (1975) argue that undertaking haphazard, poorly planned studies is equivalent to 'fooling around with people'.

In medical studies a distinction may be made between procedures intended to benefit the individual patients and procedures undertaken in order to contribute to medical knowledge generally (Committee of Privy Council for Medical Research, 1964). In the case of the former, the Medical Research Council guidelines indicate that the principle of informed consent should be adhered to unless the patient's doctor believes that full discussion of their condition is not in their interest. In studies aimed at increasing medical knowledge generally, full informed consent of volunteer subjects is required.

Nachmias and Nachmias note that there is general acceptance of the principle of informed consent in research involving human subjects, although they suggest that 'it is not absolutely necessary in studies where no danger or risk is involved' (1982: 328). Hill (1971) questions whether it is necessary for a doctor to obtain a patient's consent in the absence of knowledge of differences in the relative value of alternative treatments. In addition, it is necessary for a doctor to have confidence in the treatment in order to help patients effectively (Gilhooly, 1986). Medical experiments using placebo treatments entail the deception of the patient, but doctors using such procedures are expected to conform to strict guidelines (Committee of Privy Council for Medical Research, 1964). Usually, however, comparisons are made between treatments rather than between a treatment and no treatment (Hill, 1971), and Goldberg and Connelly (1982) suggest a similar solution in social care research. Apart from infringing the rights of subjects (Bulmer, 1982; Nachmias and Nachmias, 1982), deception may undermine respect for research and researchers, and interfere with the conduct and hence the conclusions drawn from the study (Bailey, 1987).

Valid informed consent must be made voluntarily by competent individuals, that is, persons with adequate mental capacity and in a position to exercise self-determination, and be based on appropriate information, adequately understood (Gilhooly, 1986; Nachmias and Nachmias, 1982). Obtaining informed consent in studies of elderly people is complicated by problems of comprehension. Stanley et al. (1985) report that elderly medical patients showed poorer comprehension than younger patients, although they could generally make equally reasonable treatment decisions in terms of risks and benefits. However, patients with a moderate degree of senile dementia exhibited a significant impairment in competency to consent to research. In practice it is impossible to provide participants with complete information, partly because, as Nachmias and Nachmias note, there would be no point in conducting a study in such circumstances, and so reasonably informed consent should be obtained, with the subject rather than the investigator deciding how much information is necessary and adequate (Gilhooly, 1986). However, overdetailed descriptions may deter subjects from participating (Bailey, 1987; Nachmias and Nachmias, 1982), as may written consent forms

(Bailey, 1987; Gilhooly, 1986); and Bailey also notes that advice to subjects that they are free to withdraw at any time may encourage them to do so. Written consent forms are mainly used in Britain for surgical treatments (Gilhooly, 1986), and in the United States for medical studies generally (Bailey, 1987), but Bailey suggests that wider use of signed consent forms is likely in the future. To some extent, such forms may reduce the liability of the investigator, although the investigator must retain final responsibility (Gilhooly, 1986; Nachmias and Nachmias, 1982).

Questions of privacy arise in relation to the collection of sensitive information from individuals, the location in which the information is collected, and the dissemination of the results of studies (Nachmias and Nachmias, 1982). As Bailey (1987) notes, charges of the invasion of privacy are made most commonly against survey research, although they can also occur in relation to experiments, observational studies and document studies, and the most extensive discussions of privacy issues tend to relate to censuses and surveys (for example, Bulmer, 1979). In surveys, issues of privacy or intrusion can arise at each stage of the process (Hoinville et al., 1978), but potential respondents may be more concerned about the source of their name than the actual questions, considering the growth in computerised databases and the mystique that surrounds these (Bulmer, 1979), and it is usually the method of obtaining the sample which determines the extent to which individual identities are at risk (Social and Community Planning Research, 1979). In contrast, experiments and, to a lesser extent, observational studies are conducted on restricted populations which are frequently defined by the treatments or services of interest, with corresponding limitations of generalisability.

Interview surveys are frequently conducted in private homes, with a consequent threat to the interviewee's privacy, while the environmental control required in true experiments may necessitate a more controlled setting than the subject's own home. Observational studies may be conducted in a variety of settings, but those in social gerontology are likely to be held in the elderly person's home, whether this is a private house or an institutional setting.

The protection of the privacy of information collected in a study depends upon the use of appropriate administrative procedures, which may have to be elaborate in large-scale studies, particularly surveys, since many people are involved in processing and analysing the information collected (Social and Community Planning Research, 1979). In medical studies patients may not be fully aware that their case is discussed at team meetings (Gilhooly, 1986), and this issue also arises in studies of social care. In addition, doctors and other professional staff may be required to disclose information in a court of law.

For large-scale surveys and censuses the information presented in reports is essentially statistical, and techniques have been developed to ensure that information is not disclosed about identifiable, but not identified, individuals, particularly for population censuses (Hakim, 1979; Nachmias and Nachmias, 1982). In smaller scale experiments and observational studies the potential for identifying individuals is probably greater, particularly in action research projects and observational studies undertaken in defined areas, as noted by Nachmias and Nachmias (1982). Individuals described in case studies included in reports of small-scale studies are particularly susceptible to identification within their community, even when presented anonymously.

Practical limitations

Apart from ethical limitations on the treatments that can be applied to randomly selected individuals, investigators are restricted in the extent to which they can determine the membership of the groups to be compared. The groups may be defined according to unalterable characteristics of individuals or by socially or societally determined characteristics, necessitating the comparison of different groups within a society or of different societies. In order to exert the necessary degree of control, true experiments often have to be conducted in an artificial environment, usually with small samples. The costs arising from the degree of control required in the organisation and collection of information for a true experiment in a natural setting may be prohibitive. In addition, attrition rates in complex experimental studies may be higher than in observational studies which make fewer demands on the subjects (Achen, 1986), although studies of social care frequently extend over several years, as noted by Thomas (1988), and can make substantial demands on clients.

An artificial environment will limit the types of behaviour that can be studied, and may produce 'Hawthorne Effects' in which the effects of being in an experiment are sufficient to alter the behaviour of the subjects (Roethlisberger et al., 1939), a threat to external validity or generalisability. In addition, the expectations of the investigator may affect the behaviour of the subjects or their judgements of the responses of the subjects. In medical studies a 'double-blind' procedure is often used to prevent the doctor and patient from knowing to which group the patient belongs but, as Kish (1987) notes, it is much more difficult, if not impossible, to hide the nature of social treatments from subjects and investigators. In some cases an investigator may be able to ensure that the assessment of the responses of the subjects is made without knowledge of their group membership.

The practical limitations on the sample size in an experiment are likely to affect the types of human behaviour that can be studied. Bailey (1987) notes that an experiment is most suitable for studies of individual or small-group behaviour, rather than of the behaviour of large groups. Although Bailey was referring to laboratory experiments, the same restrictions would appear to apply to experiments conducted in more natural settings. For example, the study by Goldberg and her colleagues (1970) was concerned with social work with individual clients. However, if a study is also concerned with a local system of interacting agencies, comparisons necessarily have to be made between 'similar' areas. In such cases the investigator is more likely to face the task of finding a suitable control area to match to an experimental area than being able to select randomly which area receives the experimental treatment. In practice, control areas selected for such studies are likely to have different characteristics to those of experimental areas, for example the experimental area but not the control area may include a teaching hospital district.

In studies of social and social care programmes, administrators, practitioners and clients may not be convinced of the value of a randomised study, even where there is no prior information on the relative merits of the different treatments, an argument used to justify randomisation in medical research. In social care services local politicians may be unwilling to accept the apparently arbitrary allocation of services to individuals within a locality which a randomised design would create. A quasi-experimental design, in which one area receives a new service and other areas continue to receive existing services, is likely to be much more acceptable. Despite the control imposed in randomised experiments, external factors may destroy the randomisation of individuals to treatments. For example, the personnel responsible for allocating individuals to treatments may not comply with the specified procedure but instead allocate individuals according to their own views of the most appropriate treatment for each person. Goldberg and Connelly (1982) note that if feedback of intermediate results is not given to practitioners in order to avoid altering practice during the course of an experiment, practitioners are prevented from learning and adapting their practice. In addition, Goldberg and Connelly note that random assignment of clients to experimental and control groups within an organisation such as an area office of a social services department is unsatisfactory because practitioners will discuss cases and clients will talk to each other, thereby contaminating the experiment. Furthermore, an experiment might involve additional staff, effectively relieving the control group of some of their workload. This too could bias and contaminate the experiment.

Social programmes concerned with inter- and intra-agency effects are likely to have a wide range of interested parties, each with particular interests and objectives. In discussing the approach of pluralistic evaluation, designed to handle the problems raised by evaluating such programmes, Smith and Cantley (1988) note that the objectives tend to be poorly defined at the beginning of a programme and often subject to change, making it difficult for the investigator to select appropriate criteria for success which will be accepted by the various parties. In order for evaluative studies to have an impact on policy, both Smith and Cantley (1988) and Bulmer (1986) emphasise the importance of developing an accurate model of the policy process.

Specificity of experimental inputs and the problem of their control

In an experimental evaluation of a medical or behavioural treatment in a clinical setting, considerable attempts are made to ensure that the nature of the experimental input is precisely defined, thereby enabling other researchers to attempt to replicate the findings. However, in the evaluation of a social care programme or a complex range of services the inputs, and often the outputs, cannot be so easily defined or disentangled. For example, the type, style and nature of the inputs may be deliberately varied substantially between individuals because the objective of the programme is to match levels of provision to individual needs more precisely. As noted earlier, experiments focus on the effects of a treatment rather than on the process by which the treatment affects the outcome and, where the experimental input is poorly defined, the nature of the causal mechanism relating the input to the output is likely to be even more unclear.

Close control of the input by the investigators is likely to be of particular importance in developing innovative services within large bureaucratic organisations, since there are likely to be powerful pressures to fit the new service into the pre-existing methods of working. For example, in the innovatory Community Care Schemes in Kent and Gateshead (Challis and Davies, 1986; Challis et al., 1988a) the researchers were responsible for working with small teams of staff in defining very precise features of a new form of service delivery and ensuring that the new methods were accepted by a sometimes reluctant organisation, unwilling to change its habits. In such situations the role of the researcher may include ensuring that the planned input is actually delivered during the course of the experiment. Furthermore, there may be an important trade-off between the size or scale of a project and the degree of influence or control which can be exercised, and therefore the degree to which there is input variation. In a large-scale project, those conducting the evaluation are likely to have less control over the inputs as well as less understanding of the process by which the inputs influence the outputs. In consequence, larger-scale evaluations may become purely outcome or 'black-box' (Sheldon, 1988) evaluations. In some American studies large teams have been responsible for evaluating substantial numbers of projects but, being geographically distant from them, the investigators have had little control over the activities and inputs and also relatively little understanding of the processes operating (Davies and Challis, 1986). In contrast, studies in the United Kingdom have been smaller in scale and the researchers have tended to be much closer to the service under investigation.

The importance of specifying inputs precisely in order to examine the relationship between inputs and outputs is illustrated by Goldberg (1984), reviewing evaluation studies. Where there is no relationship between inputs and expected outputs, studies cannot be expected to show significant changes. In her review, Goldberg compares the findings of Kent Community Care Scheme (Challis and Davies, 1986) with the findings of studies of volunteer support to elderly people in the community and residential care (Power and Kelly, 1981; Power et al., 1983). In the Kent scheme, clients received very substantial levels of support several times a day, but in the studies of volunteer support, perhaps only weekly contact. Similar measures of psychological well-being were used in both cases, and it is unlikely that such indicators would be influenced by only occasional contacts. In relation to the studies of volunteer support, Goldberg concludes: 'Thus this study raises starkly the question of realistic aims and appropriate measures.' A similar problem can be observed in some gerontological studies which have treated changes in an elderly person's performance in activities of daily living (Katz et al., 1963) as a measure of the outcome of social care. Social care is infrequently directly related to a programme of rehabilitation, and the effectiveness of an intervention which is principally caring, rather than therapeutic, is unlikely to be reflected in changes from one client dependency state to another. In such cases it is probably more appropriate to view changes in a person's level of dependency as occurring independently of and affecting the level of caring provided, rather than viewing them as an outcome related to a care input, since care interventions will be concerned principally with a reduction of difficulties occasioned by handicap. Studies which treat changes in dependency state as measures of the outcome of social care run the risk of not identifying outcomes which can be related to the intervention (Challis, 1981).

Introducing control in analysis[1]

As noted above, the role of control in the design or the analysis assumes much greater importance in studies in which random assignment of individuals to different treatment groups is not possible. Three main forms of control are available (Cochran, 1983): technical refinements, controlling key variables, and controls in the statistical analysis. In observational studies technical refinements may include using more sophisticated recording schedules and using more highly trained personnel, even if this means that a smaller-scale study must be conducted owing to a shortage of suitable staff. However, the main forms of control involve controlling key variables and controls in the statistical analysis, although changing the design of the study has implications for the methods of analysis used.

Introducing controls for key variables involves creating groups of individuals which are similar on those variables, and exposing the different groups to the different treatments, the simplest case being a study using two groups. In randomised experiments the procedure is usually termed blocking or pairing, and in observational studies the procedure is termed matching. Two forms of matching procedure may be used to create matched groups, simple matching or precision control, and frequency distribution control (Bailey, 1987; Moser and Kalton, 1971). Precision control matching involves matching pairs of individuals with the same or similar values for the variables of interest, while in frequency distribution control the groups are matched separately for each variable. In precision control matching, individuals with no matching partner have to be discarded, and larger reservoirs of potential subjects are required to ensure that the desired sample size is achieved. Precision control matching was used in the evaluations of the Community Care Schemes in Kent and Gateshead, in which elderly people referred to the experimental service were matched with elderly people in adjacent areas receiving the usual range of services (Challis and Davies, 1986; Challis et al., 1988a). Frequency distribution control is designed to reduce the number of non-matched cases, but the published accounts of this method do not explain how the matched distributions for variables are maintained when each new matching variable is introduced.

Introducing control in the analysis may be achieved using various statistical techniques, including cross-tabulation, standardisation and regression-based methods (Moser and Kalton, 1971).

Regression-based methods, including analysis of variance and analysis of covariance, provide the main form of statistical control for analysing data from experimental and observational studies. In both types of study the purpose of the analysis is usually to determine the effect of a treatment, which normally entails the comparisons of the post-test scores for the different groups. In true experiments the random allocation of individuals to experimental or control groups, often accompanied by matching on some key variables, ensures that the groups are equivalent, except for random fluctuations of the non-matched variables. In observational studies matching can equate the groups on a few key variables and, although the selection procedure in some studies may be 'random in effect' (Lord, 1963), Reichardt (in Cook and Campbell, 1979) argues that in most studies the method used to create the groups is likely to result in non-equivalent groups. Methods of analysis which separate the effect of the treatment from selection differences are required in such cases. Reichardt discusses four methods of statistical analysis using analysis of variance and analysis of covariance for examining differences between groups. Each of these methods could be used to analyse an appropriately designed randomised experiment, and the conclusions drawn from each analysis would be compatible, given a few simplifying assumptions. However, the conclusions that would be drawn from an observational study by using different methods of analysis would not necessarily be compatible. Reichardt emphasises the importance of examining selection procedures and tailoring the analysis accordingly. Achen (1986) discusses a number of more advanced statistical techniques based on simultaneous equation methods which employ specific equations to explain the selection procedure and the effects of the treatment.

The analysis of covariance is frequently employed to adjust the groups for differences in levels of the pre-test value of the dependent variable in both experimental and non-experimental studies. For the adjustment to be complete, the groups must not differ on any other disturbing variable, and the pre-test value of the dependent variable, or the covariate, must be measured without error (Snedecor and Cochran, 1980). In addition, the same relationship must exist between the pre-test and post-test levels of the dependent variable for each group. The effect of measurement error is to remove only part of the initial difference between the groups and, for evaluative programmes designed to help disadvantaged groups, this results in an underestimate of the effects of the programme. Other problems in the evaluation of such programmes are described by Campbell and Boruch (1975). An example of the use of the analysis of covariance to adjust for differences between experimental and control group cases is provided by a quasi-experimental study of the effects of a scheme to discharge elderly patients from long-stay hospital care to their own homes, in which a significant difference in the mean level of social disturbance in the two groups was controlled for by means of covariance analysis (Challis et al., 1989).

IMPLEMENTING EXPERIMENTAL AND QUASI-EXPERIMENTAL DESIGNS

Choice of design

The choice of design of an experiment will reflect a number of features: the nature of the project; the unit of analysis, for example the individual elderly person or the social work team; the questions to be tackled; and the political realities of the setting in which the project is to be undertaken. One kind of design may preclude certain questions which other designs can tackle. Traditionally, randomised designs have been seen as the mainstay of experimental purity, particularly within the medical tradition. However, a number of circumstances can militate against the successful use of a randomised design, including the problem of achieving sufficient precision. In small-scale studies, there is less likelihood that randomisation will achieve equivalence for the different treatment groups. Quasi-experimental designs, on the other hand, place the clear burden of proof on the investigator to identify potential selection factors contributing to differences between the groups. Cook and Campbell (1979) recommend the following courses of action to ensure that such designs provide valid information: careful planning to ensure that information required for the analysis is obtained; rigorous and exhaustive examination of the data using multiple analyses; and explicit examination of the validity of the findings and the plausibility of alternative explanations. In the original Kent Community Care Study, the groups were compared on over 80 variables before they were accepted as satisfactorily equivalent for comparisons to proceed (Challis and Davies, 1986). However, implementability and acceptability are particularly strong features of the quasi-experimental design. Research in social gerontology is likely to take place outside the traditional medical setting in which randomisation is considered the norm. Researchers will have to convince local politicians of the validity and utility of their research, and to persuade them that the value of the research outweighs any potential conflicts of interest. It is much easier for a local politician to explain to his or her constituents and to colleagues that a new evaluative project is being carefully tested in one district in the authority before being extended to other parts of the authority (forming the control group), than it is to explain that outsiders allocate different types of services to different individuals within the authority as a whole using arbitrary criteria.

In the quasi-experimental design, different levels of units of analysis may be examined in parallel. Most studies which employ the randomised controlled trial treat the unit of analysis as the patient, client or elderly person. If the implementation of a new system of services is being examined, the recipient of the service may form one unit of analysis, but the analysis may also be extended upwards to cover the system as a whole. Comparisons could then be made between alternative systems in terms of the costs and benefits to the overall population in need within an area. The quasi-experimental design makes it possible to tackle issues such as the efficiency with which services are targeted to those in need and the uptake of services.

The relationship between project and research staff

We have already noted that the investigator involved in evaluative research may be a source of input definition and control, rather than the passive observer of activities. Reid and Hanrahan (1981) indicate that this may contribute to maintaining the relationship between input and outcome and to preventing organisational and bureaucratic pressures from corrupting the experiment. Otherwise, the tensions between service providers and researchers described by Illsley (1980) and Smith and Cantley (1985) may prove too powerful. Social gerontological research frequently involves the evaluation of alternative forms of providing services, which are administered by local authorities, and so the relationship between the investigators and the project is particularly important. Innovations, often subject to evaluation, are likely to be treated differently at different stages of their development within a local authority system. During the period while a project receives special, possibly external funding, a degree of protection and tolerance may be shown towards it. However, when the project enters mainstream funding, the period of tolerance is likely to end. An administrative system developed specifically for a project which does not conform to the mainstream system, and procedures giving greater degrees of authority and autonomy to staff within the project phase are likely to be submitted to fresh scrutiny, tending to force the new service into the mainstream bureaucratic system and to adopt pre-existing norms, procedures and methods of administration.

For practitioners who have worked to develop a new approach to service organisation, this can be extremely frustrating. Researchers are likely to find themselves acting as a source of support to their colleagues implementing a new service throughout the life of a project, and not just during this latter phase. Since the researchers are likely to be the only persons within or close to the organisation with a full-time shared interest in the problems faced by those implementing the new service, the relationship between the researchers and the practitioners needs to be recognised explicitly. It is particularly important that a clear understanding is reached of the types of information that can legitimately be disclosed between researchers and practitioners and those which must be kept confidential. For example, independent assessments by the researchers of those receiving the new service would be additional to the information collected by the practitioners, and thus have the potential to contaminate the study, and it must be agreed and clearly understood that information about service recipients collected by the researchers will not be passed back to the practitioners. However, this would not preclude the researchers from reporting interim results in a more aggregated form, as discussed later. Feedback is an important aid for individual workers to evaluate their work (Goldberg, 1981), and withholding feedback of interim results from practitioners will prevent them from altering their practice (Goldberg and Connelly, 1982), but feedback about the progress of clients receiving the service should be provided by a systematic monitoring exercise built into the project. Provided that the arrangements for relaying information are clearly understood, researchers and practitioners can work closely together and provide mutual support. Researchers can develop the role of an overt insider (Bulmer, 1982) and obtain a greater understanding of the project through observing fieldwork practice in operation, and of the nature of decisions made by practitioners and the pressures on them.

Maintaining control groups

Losses of individuals from samples studied over time, particularly in studies of elderly people, are inevitable, and have been discussed in detail in relation to longitudinal studies, for example by Moser and Kalton (1971) and Kish (1987). However, in evaluative studies there is a danger that greater attention will be given to the experimental group than to the control group. In particular, the provision of a new type of service, which may offer more flexible care and a wider range of types of care, may attract into the care system people who were not previously users of services of the agency concerned, for whom there would be no corresponding members of the control group. Within a randomised design this problem would not be encountered, because potential new users of the service would be randomly allocated to the experimental or control groups. Also, the new users would not be detected as differing from the existing users. However, there may be considerable hostility from potential users allocated to the control group, which may be avoided with designs involving comparisons of different treatments rather than of a treatment and no treatment. Goldberg and Connelly (1982) recommend the comparison of different treatments as a solution to the ethical problem arising when a control group receives no treatment, as noted earlier. In contrast, in a quasi-experimental design referral patterns may change in the area subject to the experimental intervention, but not in the control area. In such cases, either individuals receiving the experimental treatment for whom no control was obtained would have to be discarded, or a wider range of individuals in the control area would have to be identified. This problem arose in the Community Care evaluations in Kent and Gateshead (Challis and Davies, 1986; Challis et al., 1988a), and the researchers first had to identify changes in the pattern of referrals to the experimental scheme, and then find similar cases in the control area. Successful maintenance of a control group in such circumstances requires the researcher to monitor closely both the uptake of cases into the experimental system and the characteristics of members of the control group, a time-consuming but vital activity. Changes in the characteristics of the clients of an experimental scheme is not just of methodological interest: the successful provision of a new service to individuals excluded from the existing range of services raises questions about the definition of the client group at which the service is to be targeted, which may not be detected in a randomised design. Again, this demonstrates the greater potential of quasi-experiments to collect process information.

The role of interim results

Although feedback of information collected by the researchers about particular clients of a service should not be provided to practitioners, in order to avoid contaminating the study, the presentation of interim results should be considered, since this can be of particular value in maintaining the interest and morale of project staff, and is of even greater importance for maintaining the interest of sponsors, funders and political interests. Critical funding decisions often have to be made on the basis of interim reports, and therefore the capacity to provide these must be built into the resources and timetable of an evaluative study. However, the data available for such an interim report are often incomplete. For example, an interim analysis was undertaken based on the first 35 cases in the experimental and control areas of the original Kent Community Care Project (Challis and Davies, 1980). Although this was a small number of cases, subsequent analysis indicated that the conclusions drawn from this small sub-group were valid for the larger population (Challis and Davies, 1986). The information presented in an interim report is likely to be based on process data such as indicators of throughput rather than outcome data. In such cases the process of making crucial decisions will not follow the rational model of full evaluation followed by decision, followed by continued funding but, instead, will be more like the process of policy-making described, for example, by Bulmer (1986) and Smith and Cantley (1985). Nonetheless, the collection and analysis of process information for such a report may contribute substantially to the development of indicators for the long-term monitoring of a service (Challis and Chesterman, 1985, 1986, 1987).

CONCLUSIONS

In this chapter we have considered experimental evaluations of problems arising in social gerontology in the United Kingdom. Despite the difficulties of undertaking such research, there is room for considerable development and advancement of this approach in the United Kingdom, where relatively few resources have been applied to social gerontology compared with those employed in the United States. Investment in evaluative research has the potential for the development of a more coherent approach to the provision of services, although such new developments would be required to satisfy evaluative criteria which existing services could not, and which are only maintained by an inertia of tradition. Furthermore, if a new approach successfully passes the test of an evaluation, it faces a new and major hurdle in the process of entering mainstream provision, usually being required to adapt to mainstream procedures rather than vice versa. It is at this stage in particular that the paradigm of evaluative research should be seen as only one contribution to effective service provision, since the implementation of a new service raises questions about the influence of bureaucratic inertia, political factors and organisational process. The successful implementation of a new service must face the issues developed in the very substantial literature on implementation (Barrett and Fudge, 1981; Bulmer, 1986).

NOTES

A longer version of this paper is available (Challis and Darton, 1990).
1. This is discussed in greater detail in Challis and Darton (1990).

7

Doing Ethnography in a Geriatric Unit

EILEEN FAIRHURST

Just as gerontology is a multidisciplinary endeavour so are the variety of research methods employed. It may be thought that specific methods are associated with particular gerontological spheres so that biological gerontology favours the experimental method and social gerontology the social survey. In reality, the matter is much more complex. Choice of research methods follows from the topic to be studied rather than the reverse, with method determining the issue to be researched. Given this, particular research methods are more or less appropriate to the matter being studied.

Recognising that social ageing does not take place in a social vacuum has implications for the methods adopted. We grow old as members of and participants in a social context: in our families, in our work meetings and in our localities. It is this study of old age in context that I will focus upon in this chapter.

ETHNOGRAPHY AND BRITISH GERONTOLOGY

There is a growing body of British gerontological literature which is influenced by the anthropological and sociological traditions of ethnography and particularly observation, both participant and non-participant.[1] I want to refer to some of that literature before focusing on my own study. As Fennell et al. (1988) have recently pointed out, such research has typically been set in those special settings where old people are gathered together: geriatric wards, day centres, old people's clubs or residential homes. These locations enable the researcher to observe and/or take part in daily organisational activities. A major feature of participant observation is that it calls for close and often lengthy involvement in the ordinary activities of those being studied (see Becker, 1958).

A pioneering use of observational studies in residential settings was that of Lipman's (1967) investigation of how residents used seating arrangements to claim and delineate control over their immediate social environment. Lipman and his associates went on to study systematically the relationship between design/physical environment and interaction in a variety of old people's homes (see, for instance, Harris et al., 1977 and Harris and Lipman, 1980). A linkage between observational methods and a concern with life in residential settings is evident in the studies of Godlove et al. (1982) and those associated with the Centre for Environmental and Social Studies in Ageing (CESSA) at the Polytechnic of North London. Godlove et al. (1982) were able to compare the extent and nature of old people's activities in hospital wards, day centres, day hospitals and local authority homes. The observational studies of CESSA extend this focus on interaction by specifically linking it to quality of life. Willcocks et al. (1987) argue that aspects of the physical and institutional environment, resident mix and staff characteristics found in residential settings combine in different ways to affect the level of resident well-being.

Other British studies have placed a greater emphasis upon partici- pant observation. Both Paterson (1977) and Evers (1981, 1982) show how the meaning of care and nursing work, held by residential care workers in the former study, and nurses on acute and long-stay geriatric wards in the latter study, may have consequences for the care old people receive.

Ethnography offers the possibility of outlining how those being studied view their social world. Such a concern has been important in research which has been in settings where old people meet for primarily social activities. Concentrating upon clubs for old women, Jerrome (1981, 1986) revealed the significance of friendship in later life and what middle-class women themselves considered to be the consti- tuents of friendship.

Work by Hazan (1980) and Boneham (1989) delineates the ways in which a shared religious and cultural background may help to shape the experience of old age. The Jewish day centre studied by Hazan was a locale in which old people could construct an alternative reality to that existing outside the centre. Boneham, on the other hand, reminds us that shared background may not necessarily have the positive connotations suggested by Hazan. According to Boneham, Sikh women's experience of old age, unlike that of men, may be more isolated and not necessarily characterised by the traditional role of social mediator.[2]

THE STUDY OF HIGHVIEW

Having noted the influence of participant observational techniques upon other British gerontological research, now I can turn to an explicit focus of my own. Although the research was conducted some years ago, before many of the studies previously considered, its methodological implications are timeless.

My study was an ethnography of rehabilitation in a unit I called Highview, part of a northern district general hospital. My intention was to provide a complementary view of rehabilitation from the perspectives of those doing rehabilitation – doctors, nurses, remedial therapists and social workers who form the rehabilitation team – and of those being rehabilitated, old people as patients. As an ethnographer my concern was to pinpoint the meanings of rehabilitation to both staff and patients and to detail the social processes underlying it. The study was informed by the sociological perspective of interpretivism but ethnographic techniques are not restricted to only one theoretical approach (see Hammersley and Atkinson, 1983; Emmett and Morgan, 1982; Rock, 1979).

Whilst the practice of ethnography has come to be associated primarily with participant observation, I included other ethnographical techniques such as in-depth, audio-recorded interviews and documentary analysis.[3] I spent a total of 18 months doing fieldwork in Highview. Twelve months of this time involved me in intensive fieldwork when I spent up to six hours at any one time, and up to five days in any one week, in the field. The remaining six months of fieldwork were used as an opportunity to withdraw from Highview and during this period I compiled some patient careers.

In the mid-1970s when I began my research there was a long history of socio-medical research on the elderly in the United Kingdom but typically it had used survey methods. Although they offered some guidelines on how the researcher should conduct herself, they were inappropriate for my specific concerns with presenting an everyday life of rehabilitation, the unpacking of which could not conform to a set of rules drawn up prior to engagement with the research setting. Unlike a survey approach which rests upon non-involvement with those being studied, and arguably courts the 'protection' of the researcher from the researched, my choice of the ethnographical method called for the active involvement of researcher with the researched. As I lacked the 'protective covering' of survey methods I was faced with some of the unpleasant aspects of doing research on old age and these, in turn, confronted me with moral and ethical dilemmas. Moreover, the logical contradiction of being both participant and observer in a project set in one's own society were in evidence. Matters of creativity and personal experience then became, as for others, crucial to my survival in the field (see Bell and Newby, 1977; Agar, 1980; Hammersley and Atkinson, 1983; Foote Whyte, 1984; and Punch, 1989).

My examination of these issues centres upon the themes of gaining access to Highview and the establishment of personal relationships upon which 'successful' fieldwork is based. In doing so I will compare my expectations of these matters prior to entering the field with my experiences of fieldwork.

GAINING ACCESS TO HIGHVIEW

Prior to gaining access to Highview I set about equipping myself with the language and concerns of those responsible for rehabilitation so that from the outset I could use organisational language when talking with Highview's staff. The literature on care of the elderly and my attendance at seminars in the University Department of Geriatric Medicine where I was employed were invaluable resources for this.

A major preoccupation was a concern with interactional skills needed to establish relationships. How should I introduce myself to staff and patients in Highview? While my reading of the literature, in directing me to the concerns of those caring for the elderly, could provide me with the basis for initial conversations with staff, such a course of action was not available vis-à-vis elderly people as patients. I pondered upon the age gap between myself and patients as a potential barrier to the establishment of relationships. I had had little personal experience of old people: I had known only one grandparent so had little background knowledge upon which to call. Similarly, I wondered how I would explain my ethnographical methods which were quite different to those commonly used in medical research. Would it be necessary to spend considerable time convincing people of the value of an ethnographical approach?

It took six months to gain entry into Highview. Matters which accounted for this included consultants' differing views of research, choice of initial research 'sponsor', and the necessity for my research proposal to be approved by Hospital Committees.

Each consultant saw research in quite different ways. While one cast research in evaluative terms and believed this would result in me pinpointing the deficiencies of individual staff, the other operated with a model of research based upon the testing of hypotheses. In addition, this consultant was concerned with ethical issues relating to his identification of Highview patients as 'vulnerable'.

Subsequently, I submitted a research outline to the Medical Ethical Committee of the hospital of which Highview was a part. From then on, my active involvement in negotiating access was minimised: I had to fit in with the organisation's administration. Three months later my submission was put before and accepted by the Ethical Committee.

Having gained their approval, I contacted a senior nursing administrator to arrange a meeting between her and the ward sisters of those wards with which I would be concerned. Upon doing this, however, the nursing administrator made it quite clear that, as far as she was concerned, I would need the approval of yet another committee, the District Management Team, of which she was a member. I had little option but to seek it.[4]

This encounter with the nursing administrator illustrates one of the unresolvable dilemmas of gaining entry into an organisation. Since only one member of an organisation can be the first person to be approached as a research sponsor, whoever is approached may not be the appropriate person as seen from the perspective of other potential sponsors.

DOING ETHNOGRAPHY

Initial steps

Gaining entry to the hospital, while obviously welcome, did nothing to diminish my apprehension about taking the big step of getting started. If anything, it was heightened because I now knew I had to do something. When Highview's Senior Nursing Officer (SNO) contacted me, I seized the opportunity to resolve my dilemma for it would have been impossible to ignore her approach.

We arranged that the SNO would show me around Highview so that I would become familiar with its geographical layout. A further purpose of this 'tour' was to introduce me to ward sisters. That the SNO saw my presence in Highview as related to research was evident in her introduction of me to ward staff which was in terms of 'Mrs Fairhurst who's doing research on the rehabilitation process'. A fortuitous outcome of the SNO's initiative was that my first meeting with nurses was alongside another nurse. Though my access to Highview had been granted primarily through the sponsorship of doctors I wanted to avoid my research being seen as conducted on their behest. I was reluctant to be introduced by them to ward staff. Fortunately, the SNO's contact with me skirted this issue.

I spent the first few days of my research meeting ward sisters and, when doing so, I emphasised my university affiliation as opposed to one with the National Health Service. My intention was to minimise being seen as somebody 'checking up' on nursing activities. In addition, I stressed that my time in their wards would not require any extra work from them: my interest was in the normal routine of events. Sisters sought more information about what I was doing and I was usually asked if I was a trained nurse.

The SNO's willingness to introduce me to sisters allowed me to start fieldwork but ward staff include more than sisters. In order to get to know the remaining ward staff and so that they would become used to me 'being around', I spent the first few weeks making plans of wards and sampling ward routines at different times of the day. On reflection there were two immediate benefits of this course of action: not only was I able to introduce myself to individuals working in Highview but also I became increasingly familiar with its geographical layout. I began to feel less of a stranger.

Successful fieldwork is predicated upon personal acceptance. This, in turn, requires that the researcher who is initially a stranger to those being studied becomes a non-stranger, if not a 'friend'. When I first started fieldwork I was struck by how ward staff, such as nurses, cleaners and ward clerks, did accept a researcher's presence. I found that rather than having to be taught how to be studied, they were very willing to tell me, even without knowing who I was, about themselves and their jobs.

On the other hand, my experience could be said to reflect the hierarchical nature of authority relationships found in a hospital. Since nurses, cleaners and ward clerks have little, if any, say in what happens in hospitals it is not surprising, perhaps, that they talked to me without knowing who I was. But, on the other hand, my experience allows me to make a more important general point. While my observations could be put down to ethnographic inexperience, or even to sociological naivety, more than these two matters were involved. My reading of the research literature in the mid-1970s had not alerted me to the possibility of being taught how to be a researcher by the individuals I was ostensibly studying. Thus, my pre-fieldwork concern with 'convincing people of the value of an ethnographic approach' was far too simplistic: some individuals needed convincing but others did not.

Far from having to teach people how to be studied (see McCall and Simmons, 1969) I learnt quite the opposite from my experience. Research relationships cannot be reduced to applying the 'right' approach by simply acquiring and slotting into a role. Each location and any change of staff call, then, for the establishment of fresh relationships.

Relationships with staff [5]

Given that the literature had not 'told it like it was' what did I do as a researcher in Highview? Following Schatzman and Strauss (1973), I sampled life in Highview according to the dimensions of time, space, people and events. I observed and took part in events at different times of the day and night and on every day of the week. I spent time on wards with nurses, accompanied occupational therapists, physiotherapists and social workers when doing their work either on wards or in their respective departments, and attended case conferences, ward rounds and rehabilitation review clinics.

While on wards I conducted myself in a 'serviceable manner' by assisting with the distribution of food and drinks at meal or coffeetime or getting bedlinen or clothes for patients. Although there were some instances in which I was seen as an 'extra pair of hands', I also confused existing stereotypes of what people 'working' on wards do. While there were instances in which I would be asked if I would 'lend a hand', it was accepted, nevertheless, that I could go into the ward office to look at ward registers. Now the point about working on a ward is that staff do not regularly frequent the ward office: nursing staff are on the wards to do ward work.

Though there were volunteers on Highview wards there were two matters, in addition to my perusal of ward registers, which distinguished me from them. Firstly, I did not wear any kind of overall, or uniform; I wore ordinary clothes. Secondly, in times of staff shortage,

I would help in the preparation of drug rounds by writing patients' names on slips of paper and inserting them in appropriate containers.

Just as there were times on wards when I observed rather than participated, so there were when spending time with occupational therapists or physiotherapists. Clearly, I did not possess the technical qualifications to take part in assessment of patients but I often assisted occupational therapists when they were doing diversional activities with patients. Thus, I handed out bingo cards or materials for doing craft work. That a time came when I felt able to do such things, suggests I had begun to penetrate Highview's culture for I was becoming '. . . able to pass as a native' (Halfpenny, 1979: 819). Similarly, since I lacked technical knowledge, I did not actively take part in ward rounds, case conferences or review clinics. At those events I took notes of the proceedings and functioned primarily as an observer.

Junker's (1960) classic typology of the four roles an ethnographer may take was an attempt to outline a variety of possible roles for fieldwork. The 'complete participant' and 'participant as observer' demand much more involvement with the researched than the more detached 'observer as participant' and 'the complete observer'. A difficulty with this approach, though, is that it conveys the idea that a research role is adopted for a particular study. On the contrary I had many roles: the way I conducted myself depended upon the particular location I was in and the specific purpose of a member of staff. Rather than fieldwork requiring a linear progression from observer to participant, there occurs a constant interplay between the two and one moves, imperceptibly almost, from observer to participant and back again.

The point is that what one does as a researcher is influenced by what is appropriate to particular circumstances. Thus, I would have been conspicuous if I had stood or sat rather than offering help when wards were short-staffed. I also felt it was important to give of myself rather than just accept what staff said. Though there was an acute shortage of nurses at night, I spent most of that period of fieldwork observing, listening to and talking with nurses. Since night staff were used to shortages, they had a well-developed organisation of work. It would have been inappropriate for me to have pressed offers of help on them because not only would that have emphasised my 'outsider' status but also it would have intruded on what they normally did. Whereas day staff were used to volunteers who offered help, night staff had no contact with them at all.

It is through these various ways of presentation of self that I sought to share the cultural life of staff at Highview. I was not entirely 'of it' (see Bruyn, 1966), however, because there were times when staff noted I was privy to matters they would not discuss with colleagues. Some of the social work and occupational therapy staff saw me as somebody with whom they could discuss difficulties experienced during the course of their work. Often these centred around disaffections with colleagues and it was not unusual for such talk to be formulated with reference to me being an 'outsider' as I was not employed by the hospital.

I make no claims that my initial presence in Highview may not have affected events. The novelty of a researcher's presence, however, cannot last, if for no other reason than that organisational work has to be done. People have too many pressing work tasks to be achieved to be constantly concerned with a researcher's presence. That this is so was indicated by staff's acknowledgement that they could trust me for they 'knew' I would not report observed events to their superiors.

Relationships with patients

The study of individuals who are relatively powerless raises ethical matters; particularly that they should be involved in consenting to be studied. Though aware of, and sympathetic with, such a view it seemed to me impossible to incorporate this approach in gaining access to Highview. From a practical point of view, doing the research depended upon the permission of those in authority and patients had none. It was only with the former's agreement that I could do my study through which I would have the opportunity to portray the patients' perspective. This is not to say that ethical dilemmas did not impinge on me as a researcher but we will return to them subsequently.

Before starting fieldwork I was concerned that the age gap between patients and myself would hinder the initiation of contact. In the event the major difficulty was not initiating but rather sustaining interaction. As I recorded in the early stages of fieldwork:

> Frequently, patients will raise the issue of how 'it's terrible to become dependent upon people when you get old' or mention their present fate. They see being in hospital as a poor reward for having spent their lives working. I find remarks like this very distressing and do not know what to answer. Whenever this situation arises I try to change the topic of conversation. (Fairhurst, 1975: 9)

Nor was my distress about such remarks lessened as fieldwork progressed. Although I managed to tolerate the smell of urine, I found I could never cope with elderly people bemoaning their fate. More often than not, I still attempted to change the topic of conversation. It is interesting to note that when I tried to close conversations with patients some of them raised a new topic. In such circumstances, I had little option but to continue talking for to have done otherwise would have transgressed social conventions. Any attempt of mine to curtail the conversation abruptly could have been interpreted as 'rudeness'.

I came to know many patients very well and they were interested to know about my family life and what I did when I was not in the hospital. My university affiliation was taken as an opportunity to tell me about the educational achievements of children and grandchildren. On the whole, patients saw me as somebody with whom they could talk: as someone in whom they could confide. They also viewed me as someone who would do things for them. It may be that patients told me about themselves precisely because they came to realise I would buy sweets, stamps or writing materials for them. In this way it could be said there was some kind of exchange relationship between patients and myself.

At first, patients addressed me as 'nurse' but this reflects less their perception of my function than the distinction generally made by old people in Highview between staff. In general, patients operated with two categories of staff – doctors or nurses. Physiotherapists, occupational therapists and social workers often remarked upon their being called 'nurse' by patients. Once patients knew that I was doing research, they would tell new patients that I was not a nurse. This usually occurred when a new patient would ask me to help him/her out of bed or accompany him/her to the toilet. While I often assisted a nurse to do such tasks I was reluctant, given the frail condition of many patients, to do so unaided.

One important difference between my relationships with patients and staff cannot be ignored. While I could do some of the work undertaken by remedial staff or nurses, I could not 'do' being an old person. This was put into sharp perspective for me after I had been on holiday during fieldwork. I noted that this had relevance to understanding how patients might feel about being in hospital for a lengthy period. My field notes continued:

> I have been able to have a holiday. The choice has been mine to remove myself from the situation but the patients have not got this choice. I really felt as though I just couldn't go on any longer doing fieldwork and it was absolutely necessary for me to get away. The patients, however, are not able to do so. Stressing the fact that I had the choice to remove myself from the situation does of course raise the problem of the extent to which my account can fully reflect an empathy with patients. Clearly, because I have the option to remove myself from the situation, then my account can never fully reflect an empathy with patients. However, the fact that I had found it necessary to remove myself from the fieldwork situation does, I think, serve to emphasise exactly how boring and oppressive and how harrowing the hospital might be for many people. In this way I have been able to get the feel of at least some of the monotony and routineness which you find in much of hospital life of geriatric patients.

It could be argued that the difficulties of a younger researcher being unable to 'do' being an old person can be accounted for by the disparity in chronological age between the researched and the researcher. But if this were so how could we reconcile this with notions that, despite a gulf in age, grandchildren and grandparents often 'get on well together'. I would suggest that the difference in my relationships with staff and patients relates to general matters of personal experience and conducting research on unpalatable topics and it is to these we must turn now.

PERSONAL EXPERIENCE AND ETHNOGRAPHY IN ONE'S OWN SOCIETY

Since my study was set in a hospital, some of the more extreme consequences of old age for individuals confronted me daily. Some of the results of declining physical functioning such as incontinence, brain damage and ulcerated legs are unpleasant for one human being to witness in another. Given this, research on old age, especially on the hospitalised elderly, may be said to involve focusing on an unpalatable topic. As such it presents a researcher with moral and ethical dilemmas.[6]

In this section I want to refer much more extensively than I have done previously to my field notes. Specifically I shall use comments from them which I made two months and then twelve months after I had been in the field. The first extract notes:

> It is quite evident from these notes that the whole geriatric set up has really got to me and I have hit a low trough of depression in fieldwork. One often reads about this in accounts of fieldwork and in many ways one is sceptical about it. However, having experienced this and no doubt I will experience it again while doing this research, it is perhaps worthwhile to record my views on the matter. I have noted how being a participant observer raises questions for me personally and I have compared this with the role of the social anthropologist in, for example, an African society. The thing is of course that in my research I know people who are of the same age as the people in my study. I think it could happen to them or my parents or even me. There is no way one can get away from this set up as it is my society.

In the early stages of fieldwork, then, I became aware of the ramifications of conducting anthropological-style work in an untraditional anthropological setting. As I thought, the stressful nature of fieldwork did confront me again in my research and now I want to examine that topic further by focusing on field notes written twelve months after being in the field. These specific notes also allow me to illustrate particularly what might count as 'stressful'. My notes began:

> It is with the utmost effort that I am writing today's notes. I really feel like walking out of the hospital and never going there again. I might even go as far as to say that I have arrived home tonight feeling the most depressed that I have ever felt.

On that day, three events relating to three separate individuals, which disturbed me, occurred. The first concerned a woman whose sister, without asking her but on the advice of her GP, had given up the tenancy of her home and sold her furniture. I was distressed by this because the woman was due for discharge a few days later. I mentioned the matter to the ward sister and expressed my surprise. The ward sister agreed but she added that, in her opinion, the patient would not be going home anyway. It interested me that she did not pick up my comment about the patient not being consulted about giving up her home.

The second incident focused on a woman whom I had got to know very well during my period of fieldwork. She had been in hospital for almost nine months before she had been discharged to an old people's home. She was attending the day hospital attached to the geriatric unit. I asked her how she was finding the home. She told me she was very unhappy there. She was of the firm opinion that it was not 'a home'. She was terrified at the thought of having to spend the rest of her life there. She detailed the conduct of the manageress of the home and how, all in all, she did not like it.

Finally, there came an incident akin to the proverbial straw that broke the camel's back. One of the men I asked to take part in my study of patient careers refused for 'everything gets back to the nurses'. Despite my assurances of confidentiality he was adamant he did not want to take part. Apparently one of the nursing staff had challenged him about complaints he had allegedly made about nurses on another ward. I had the impression he thought I was involved in the matter in some way. Fortunately, I succeeded in convincing him otherwise but he was still unwilling to be interviewed for he did not want to be called a 'troublemaker'. I found our conversation very distressing not only because of the content but also because he was stammering when talking to me.

My dilemma in this case was twofold. On the one hand, I had great sympathy with the man for I found it intolerable that he should be treated in the way he had been by nursing staff. On the other hand, however, I realised that informing a ward sister or nursing officer of the incident might have had exactly the opposite consequences for the man than I had intended: my action could have been interpreted as confirming him as a 'troublemaker'. The point is I did not have to live in the hospital. Whereas I left the hospital each day, the man was there until his discharge or death. To cope with this dilemma I left the hospital shortly afterwards and this, or going to another part of the hospital, were the ways I usually responded to such events. That I, like staff, did leave the hospital, sharply differentiated my daily life from that of patients.

Moreover, just as some staff's actions caused me ethical dilemmas so did my own. I earlier described the strategies adopted when patients bemoaned their present state. Over and above the practical problems they presented me with, they also highlight the ethics of taking certain information from individuals and yet, at the same time, attempting to forestall the airing of their own grievances.

I would suggest that two general points can be drawn from my fieldwork experience. Firstly, research on unpleasant topics may, and in my case, did, have personal implications for the researcher. As my field notes indicate, patients' experiences of Highview took on a special significance. The very fact of Highview being set in my society brought home to me that other people I knew, especially my parents or even I myself, might share such experiences. My reluctance to act as an advocate for patients in those instances where I found their treatment distressing placed me in a difficult moral position for I felt as though I was in some ways a party to the whole set-up. We have here in stark reality the logical contradiction of being both participant and observer.

The genesis of this contradiction derives from the geographical proximity of the researcher's 'field' to her own arena of life. Agar's (1980) discussion pinpoints the fuzzy line between fieldwork and home life. Whereas traditional ethnographies involve travel to another country with consequent clear distinctions between home and the field, ethnographies in one's own society involve frequent and more rapid movement between home and field.

Doing research close to home, then, has consequences not only for the researcher as an individual but also for the relationship between the researcher's experience and the research findings. It is precisely because unpleasant aspects of doing research concerning elderly people, particularly those in hospital, are inextricably linked with the notion of personal experience that arguably accounts, at least in part, for the relatively few ethnographies of old age. The concern with resource allocation, be it in terms of medical or social services, in many studies of old age is an example of what Roth (1962) has termed 'management bias' on the part of social scientists. Studies focusing on the experiential aspects of old age should acknowledge and confront the crucial matter of the researcher's own experience. I would not claim my experiences offer any special solution about how to do research on unpleasant topics but I believe those experiences were an integral part of my data.

RECORDING AND ANALYSING ETHNOGRAPHICAL DATA

The dynamic nature of ethnographical research has implications for both its doing and its recording. The continual move from observation to participation has consequences not only for roles adopted but also for the recording of field notes. As I acknowledged earlier, when I functioned primarily as an observer I was able to make notes while at Highview. Apart from those instances, I followed the conventional practice of ethnographers of compiling my notes at the end of each day. I dictated them on to a tape-recorder for transcription by my secretary. Each page of transcribed field notes was dated and individually numbered.

Given that eighteen months of fieldwork yielded hundreds of typed pages of field notes, how did I analyse them? At the time of my research Glaser and Strauss' (1967) notion of grounded theory was an influential analytical approach among ethnographers. They argued for the generation of theory from comparative analysis of similar and dissimilar events. Consequently theory is continuously generated during analysis which takes place during the course of the research. I found this comparative approach useful in directing me to look at the same theme in different parts of the organisation, for instance, the way different occupational groups within the rehabilitation team had different views of an ideal rehabilitation patient; how ideas about nursing work differed between night and day staff and how old people as patients viewed their experiences (see for example Fairhurst, 1981a, 1981b and 1983a).

As a lone researcher, though, it was not always possible to adhere strictly to Glaser and Strauss' canons of analysis throughout fieldwork. I did give a number of conference papers based upon the study whilst still doing the research. The major part of my analysis, however, was done after completing fieldwork. I made an index of field notes on cards which listed major themes and events and their location in my notes. These became the basis of my analytic categories.[7] The advent of personal computers, of course, facilitates quicker retrieval of analytic categories.

CONCLUDING REMARKS

In this chapter I have examined the potentialities of an ethnographic approach for gerontology with special reference to the experiential aspects of old age. An important feature of such endeavours is the confrontation of issues emanating from conducting ethnography in the researcher's own society. In presenting them I focused upon the establishment of relationships with individuals in Highview, and compared those matters, which prior to beginning fieldwork I envisaged would impinge upon fieldwork relationships with my experience once in Highview. This approach enabled me to suggest that fieldwork relations, rather than being based upon clear distinctions between observation and participation, call for continual movement between these two states and this is a process influenced by the contingencies of situations in which a researcher finds her or himself. In addition, the consequences of the tensions between being both participant and observer in one's own society directed attention to personal experience as an integral part of the researcher's own conduct *qua* researcher. I have described the ways I sought to penetrate the culture of Highview. It would be naive of me to claim I have totally understood it. Beattie's (1964) longstanding advice to social anthropologists about the unattainability of perfectly understanding other cultures is pertinent to ethnography in non-traditional settings, not least because what we study, even though part of our society, is just as strange to us as that of any pre-industrial society studied by a social anthropologist.

NOTES

I should like to acknowledge the financial support of Ciba-Geigy, the support of my former colleagues in Department of Geriatric Medicine at Manchester University and the patients and staff of Highview who, despite some of the topics raised here, helped to make my fieldwork enjoyable. My thanks also to Jean Biggs for typing this manuscript.

1. Although not a major focus of this paper, the reader should be aware of the existence of a debate within anthropology and sociology about the distinguishing features and theoretical and logical underpinnings of ethnography. See, for example, Becker (1958); Bruyn (1966); Glaser and Strauss (1967); Schatzman and Strauss (1973); Johnson (1978); Agar (1980); Burgess (1982); Hammersley and Atkinson (1983); and Strauss (1987). Given this debate the reader should note that not all ethnographical studies necessarily share the same theoretical framework (Halfpenny, 1979).

2. For some North American ethnographies of old age see, for example, on residential settings, Gubrium (1975, 1980), Hochschild (1973) and Ross (1977) and, on day centres, Myerhoff (1978).

3. In, for example, Fairhurst (1979, 1980, 1983b, 1987, 1988) and Fairhurst and Lightup (1982), I used ethnographic interviews and documentary analysis in a study of middle-aged men and women.

4. Some of the functions and roles, such as District Management Team and Senior Nursing Officer, in use in the NHS at the time of my study, no longer exist.

5. This section relies heavily upon part of Fairhurst (1983a).

6. For some recent discussions of ethical issues involved in research other than on old age see Punch (1989) on police deviancy and Cannon (1989) on breast cancer.

7. Since the 1970s increasing attention has been directed towards the analysis and writing of ethnography. See, for example, Gubrium and Silverman (1989), Hammersley and Atkinson (1983), Punch (1986) and Strauss (1987).

8

Triangulating Data

LEONIE KELLAHER, SHEILA PEACE
AND DIANNE WILLCOCKS

It is a fact that much of the research carried out during the 1970s and 1980s concerning older people is evaluative research, aimed at examining the delivery and effectiveness of certain services. The focus of this chapter is upon just one of the trends to have emerged in evaluation over the past decade or so. This is an approach to evaluation which has been referred to as a 'pluralistic' one; that is to say, more than a single perspective is taken in approaching a particular area of service provision. Indeed, several approaches may be adopted, and many different categories of informant may be involved in data collection (see Smith and Cantley, 1988). These kinds of strategies clearly differ from the traditional large survey approach in that they entail a range of methods and sources, rather than a single pathway.

Multi-method or pluralistic evaluation has evolved partly as a response to circumstances which have changed somewhat since the 1960s when the larger-scale survey method was predominant in social policy research. Firstly, there has been an increasing emphasis on social processes. This goes beyond the traditional 'black box' model of research concerned with simple ideas of inputs and outcomes. Thus, the consumers' experiences and their accounts of service provision move into sharper focus. It is no longer seen as sufficient to measure gross 'satisfaction' levels amongst older people as users of services. The obstacles and pathways towards take-up of a particular service have increasingly come under examination, and this has demanded innovative ways of eliciting information that are, inevitably, more complex.

Secondly, the idea of a user being a single individual, who can be considered at some distance from the contexts of social, political, geographical and material settings, has given way to an acknowledgement that users act and make choices in relation to, and within, all of these settings, and that a more rounded picture is necessary if services are to be shaped in ways which are acceptable to older people themselves. Correspondingly, where the providers of services are concerned, the assumption that planning processes are rational enough for service delivery to be evaluated from a cross-sectional, snapshot view of bureaucratic or organisational activities and statements of intent, can no longer be held. Qualitative or longitudinal strategies are frequently adopted to understand better the discrepancies and dislocations which exist between policy statements and service outcomes.

An approach to evaluation thus becomes necessary that acknowledges a wide range of group interests; that reorganises unequal power relations and that responds to varied definitions of what constitutes successful service provision. Hence, a multi-dimensional approach to data collection is now often advocated. But what is a multi-dimensional approach; what does it constitute, and how is it constructed? Is it something more than a simple hedging of bets? Is it a version of the ethnographic method of research? How is complex data analysis undertaken? And most crucially, what does it achieve in terms of service evaluation and in terms of improved service provision for older people? This chapter considers these questions in relation to a particular case study in which local authority residential provision for elderly people was evaluated using a range of methods of data collection, a particular approach to analysing and meshing findings, and a series of dissemination 'products'.[1]

THE NATIONAL CONSUMER STUDY IN 100 LOCAL AUTHORITY OLD PEOPLE'S HOMES

The research in question was a study of consumers in 100 local authority old people's homes, commissioned by the DHSS (Works Division) in 1980. Since this was a piece of commissioned research, two sets of definitions concerning the problem to be investigated – those of the sponsor and those of the research team – emerged at the outset. The sponsors were professional architects at the DHSS whose broad objective was to encourage local authority architects to design residential homes which would offer improved living environments for elderly people in care. Their vehicle for achieving professional architectural influence was the *Local Authority Building Note No. 2* (DHSS and Welsh Office, 1973) which offered guidelines rather than mandatory instructions. This document was to be revised and the research findings were to inform that revision.

Many assumptions – only partially informed – were made by the sponsors about the kind of research appropriate to the task. In submitting a proposal, researchers set about an explicit redefining of the objectives. The sponsors were working in the traditional administrator's mode, which meant that they wished to obtain reliable information on which to base professional design and management; policy and practice. However, the researchers proposed a more elaborate model which insisted that any understanding of service provision which aimed to promote consumer satisfaction in residential care needed to take account of the following interacting factors:

- the physical environment of homes – design and layout
- the institutional environment – regime and social interaction
- the characteristics of the users and of those working with them

The operationalisation of this model was to be achieved through the identification of specific aims around which the research strategy could be developed:

- to assess the reaction of elderly residents in local authority homes to their present environment and to interpret the practical implications this may have for planners and architects;
- to explore the attitudes of old people to residential care and identify consumer preference, or aspirations for environmental improvement amongst the users;
- to investigate attitudes and experiences of staff, and to look at the impact of physical features of the home on working life;
- to determine the way in which quality of life may be influenced by a range of factors relating to physical environment, institutional environment and residential mix;
- to determine the importance of locational factors, and the extent to which the convenience and proximity of the home to local services and accessibility to family and friends may contribute to social and psychological well-being for both elderly residents and staff.

In order to meet most of the needs of the sponsors, the use of a fairly straightforward cross-sectional survey approach seemed to suffice. However, in order to obtain information on processes and interactions concerning the actual use of the buildings being evaluated it was necessary to adopt other methods (see Willcocks et al., 1987). In the event, the following research strategies were adopted.

Collection of data through surveys

Survey data was collected at various stages in the project. First, a postal questionnaire was sent to all local authorities in England to discover the crucial parameters of residential provision. This data was used in the stratified sampling of 100 homes for further study. Within the hundred homes, interviews were carried out with 1000 residents (ten from each home) and 400 staff (four from each home). Interviews with staff and residents concentrated on their views about the physical environment in which they lived and worked. Questions asked of the elderly residents also looked at how and why they had come to live in residential care and at other aspects of life in the homes. This survey also included measures of psychological well-being, even though the researchers recognised the problems of administering these kinds of scales with older people living in care settings (see Peace, et al., 1979). Where staff were concerned, interviews looked especially at interactions between staff and residents; aspects of staff routine and staff characteristics. In addition to the structured interviews a visual technique was employed at the end of each resident interview. This procedure was developed to encourage residents' responses in prioritising their preferences on more than 20 aspects of the institutional environment, which were depicted on a series of cards (Willcocks, 1984). The interviewers who carried out the two surveys also completed a schedule giving their impressions of the homes they visited. Finally, a detailed appraisal was carried out of the physical environment of each of the 100 homes by one of the researchers.

Collection of data through detailed study

Detailed studies were carried out in a sub-sample of four homes: an observation study examined social interaction patterns and the daily routine within each home; a location study explored the relationship between residential homes and the local environs. A week was spent at each home for each study. Pilot work was carried out in one home (chosen from eight pilot homes used for the surveys), before embarking upon detailed investigations in three other homes. The rationale for selection was the coverage of the widest range of features across a small number of homes rather than a concentration upon similar features, and on a comparison between homes.

The observation study

The relative strengths of observation over survey approaches can be argued in the following ways:

Observation studies have:

- the capacity to take account of sequences of events;
- the capacity to study actions rather than reports of actions. Additionally, observation allows the possibility of discovering 'deviant' behaviour which may represent informal institutional organisation. Discrepancies between reported and observed behaviour and formal and informal organisation may be explored using observational techniques;
- observation studies place emphasis upon whole configurations of actions, upon contextual interpretations and upon process as well as service inputs and behavioural outcomes;
- groups rather than individuals may be investigated, since observation gives direct access to encounters and interactions between people and things.

After a period of pilot work, an approach was developed which would permit some systematic comparison of material observed in the four very different homes. At the same time, scope for a responsiveness to the unique features of the regime of the particular homes was to be maintained. Two instruments were devised. First a *log-journal* – a sequential account, covering seven days or around 100 hours, of observed events. This represented a temporal or linear aspect of observation. Very brief notes were made during the day and expanded at the end of each day's observation. Secondly, *field-logs* were taken for six days. These were notes taken twice a day at those times when institutional routines allowed residents some measure of choice about where to be and what to do.

In addition to these measures, four activities or domains which had emerged as pivotal to residential life were selected for particular record. They were:

– mealtimes – representing the daily cycle of the residential process;
– bathtimes – representing a focus for the weekly cycle of residential life;
– attitudes to the management of incontinence;
– attitudes to physical deterioration amongst residents and to death.

The residential life and its processes were thus observed and charted along temporal and spatial dimensions, and also in relation to attitudes and practices which, it was argued, permeate the residential process as a whole.

The location study
The location study, which was concerned with the home in its community and neighbourhood contexts, also combined a range of research techniques. These included a mapping exercise of the home's location and the site. Taped discussions with groups of residents and staff in the four homes were undertaken to discuss their experiences outside the home. These included journeys to work; local amenities; use of the grounds and views from the windows. A small community survey was carried out at each site to obtain the attitudes and opinions of those living in the immediate vicinity of the home; that is to say along the boundary. Finally, for each home there was a series of taped, in-depth, interviews with at least three professionals who had been involved in the design, planning and siting of old people's homes for each of the four authorities. This included interviews with architects, planners and members of social services staff. The group discussions and in-depth interviews were carried out with the aid of a topic list rather than a questionnaire, in order to allow conversation to flow more freely. Thus, a complete profile was developed for each of the four homes giving data on patterns and interactions inside and beyond the establishment's physical boundaries.

DATA ANALYSIS

Given the constraints of the original 18-month contract, the possibilities for cross-fertilisation between the wealth of quantitative and qualitative material which had been collected were severely limited once the writing-up stage was reached. Inevitably, it is difficult to achieve full exploitation of the data, in the first instance, when the sponsor is pushing for 'results' and immediacy is paramount. At the first level of reporting back to sponsors, the qualitative material served mainly to spotlight several of the possible paths through the mass of quantitative data and to illustrate certain key points. The point really to be made here is that, whilst it could only be advantageous to adopt qualitative strategies, in addition to quantitative ones, the researchers did not anticipate at the analysis and report stage how the two kinds of findings could be meshed. Nevertheless, in the later drafting stages, which involved the three principal researchers, each of whom had taken responsibility for one of three data sets, it transpired that findings from across the three data sets were being used to illuminate findings and to make or support arguments.

The question arises here whether this is what is meant by the term 'triangulation', or whether such meshing of data was simply the consequence of a multidisciplinary team; sociologist, social anthropologist and social geographer, working in close collaboration on the same topic and material? What it might reveal is the extent to which triangulation might operate in ways that are more or less visible and explicit; sometimes relating to different professional or disciplinary perspectives and this, in turn, linked to different methods which may be embedded in different research contexts. Importantly, triangulation essentially implies a meeting and meshing of different boundaries for a given topic which enables questions to be posed in new ways, leading to fresh insights and understandings.

Triangulation of methods

It has frequently been argued, for example by Campbell and Fiske (1959), Moser and Kalton (1971) and Denzin (1970), that investigation in the social sciences should adopt a range of research methods; particularly that quantitative and qualitative approaches should be combined in complementary ways. However, research practitioners engage – not infrequently – in spirited debates concerning the merits and deficiencies of each approach. Yet a complete separation of so-called quantitative and qualitative approaches hardly seems possible. For in quantitative work, categories for investigation and analysis must first be distinguished through pilot work, and this is likely to consist of qualitative, unstructured explorations, such as observation in the natural setting. Conversely, in qualitative work some quantification is

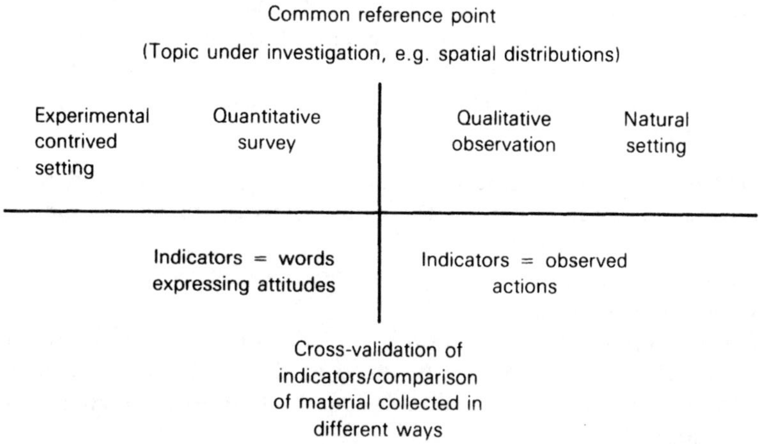

Common reference point

(Topic under investigation, e.g. spatial distributions)

| Experimental contrived setting | Quantitative survey | Qualitative observation | Natural setting |

Indicators = words expressing attitudes   Indicators = observed actions

Cross-validation of
indicators/comparison
of material collected in
different ways

Figure 8.1 *A framework for linking data*

necessary, if only to note the length of stay in the field. Thus it can be argued that all social research rests upon some commonly accepted reference points by which researchers can transmit and translate their particular observations more widely to others. In order to achieve the highest standards of reliability, validity and replicability researchers would expect to share data in ways that correspond to real-world concepts of frequency of activity and experience of everyday events, that is, both quantity and quality.

The necessity of using indicators in every method of research is therefore an ever-present foundation for integration. In a survey, the basic indicator is a form of words which reveal attitudes, goals, etc. and which may refer to habitual or ideal actions. In observation the basic indicators may be units of activity by which the subject's goals are, perhaps indirectly, revealed. These goals may only be inferred from the choices of action the subjects appear to prefer, and those options they refuse. The difference may be between covert and overt behaviour. The whole methodological repertoire might be conceptualised along a continuum ranging from the experimental or contrived setting at one extreme to the natural setting at the other. Quantitative and qualitative methods can similarly be conceived as lying either side of a common reference point, both methods contributing indicators which we might expect to inform the topic under scrutiny or consideration (see Figure 8.1). But the adoption of a multi-method approach does not simply mean the collection of more data; rather, it should permit a sharper focusing upon the reference points around which research is constructed.

Triangulation then, is more than just combining methods. In *Linking Data* by Fielding and Fielding (1986) the authors refer to triangulation as 'using a number of data sources (self, informants, others in the setting) or a number of accounts of events (the same person regarding an event from several "angles" for different audiences)' (1986: 24). Denzin, writing earlier, in 1970, specifies four possible forms of triangulation:

- data triangulation – including triangulation in time, space and person;
- investigator triangulation – the same situation being examined by more than one person;
- theory triangulation – using different theoretical perspectives to examine a situation;
- methodological triangulation – including 'within-method' approaches (e.g. same method used at different times); 'between-method' approaches (e.g. different methods used in relation to the same subject).

How this range of material is analysed, combined and used in data analysis and reporting has been less widely discussed (Fielding and Fielding, 1986). At one level it is obvious that the use of several approaches represents an insurance policy – data overlooked in one approach may be retrieved from another, each compensating and complementing the other. In *Linking Data*, Nigel and Jane Fielding argue that the important feature of triangulation is not a simple combination of different kinds of data but the attempt to relate these different kinds of data so as to counteract the threats to validity identified within each. In this way, the differences between data sets can be as illuminating as the areas of overlap. The aim is thus to add breadth and depth to analysis.

But what kinds of data should be triangulated? And in practical terms how is it done? Again, Fielding and Fielding suggest that as many guides as possible should be employed to home in on the topic or theme. In particular, they suggest that at least one method that reveals the structural aspects of a problem should be used; and also a method that looks at actual interactions. This way the meaning of events or features for all those involved can be considered (1986: 34). This all seems sensible and prudent and, given sufficient resources and the appropriate research skills, few would argue with such a strategy. However, there are a number of important questions to be raised. How is the move from the ideals of multi-methodology to practical tactics made? That is, how is data collection to be designed? Then, how is data to be handled when two or more approaches are adopted? Is it enough to aim to transform qualitative data into quantitative data? Does this not defeat the object of the qualitative approach of aiming for a holistic view of phenomenon? What is the status of comparison across and between approaches where data are of such divergent complexions? Indeed what of the different status accorded to quantitative and qualitative methods? How are we to take this into account?

Fielding and Fielding (1986) suggest that there are three ways of considering the comparability of data:

- data combined – using different methods to explore analytic themes or 'frames', data treated cumulatively;
- data in conflict – data from one methodology may conflict with another, identifying points of dissonance;
- indefinite triangulation – here they suggest that the inevitability of different versions can be used analytically not to highlight dissonance but to highlight how various interpretations of events can be assembled from people having different physical, temporal and biographical experience of the situation.

These three frameworks can be applied to the case study being considered here to examine some of the ways in which the data relating to the residential life of old people have been treated.

Data combined
The most systematic attempt at data triangulation in this study of 100 old people's homes took place in the period of secondary analysis of the data during 1983–5 which was supported by the ESRC (Peace et al., 1986). The main objective of this analysis was to develop a model of residential life for old people which could predict those aspects of residential life which had most influence on resident well-being.

Much of the secondary analysis concentrated on the creation of a home-based file for the 100 homes, which involved aggregating and linking survey data from the staff survey, the residents' survey and the studies of physical environments. In order to make manageable the analysis of what had started as a great many simple variables, a number of derived or aggregated variables were created. This exercise rested heavily on the knowledge and experience which the researchers had gained in the course of fieldwork and was also informed by other authors writing in the same area (for example Goffman, 1961; Raynes et al., 1979; Moos, 1980; Lawton, 1980). Data was taken, then, from several sources in order to create derived variables (see Willcocks et al., 1987). In Figure 8.2 an example is given of the variable STAFFSAT (resident satisfaction with staff) developed through combining the responses to a number of questions contained in the questionnaire administered to residents.

Initial analysis using correlation techniques showed that institutional effects were not the only determinants of resident or staff well-being or satisfaction. In order to take this further, multiple regression analysis was used to try and predict aspects of resident well-being. A range of independent variables concerning the physical environment, the organisational/social environment and mix of residents was used to predict resident well-being as measured on a number of scales (see Peace et al., 1986).

Variable Name: - STAFFSAT

Definition: - Resident satisfaction with staff

Items: - Resident questionnaire, residents asked Do you ever feel that:
  - staff don't spend enough time talking to you?
  - staff are always telling you what to do?
  - there are not enough staff in the home?
  - you do not get to know the staff?
  - staff are always changing?
  - staff spend too long with particular residents?

Figure 8.2   *Derived Variable – Resident Satisfaction with Staff*

The results are best explained in relation to three measures of outcome: adjustment to home life; adjustment to ageing; and average resident satisfaction with life. In each multiple regression model the researchers were able to explain approximately 40 per cent of the variance on the basis of 18 variables. However, in each case, six or seven variables accounted for the greater part of this variation (32–3 per cent) with one variable 'STAFFSAT' (outlined above) being prominent in each case (see Peace et al., 1986). This analysis led to the question of whether any further light might be shed on these relationships by a systematic consideration of the qualitative data. It seemed necessary to turn to the qualitative data since, despite the construction of a plausible multivariate model, there remained uncertainty that the aggregated data were in fact reliable. The difficulty of administering those parts of the resident questionnaire concerning well-being had already been acknowledged. So the unreliability of this and other data would have been compounded by aggregation in order to produce derived variables and variables at the level of home.

In turning to the qualitative data, a method of linking and comparing data sets was possible, and subsequently a strategy was developed whereby the qualitative material was structured and, in effect, quantified. Although the researchers were unable to develop this technique across the whole qualitative data set, the analysis started by taking the questions from the derived variable 'STAFFSAT' to develop the categories for a content analysis of the chronologically written observations covering periods of seven consecutive days in the detailed observation study. The following categories were developed for content analysis:

- Incidents where staff were carrying out a task and ignoring residents; residents' wishes not respected or acted upon;
- Staff engaged in interaction which could be seen as authoritarian behaviour – coercion, manipulation;
- Resident in need, but staff absent;
- Resident does not need staff assistance, but staff present;

- Resident and staff unfamiliar with each other;
- Resident uncertain of staff role;
- Staff seem to have favourite resident(s) and behaviour is detrimental to other residents.

Using this coding system content analysis was carried out by two researchers, independently. Each paragraph of reported observation was used as a unit of analysis. Results showed a high level of agreement between researchers (60–70 per cent). The most common areas of behaviour recorded related to items 1 and 2, staff ignoring residents and being authoritarian. This exercise proved very useful in charting the nature of interactions of staff and residents over extended periods of time. As expected, there were variations between the homes on aspects of staff/resident relationships and this meant that it became possible to look at the unique differences between home types that had been lost in the aggregation of data.

Data in conflict
The best examples of conflicting data being used to uncover residential realities arose in the comparison of stated policy and actual practice. Comparison was made across the survey of staff, the survey of residents; observations and field-logs in a small number of homes, and the examination of official guidance documents from the local authorities. The theme of 'territorial control' in homes may illustrate the value of considering material that appears to be at odds. In the 100 homes, the survey of residents showed that just half the residents occupied a room of their own; in principle, therefore, they had the possibility of retaining individual identity in personal space. But what did this particular residential reality actually mean? When staff were asked 'Can residents lock their own rooms?' only eight homes emerged where this was even said to be possible. This raised the question of whether space that is not 'defensible' could ever be truly personal. However, when asked 'Do residents have somewhere to lock up their personal possessions in their rooms?' this appeared as a possibility for over half the residents (52 per cent). When actual practice in the four homes studied in detail was considered, however, the following procedures were observed: in one home doors could be locked and keys were available, but these were allowed only to certain residents and doors could only be locked from the outside, so only possessions could be secured. In the other homes doors were fitted with locks that served no function whatsoever. In one case the keys had long since been mislaid; and in others, residents were not issued with keys. Thus the emphasis in practice was upon securing property rather than upon residents securing themselves or their territory. This conclusion was endorsed by statements made by senior staff, and also in local guidance documents where no mention was made of locking rooms, though a great deal of space was devoted to 'safety of property'.

A second important theme in residential care is 'privacy'. In official guidance privacy appears to represent an ideal goal of policy – yet at the time of the study, in 1981, little evidence was found of practices designed to operationalise 'privacy' in any real way. In general the researchers found that staff expressed the certain belief that residents did have privacy. Eighty per cent of staff thought residents had privacy whenever they wanted and an even higher proportion of staff (91 per cent) said that residents generally had privacy for entertaining visitors. Yet there was a high degree of disjunction between the various sets of information concerning territory and privacy. The field logging exercise in the four detailed study homes showed that only 10 per cent of residents in these homes moved from their customary place in the lounge during the course of an eight-hour period other than to go for a meal, to the toilet, or for a routinely organised bath. Such documentation of areas of mismatch between policy and practice proved crucial when it came to putting across findings to practitioners and policy makers and, particularly in helping staff and managers think about making changes in residential practice (see CESSA, 1986).

Indefinite triangulation
An example of indefinite triangulation was the way in which a picture was built up of the importance of environmental control to residents that was to be the mainstay of the final argument and recommendations to the DHSS concerning the design of residential care homes (see Willcocks et al., 1982b, 1987; Peace et al., 1982). Although at the time of making recommendations this argument developed in an apparently spontaneous way as the three researchers worked together, on reflection it is possible to see how material from several sources contributed to the formulation of the argument and to its strength. A major recommendation concerning the protection of personal space, which found concrete expression in the discussion of the proposed 'residential flatlet', can be traced to material which came from the following data sets:

- residents questionnaire – data concerning the residents' desire for single rooms; the fact that residents with rooms of their own made more friends;
- visual game – how residents ranked highly those aspects of environment that were 'normal, unexceptional, uninstitutional' such as temperature, single rooms, ordinary baths;
- staff questionnaire – data concerning staff's desire for resident privacy and autonomy even recognising the conflict with staff needs for 'the organisation to run smoothly';
- observational material – residents' use of space; gender differences in the use of space; how space was used to control surveillance of residents and how this affected resident behaviour.

CONCLUSION

In the course of the question which has been posed in this chapter –
whether triangulation 'exists' – terms like 'process', 'input' and
'outcome' have been used. By way of conclusion the authors would
argue that a set of research strategies have been employed in the study
of 100 old people's homes which is something more than a collection
of assorted techniques and methods for the collection of data.

Triangulation as a methodology, rather than as a method, is founded
upon a combination of complex elements which come into play at
different stages during the course of a research programme. In other
words, triangulation occurs in relation to the stages of:

input
process
outcome

The kinds of *input* which promote triangulation are associated with the
presence of certain conditions. These will include sufficient diversity
within the researcher or the research team to allow material/data/
research questions to be framed in ways which are qualitatively
different to the ways which are likely to be generated when there is
a more unilateral approach. This qualitative difference might be a
consequence of having a multidisciplinary team, or of there being an
individual researcher with a breadth of intellectual and/or practical
interests and skills. This in itself should introduce different theoretical
and practical challenges. Apart from these multi-faceted aspects within
the research team, there is a corresponding multiplicity of interests
amongst those being researched; these interests, if acknowledged and
then addressed in research terms, will provide the chances of triangulation.

The *process* of the research is likely to be a triangulated one where
different structural influences within the research question are again
recognised and come to inform the way the research is carried out.
Such influences in the case study described here come under headings
such as:

political/ideological
economic
professional
temporal

Whilst it may not always be feasible to take a broad view and
approach, the wide range of influences described here will always be
present within an issue under investigation. The critical path to
triangulation will, however, depend upon resourcing, time and a willingness or capacity on the part of researchers to think broadly around
the issues.

When considering the *outcomes* of research which claims to be triangulated, it is helpful to look back at the categories suggested by Fielding and Fielding (1986). They note that research can confirm and elaborate previously known facts. It can elicit information which is in conflict with what is already known, or it can provide inconclusive data. Here the authors propose a simple nomenclature based upon differences in the kinds of evidence which arise out of a multi-method approach to an issue or a problem.

- *Confirmatory evidence*: for instance the study of old people's homes confirmed the observations of policy-makers and practitioners that residents did not make many decisions about moving around the home, outside the influences which could be classified as institutionally determined.
- *Disconfirmatory evidence*: residents expressed views about the grouping of chairs in the public lounges which were opposed to the views put forward – as the residents' preference – by staff.
- *Circumstantial evidence*: this kind of evidence informed the principal recommendation to arise out of the study, namely that in redesigning and reorganising residential homes for older people, there should be a reversal of the kinds of spatial balance which had been observed, because the resident evidence, though muted, gave sufficient weight to the conclusion that greater investments should be made in personal and private space, at the expense of public space.

In other words, different kinds of evidence emerge in novel ways which can successfully challenge powerful assumptions that may be defended by powerful interest groups or agencies. All the examples given regarding the three categories established by Fielding and Fielding show how myths and misunderstandings about residential care, whose origins can be traced to the poor law and to professional protectionism, can start to be unravelled by triangulated data that is so compelling it just will not go away.

NOTE

1. For further details of the dissemination of findings from the National Consumer Study in 100 Local Authority Old People's Homes see Chapter 13.

9

Researching Very Old People

MICHAEL BURY AND ANTHEA HOLME

INTRODUCTION

Background to the study

The cumulative effect of declining death rates combined with a bulge in the birth rate in previous years has meant that the numbers and proportion of the elderly aged 85 years and over has increased steadily and will continue to grow over the next 20 years.

At the time the present study began in 1986, the changing balance between these very old people and the young elderly in this country was sometimes noted both in official statistics (Craig, 1987) and demographic research (see for example Walker, 1986a). There was, nevertheless, a tendency to treat the very old as a residual group. This tendency, particularly in policy debates concerning care and the elderly, has persisted. Consequently the health and social circumstances of the very old have received little attention in empirical social research on ageing.

Aims and objectives

In the present study[1] we aimed to redress this imbalance of interest. At the same time we hoped to cut through the stereotypes of 'burden' and 'elite group' or even that the very old represent 'a challenge', and we suspected that, as with any age group, there would be heterogeneity. Whilst the choice of 90 as the lower age limit is arbitrary in one sense we thought that it would set an appropriate boundary within which some important features of the experiences of very old age would emerge.

In investigating, therefore, the health and quality of life of people aged 90 and over we had five objectives. First, to discover what kind of lives they led; the proportions, for instance, for whom life still held much to enjoy or for whom, because of senility or inability to cope with the adversities of extreme old age, it held little or nothing.

Secondly, and clearly of great relevance to the first objective, was the need to examine the extent of care, and the nature generally of the informal and formal support they received or needed. Thirdly, we hoped to identify at least some of the possible influences – genetic, social and cultural – that had brought them through to their tenth decade and beyond. Interrelated with these three main objectives was a fourth – to see how feasible it was personally to involve people of this great age in such a study. Finally, we hoped that our findings might have implications for future policy and research.

Scope and design

The various imponderables meant that the study would be an exploratory one but unique, we believed, not only in the choice of age group but also in its general scope. Although the sample would be small, it would include people from different geographical locations, those living at home as well as in institutions of one kind or another, and of all shades of physical and mental capacity. This last, of course, could necessitate the use of proxies for interviewing.

The emphasis of the study was on the views and self-assessments of the elderly people themselves. The questions covered a wide range of topics, but focused mainly on health status and health care, morale and well-being, social support and personal and family history.

Wherever possible, a person identified as the key carer was interviewed. The chief objective here was to supplement the information obtained from the main interview, though we are of course aware of the difficulties and stress that carers all too often have to face.

In what follows we first discuss the process and problems of identifying the 90-plus population and selecting the sample to be studied. We then briefly describe the achieved sample and its representativeness. Thirdly, we examine the method. This, after reference to the pilot study, is followed by an account of the interviewing procedures, which includes the method used for approaching the subjects, which we considered of great importance. Finally, we summarise the outcome.

THE 90-PLUS POPULATION

Selection of the areas

In order to achieve a representative sample it was necessary to give every person aged 90 and over in England an equal chance of being selected and yet confine our interviewing to defined areas. With advice from the Office of Population Censuses and Surveys (OPCS) we adopted the method of area selection based on the principle of 'probability proportionate to size' (PPS) (Hedges, 1977), using local area data for those aged 80 and over (OPCS, 1984). Initially, we aimed to interview in 12 areas and, through the PPS method, were able to select the areas, which included two London boroughs.

We then, however, met two major difficulties in moving forward. The first of these concerned one of the London boroughs where coincidentally we were piloting the questionnaire. Some of the professionals and service providers with whom we came into contact were extremely helpful and interested in the research. Others, however, erected insurmountable barriers in our path which forced us to abandon the area.

By this time we recognised that there was a wider problem with our design. We had taken on more than we could handle, with limited staff and finances; eight areas was the maximum number that could be covered in the research. In order to capitalise on the preparatory work already under way, these were chosen at random from the eleven areas already identified (excluding the abandoned London area). It is these eight areas which form the basis of the study.

We think we have gone much further than most research in establishing a representative sample of the oldest old, though we regret the absence of a London area. Nonetheless, we are able to present findings from respondents in a wide variety of urban and rural settings and in a diversity of social contexts and circumstances.

Method of identification

Having selected the areas, the next task was to identify the chosen population. Identifying by name all those aged 90 and over was essential to avoid the risk of counting twice. In order to collect these names, we decided to approach all the services and agencies which might be concerned with very old people in their locality, or have knowledge of them. These included GPs, Family Practitioner Committees (FPCs), the hospital and community health services, social services, housing departments, private and voluntary residential and nursing homes, voluntary agencies, the church, and, where appropriate, the local press and radio. There were a number of reasons for this choice of approach. GP lists when used on their own are notoriously unreliable (Shearer, 1987; Bowling et al., 1988). OPCS statistics for our chosen age group were not available at a local level. Furthermore, the Department of Health and Social Security (DHSS) were not prepared to allow us to obtain names from records of pensioners.

By seeking saturation coverage we could hope to minimise the potential obstacles of non-co-operation. Visits to each area by the research officer, who had meetings and discussions with representatives of the various services and agencies, also greatly helped in this respect.

Compiling lists of named persons, however, presented major difficulties. It was not only the DHSS that would not disclose names. We also sometimes met resistance from other agencies. Concern about confidentiality has undoubtedly increased in recent years. Some professional care agencies as well as administrators, when asked to provide names, were reluctant to do so, arguing a lack of authority.

In one or two instances we were unable to overcome the resistance, and, where we did so, the assurances required and the committee procedures involved usually caused considerable delays.

In the event, we surmounted the various difficulties of identifying the 90-plus population and were reasonably confident that we had come close to establishing the total live population of men and women aged 90 years and over living in the eight areas at the time of identification. Unfortunately, we also identified a number of people who, it subsequently turned out, were no longer alive. From many of our 'sources' the information provided at the time was reasonably reliable. From some, however, which included FPCs, GPs and social services departments, it was often seriously out of date. It seemed to make no difference whether their lists had been compiled by hand or computer; if anything the latter were worse than the former. Quite why GP, and for that matter FPC, lists are an unreliable source of information on their patients is something of a puzzle. Exactly where the difficulty lies is hard to establish. The various chains of notification of deaths are clear and, for the most part, mandatory. But somewhere along these chains the links are often weak. The problem appeared often enough to cause concern, and not just from the viewpoint of the present study. The fact that the National Health Service Central Register is used for much epidemiological, mortality and morbidity social research makes poor notification particularly worrying, though it may be that the failure to keep lists up to date occurred only at *area* level. Whilst we can only report our experience of relatively frequent individual errors discovered in the process of our own identification procedures, we think the problem is significant enough to warrant further attention.

These various notification procedures – obligatory or otherwise – within the health service do not of course apply to the domiciliary social services. Here they must keep their own lists up to date although this is not always easy. In the present study we found considerable differences between the areas in the reliability of the lists. Not surprisingly, information obtained directly from the various residential institutions, statutory or private, was up to date, except occasionally from a hospital. Response to our initial request for names was lower in the case of private residential homes and nursing homes. The proportion of non-replies, varying from area to area, amounted to 30 per cent of the residential homes and 15 per cent of the nursing homes. Follow-up telephone calls revealed a number of expected reasons – too busy to reply, our letter not received, and, most usually, nobody aged 90 and over.

Nearly all responded to the follow-up and, among the few who did not, we could discount the risk of losing more than the possible odd name because of coverage from other sources. We were not in a position to investigate the few which remained persistently incommunicado. We therefore cannot say if this was an indication of

Table 9.1 *90+ population by sex and area (original estimates)*

	Women	Men (nos)	Total
Broadland	262	74	336
Chichester	787	230	981
Dudley (est.)	725	150	875
Maidstone	364	72	436
New Forest	790	225	985
Sefton	1134	221	1355
S. Shropshire	164	42	206
Wear Valley	193	46	239
Total	4383	1060	5443

dubious practices, or simply dislike of research on the part of owners and managers, or a sense of protectiveness towards residents or patients.

Reliability of the identified populations

Table 9.1 gives the male and female 90-plus population as estimated from our original identifications. The estimates, however, must be viewed with caution in the light of the later discovery at the field stage of the many pre-identification deaths. For the sake of accuracy, using the pre-identification figures, we attempted a revision of the estimates. This age group is notoriously difficult to 'pin down', particularly as the numbers diminish with every advancing year as a result of high mortality. The true picture is probably somewhere between the two estimates but we have been advised by OPCS to let the original ones stand.

As is well known, in the older age groups women far exceed men. We were pleased to find, as can be seen in Table 9.2, that the male/female proportions in the present study reflect those of the population aged 90 and over in England and Wales.

Selection of the sample

In Chapter 5 of this book Graham Fennell discusses various methods of sample selection. Where the sample is small and taken from elderly populations, he stresses the advisability of stratifying it so that the age and gender groups may be adequately represented. In our defined group, because of the shortage of men, and particularly older men, we chose a four-cell stratification: women 90–4 and 95 plus; men 90–4 and 95 plus. This of course entailed weighting in the analysis in order to obtain estimates for the position of those aged 90 and over as a whole, that is, to re-establish a representative sample. Given the discrepancies

Table 9.2 *Comparison of 90+ population sex and age proportions (%)*

	90+ population	
	Present study: as estimated in the 8 areas; 1987	England and Wales, 1986[1]
Women		
90–4	61.0 ⎫ 80.5	61.6 ⎫ 80
95+	19.5 ⎭	18.4 ⎭
Men		
90–4	14.8 ⎫ 19.5	16.6 ⎫ 20
95+	4.7 ⎭	3.4 ⎭
Total	100 (5443)	100

[1]*Source:* Unpublished OPCS estimates

in our own figures we used 1986 population estimates (OPCS, 1986) for this purpose.

The target sample size was 200, but we clearly could not hope for 100 per cent response. To allow for a reasonable failure rate, therefore, we selected a sample of 260 – 65 per cell – by the appropriate interval from a randomly selected starting point.

THE SAMPLE STUDIED

The achieved sample

In a randomly selected sample, it is legitimate to substitute for those who are no longer alive or who otherwise do not 'qualify' for inclusion in the study – a group that we have designated 'out-of-scope' (Morton-Williams, 1979). Finding substitutes, however, and substitutes for substitutes, involved reviewing hundreds of names. The problem became unmanageable and we eventually abandoned the search. This left a target sample of 222 rather than 260 individuals who were designated 'in-scope', and therefore ready to approach.

The response rate

Table 9.3 shows the response rate of the in-scope sample and how this was distributed between the four cells.

For people of such an advanced age we regarded a response rate of more than 82 per cent as satisfactory. It was, we think, partly a result of very careful preparation for the interviewing. In fact, it was the women, particularly the 'younger' women, who exercised their right of refusal in greater proportions than the men. In some cases, of

Table 9.3 *The selected sample: response rate by sex and age*

| | Women | | | Men | | | Total | |
| | 90–4 | 95+ | Total | 90–4 | 95+ | Total | | |
	(nos)		%	(nos)		(%)	(nos)	(%)
Interviewed	46	47	78.2	54	36	87.4	183	82.4
Refusals/denials of access	14	12	21.8	9	4	12.6	39	17.6
Total	60	59	100 (119)	63	40	100 (103)	222	100

course, refusal was not necessarily an individual's choice; family members or other carers might also be involved.

Representativeness

The re-weighting of the stratified sample cell numbers in the analysis is based, as we have seen, on the assumption that our selected sample is representative. Other factors however must also be taken into account in making such an assumption, not least the proportions living at home and in residential accommodation.

An accurate picture of the level of residential, nursing home and hospital provision for elderly people is still difficult to get (Challis and Bartlett, 1987); for our age group, virtually impossible. It is clear, however, that the percentage of the elderly population in institutional accommodation increases markedly with age. Laing (1988), for instance, suggests that about 15 per cent of the English population aged 85 and over are in residential homes compared with just over 3 per cent of those aged 75 to 84. With such a rapid rate of increase a considerably greater rise would be expected for those aged 90 and over.

For people resident in *all* types of establishments, Laing puts the figure at 20 per cent for those aged 85 plus. It would therefore not be surprising to find that something in the region of 40 per cent of people aged 90 and over would no longer be living in their own homes. The proportion in this category among our selected sample was 47 per cent (87 per cent of whom were interviewed), which is in line with these estimates.

The absence of a London borough in itself means that we must exclude London from an otherwise nationally representative sample. The extent, however, to which this means a bias in terms of social class, income level and tenure needs further analysis. As far as health status and social circumstances are concerned, the lack of data from an inner-city setting may detract from the general representativeness of the sample. Against these limitations, there is, however, some evidence (Bowling et al., 1988) to suggest that the oldest old share many common features, particularly in attitudes, irrespective of their place of residence, and even though they may belong to different social strata.

THE PILOT STUDY

The pilot exercise was not only important in the design of the questionnaire and the conducting of the interview. It also gave us invaluable insights into all the preliminary procedures. Despite the obstructions and difficulties in the London area already referred to, over 50 per cent of the expected population were identified and some pilot interviews conducted. In the second pilot area, a mixed urban–rural district in the south of England, the response of the medical, hospital and community health services was excellent. The release of names, however, was the sticking point with the Director of Social Services. This area was, in fact, one of the eight later selected for the main study, and the problem was eventually circumvented by good will. By comparing our list from other sources with theirs on computer, a member of the social services department was able to supplement ours, but without using names. These anonymous subjects thus formed part of the total population, from which the selection for interview was made.

When we came to the main study, to maintain anonymity, this same member of the social services department was designated by the Director to carry out the interviews of anyone on their lists, approaching the respondents by the same method as generally in use and using the same questionnaire. He attended the interviewing briefing session and followed the same procedures as the other interviewers.

THE INTERVIEWS

Proxy interviews

We decided to use proxies only where absolutely necessary in order to make the sample as representative as possible of the defined age group. In the event, as can be seen from Table 9.4, the proportion of subjects for whom we had to use a proxy for the whole interview was relatively small. Among the older men, for instance, this was as low as just over 5 per cent. In a further 28 per cent of interviews with this group a proxy helped. Thus 67 per cent were solely with the subject, a proportion topped – at 76 per cent – by the male 90–4 age group, reflecting the fact that the latter group tended towards 'better' health and greater independence than the other three.

Sometimes a subject needed the help of a relative or member of staff to act as 'interpreter'. This might be because of severe deafness, some memory loss or confusion, or general frailty. The interviewers' manner

Table 9.4 *Subject/proxy interviews by sex and age (%)*

| | Women | | | Men | |
	90–4	95+		90–4	95+
Subject	65.2	48.9		75.9	66.7
Part proxy	17.4	31.9		14.8	27.8
All proxy	17.4	19.2		9.3	5.5
Total	100	100		100	100
	(46)	(47)		(54)	(36)

of handling these joint interviews varied according to the degree of intervention necessary to get a reply that was as full as possible yet remained 'uncontaminated' by the proxy's own views. Wherever possible, the elderly person was questioned directly. Sometimes, if there was no response or only a limited one, the proxy might need only to act as a memory jogger. Sometimes, in the event of extreme deafness, for instance, the question might be rephrased by the proxy; sometimes, actually answered. In this case, the interviewer would have to decide if the reply could be considered valid, in the light of its factual content and the proxy's knowledge of the respondent. Substitute *opinions* would be invalid. Such joint interviews were often full and satisfactory, unlike those where reliance was entirely on a proxy. It must be accepted that the corollary of sole proxy interviewing is an equivalent number of incomplete interviews.

Carer interviews

Carer interviews – 158 in all, 86 per cent of the main interviews – were usually arranged at the time of the main interview, and only carried out with the respondent's agreement. There were a few instances where the interviewer could find no appropriate person; others where the respondent objected to such an interview. In one or two particular cases the interviewer rejected the idea of such an interview as 'insulting' in the light of the elderly persons' obvious ability to look after themselves.

The interviewers

In a study of this kind the interviewer is all-important. Patience and sympathy are essential qualities and we were fortunate in having these in good measure among the 12 women and 1 man who made up the team. Above all, they were experienced and trained and also, for the most part, familiar with their localities. After an extensive briefing session, each interviewer was asked to complete a mock interview. These not only clarified certain difficulties for the interviewer but revealed the need for minor amendments to the questionnaire. Throughout the interviewing period the research officer was continuously in touch with members of the team.

The instrument design

The main questionnaire was initially designed with three issues in mind. Firstly, we assumed that a more than usually high proportion of our respondents might have difficulty in sustaining a long interview. Secondly, we felt that there might be problems for many in understanding even relatively straightforward questions. Thirdly, and connected with this last point, we assumed that deafness or problems with comprehension might induce the need to repeat a question, at least in a proportion of our interviews. Rephrasing might help understanding. So, though the questions, with one exception, were formulated as direct questions demanding a reply, interviewers were allowed to use different wording, provided, of course, that the sense was preserved.

The questionnaire combined structured and semi-structured components. The main exception to the question/answer formula was a request at the beginning of the main central section of the questionnaire that they describe a typical day.

The idea of trying to open up the topic of everyday life, providing little by way of guidance other than prompts, was only partially successful in the aim of motivating a spontaneous response. Bucke and Insley (1976) had used this method successfully in their small study of centenarians. But they did the interviewing themselves. In our study a few people rattled through their day, with evident pleasure, needing little prompting. With some the exercise had to be abandoned, and in between was a range of responses calling for greater or less prompting. The results were mainly useful in providing illustrative material, but they were not full enough to be subjected to more systematic analysis.

In designing the study we attempted to strike a balance between a research instrument that would allow us to explore a range of subjective views, yet provide a profile of the sample which would give us the basis for comparing individuals and the different groupings within the sample.

Where possible, as is common practice, we drew on tried and tested questions from elsewhere (see Note 2, p. 142). Similar patterns of response have already emerged from the different strata of the sample, indicating a reasonable degree of reliability. On the whole interviewers did not report widespread difficulties as the result of ambiguities or confusion with the questions.

We attempted to build in 'validity checks' (de Vaus, 1986) on the information gathered from each respondent, by two means. First by the comparison of 'internal' replies and secondly, by 'external checks' (Oppenheim, 1966) through the carer interviews and an additional assessment by the interviewer.

Approach to the subjects

The procedure was as follows: letters briefly explaining the project and asking for an interview were prepared for each selected subject – to eliminate bias, with similar wording for all – and sent to the person from whom we had received the subject's name. If we had heard from more than one source – a GP, for instance, and an area social services officer – we chose the one we believed to be best known to the respondent as our means of communication, and sent a courtesy letter to the other. Our covering letter to the GP, or whoever, reminded them, with appreciation, of their promised co-operation, asked them to sign the letter to the subject (or letters if more than one) and send it off in the stamped addressed envelope supplied, together with a printed reply slip and a stamped return envelope addressed to the research officer of the project. No one failed to undertake this on our behalf. The fact that the letter came from someone they knew, undoubtedly, in our view, helped to promote the atmosphere of goodwill in which nearly all the interviews were conducted, as well as encouraging an initially positive response. One male resident in a local authority home was reported by the warden as being 'very aggressive; he nearly blew a fuse when the letter was read to him. Sorry!'. For the most part, however, the refusals or denials of access by relatives came as a tick against the 'no' on the return slips. These were often accompanied by an apologetic little note, just as the acceptances often included a welcoming one.

The interviewers had been provided with a list of the selected subjects for their areas giving as much information as possible about each. They were immediately notified by the research officer of any acceptances or refusals or of any intimations that the person had died or left the area.

This information came either directly from the source or from someone at the address written to. In the event of the individual being 'out-of-scope' we then selected the next randomly chosen subject on the list and started all over again – sometimes with the same source and sometimes with a new one. In the case of acceptances, it was for the interviewer at this stage to take matters further, either telephoning or calling to make an appointment. After a reasonable lapse of time, if no reply had been received by us concerning an individual the interviewer was asked to follow things up, either by contacting the source or by calling at the given address. If non-availability was discovered, the research officer was notified and the substitute-seeking procedure followed. We often had to resist pressure from the GP or other source to take the next person on *their* list by explaining to them the nature of random selection.

These, as can be imagined, were busy weeks, for our aim was to conduct the fieldwork simultaneously in all the areas. Interviewers were able to start interviewing while substitute seeking proceeded and the bulk of the interviewing, in fact, lasted for only eight weeks.

Presentation of the questionnaire

Presentation of the chosen instrument is as important as design, particularly with a study group such as ours. Elderly, often frail, people are especially vulnerable to the sins of commission and omission of run-of-the-mill survey techniques. Of considerable importance is the manner in which the interviewers introduce themselves and the topics to be discussed once they are face to face with the respondent. Great care, therefore, was taken in the wording of the introduction on the questionnaire which, unlike that of the questions, the interviewers were asked not to deviate from.

Use of tape-recorders

Reference is made in the questionnaire introduction to the intention to tape-record the interview. Experience has shown that an assumption of acceptance of this idea was rewarded in fact with untroubled agreement, whereas a tentative 'would-you-mind' approach resulted quite often in refusal. Only one of our respondents raised an objection to the idea and on two occasions we were asked for a copy of the tape. The main object of recording the interviews was as source material for quotes and case histories. Furthermore, listening to the tapes has given us considerable insight into the nature of the response and the personalities of the interviewees, as well as the process of interviewing itself.

The length of the interview

The staying power of the respondents was on the whole remarkable. Other researchers in this field will not be surprised at the fact that if anyone was exhausted by the end of the interview it was the questioner as often as the person questioned.

There was a considerable number of questions and 1000 variables in all, though naturally not all these applied to everybody. In the pilot we had found that one and a half hours could comfortably accommodate all the relevant questions, with an additional half hour or less for the carer interview. In the main study there was, not unexpectedly, considerable variation, the longest interview lasting four hours and the shortest twenty-five minutes. But the norm was in fact one and a half hours, and there were very few complaints about the length of time or indeed about anything else.

OUTCOME

The analysis of our survey material will, of course, prove to be the test of our methodology. Whilst we have been keen to develop the methodology relevant to the study of the very old, this has not been our main objective. A preoccupation with methodology can often mean having to search for a substance. Indeed, it has been our experience that method and substance are often more closely aligned than is sometimes recognised.

In the first place, the desire to establish a *representative* sample of people aged 90 years and over created many headaches for us, which reflected real problems in the field as well as self-imposed technical hurdles. The difficulties, for example, that we encountered in identifying individuals aged 90 years and over, both from national statistics and from local sources, often reinforced our feelings that the very old are indeed treated as members of a residual category. No doubt official records of people of all ages are 'inaccurate' in many ways (and there are reasons to be thankful that this is the case). But, during the identification stage, on finding that people who were thought to be alive had in fact been dead for many years, we constantly asked ourselves what did this mean for those who *were* alive?

Moreover, the quantity of letter writing (something in excess of 2000 letters) that was necessary in order to gain access to our subjects, as well as highlighting the above-mentioned problem, also revealed aspects of protectiveness towards the very old that warrant further examination. Much of the time we fully understood the concern of agencies, institutions and family members for the welfare of the individual in question. But we were not convinced that this was always the central issue. The rights of the elderly and the very old to make choices and exercise control over their own lives are as important as for any other group of adults. We are, of course, aware of the dependence of many elderly people and their vulnerability to exploitation, but these issues should not be used as an impenetrable shield against the outside world as a whole. Our experience suggests that there is often a fine line between legitimate protectiveness and over-protection.

Finally, the process of interviewing itself disclosed important features of the daily life of our respondents, in spite of the difficulties we encountered in establishing 'a typical day'. The main problems in interviewing centred inevitably on the frailty – physical and mental – of some of the respondents. Senility or severe confusion was in one sense easier to cope with than partial confusion or memory loss, since the former was usually known about beforehand and appropriate proxy arrangements could be made. The most obvious difficulty concerns deafness. In reading and listening to the interviewers' comments after the event, and even more so in listening to the interviews on tape, we were made painfully aware of the problems of communication brought about by hearing difficulties.

In short, our identification, sampling and interviewing procedures involved both technical and substantive issues throughout the months of our survey. Generally, in fact, the findings of this study confirmed those of others (for example Bucke and Insley, 1976; Ridley et al., 1979; Bury, 1986) that the ability to interview the very old, allowing for an inevitably higher incidence of severe memory loss, was comparable with that of interviewing younger age groups and that reliable information can be obtained. From this we take heart, both for the completion of our task of providing a picture of the quality of life amongst the very old, and the reassurance it gives that their marginal social status can be overcome.

NOTES

1. The study was funded anonymously, with an initial grant of £50,000 for two years from April 1986. Delays, outside our control, at the sampling stage, the wealth of data collected and the small size of the project team necessitated an extension of a further year (which the same charitable Trust has generously funded). The project is directed by Michael Bury, Senior Lecturer in Medical Sociology, Royal Holloway and Bedford New College, University of London, assisted by a part-time research officer, Anthea Holme (the joint authors of this chapter), with part-time secretarial help. This small project team was further helped by thirteen interviewers local to the eight study areas and three coders. Members of the Advisory Committee are as follows: Sir Cyril Clarke, KBE, MD, FRCP, FRS, Royal College of Physicians; Sir Richard Bayliss, KVCVO, MD, FRCP, Royal College of Physicians; Dr D. Pyke, CBE, MD, FRCP, Royal College of Physicians; Professor Margot Jefferys; Mr B. Sheldon, Royal Holloway and Bedford New College.

2. The main sources consulted for the research project questionnaire were: Copeland, J., Department of Psychiatry, Royal Liverpool Hospital (GMS study – interview schedule); Department of Sociological Studies, University of Sheffield (Family Care of the Elderly, Survey of Elderly People in Sheffield – interview schedule); Ford, G. and Taylor, R., Institute of Medical Sociology, MRC Medical Sociology Unit, Aberdeen (Styles of Ageing – interview schedule); Hunt, S., Research Unit in Health and Behavioural Change, University of Edinburgh (The Nottingham Health Profile); Wenger, C., University College of North Wales (The Elderly in the Community – interview schedule); Wilkin, D., Centre for Primary Care Research, University Hospital of South Manchester (Services for the Elderly – physical and psychological assessment schedule).

10

Doing Biographical Research

BRIAN GEARING AND TIM DANT

Since the mid-1970s gerontologists have become increasingly interested in the biographical approach to the study of old age. However, only a very few published British research studies have used a biographical method. Consequently, this chapter is about an approach and style of gerontological research whose methods are still developing. We aim to clarify the distinctive nature of the biographical approach; to trace some of its origins; and to discuss some of its uses.

MARKING OUT THE BIOGRAPHICAL APPROACH

We begin with the paper whose publication in 1976 stimulated an interest among British gerontologists in the biographical approach. Malcolm Johnson's paper, 'That was your life: a biographical approach to later life', marked out a number of positions which help us to clarify what is distinctive about a biographical perspective in old age. Johnson criticised the discipline of social gerontology which had emerged in America, Australia and Western Europe for its lack of attention to older people's own subjective concerns and life experience.

He argued that the social theories of old age developed up to that time had emphasised only the common features of older people's lives (rather than the differences between older individuals and varieties of lifestyle). Equally unsatisfactory, he contended, were the majority of research studies in gerontology which merely described and quantified the circumstances and problems of older people. Whilst usually presented as objective by researchers, these studies were typically based on concepts of 'need' which derived from existing categories of service provision (for example the 'need' for a home help), or related to the standard basic amenities (for example housing needs); or they sought to quantify a limited range of problems and pathologies (such as loneliness or disability) as defined by an external observer. In short, in the 1960s and 1970s, both gerontological research and professional assessments had become fixated on discovering and rediscovering a very limited range of *dependency needs*. Older people themselves were rarely consulted about what *they* wanted from health and social service agencies, or from life in general. On rare occasions when a researcher did ask for their views, the research approach was circumscribed by the inflexibility of the survey method which standardises questions in advance, tries to eliminate interviewer bias, and uniformly categorises subjects' responses. A distinctive feature of Johnson's critique was that it encompassed both theory and research, on the one hand, and social service provision on the other:

> Just as the social workers who disburse these benefits are constrained by the nature of existing provision, so are many researchers, who cast their studies in the terms of what is, or might easily be, available. Thus there is a reinforcing process which lends a spurious legitimacy to giving older people the nearest thing you have from a minute range of provisions. One of the major flaws in this allocation process is the failure to properly diagnose the elderly person's true 'needs' . . . (Johnson, 1976: 154)

This dual focus – on the study *and* practice of gerontology – has remained a feature of the biographical approach as it has developed in the past decade. In this chapter, we try to reflect this multi-faceted approach by discussing the main ways in which the biographical approach is used – in therapy (for example reminiscence work), in health and social care (as a method of assessment), as well as in research. Central to all these approaches is the biographical interview in which older people are encouraged to reconstruct their past lives so that their current needs and preoccupations can be better understood.

THE ORIGINS OF THE BIOGRAPHICAL APPROACH

Underlying Johnson's critique is a view that old age theory and research are flawed by social gerontology's functionalism and empiricism. In embodying these characteristics much of gerontological research has ignored the *meaning* of older people's lived experiences and denied them a part in defining their own needs. Johnson's alternative approach drew on the strengths of two related social science traditions in the United States: symbolic interactionism and the life history approach in sociology.

Central to Johnson's version of the biographical approach is the interactionist concept, *career*. He invokes Roth's formulation of career as being

> a series of definable phases of a given sphere of activity that a group of people goes through in a progressive fashion (that is one step leads to another) in a given direction on the way to a more or less definite and recognizable end point or goal or series of goals. (Roth, 1963 cited in Johnson, 1976)

Johnson proposes that the many intersecting careers an individual experiences in a lifetime and which may be shed compulsorily or voluntarily in later life, may in any case have differing degrees of significance for the individual. This significance is more likely to be known to the person concerned than to any outside observer, but it suggests an approach to unravelling and integrating something varied and complex – the biography of the older person. By identifying main strands in a life ('careers'), how they have shaped and been shaped by significant biographical events (family, upbringing, marriage, work, parenthood, retirement, widowhood, and so on), we will better understand the way the individual concerned experiences 'old age', and his/her present needs, satisfactions and problems.

The other strand of sociological research which has influenced the biographical approach is the life history tradition in American sociology. Like symbolic interactionism it stems from Chicago in the early decades of this century, and, in particular, from the classic study by Thomas and Znaniecki, *The Polish Peasant in Europe and America* (1958), which used 'human documents' – a major life history, newspaper cuttings, diaries, letters and so on – to study a public issue of the time. A clear account of the life history approach is given by Ken Plummer in his valuable survey of the method *Documents of Life: An Introduction to the Problems of a Humanistic Method* (1983).

The biographical/life history perspective has also been influential in the work of European sociologists, such as Kohli (1978) who used it in studying the compulsorily early retired in West Germany and Bertaux (1981) in studying the experience of French bakers. Rosenmayer (1981) traces the significance of biography in understanding old age beyond the interactionist sociologists to the historical philosopher William Dilthey. In the United States, Glen Elder (1974) has studied the formative influence of being a child at the time of the Great Depression on a cohort of older Americans; Graham Rowles has used a biographical approach to understand the geographical dimensions of ageing (1978); and, recently, Sheila Matthews has used oral biographies in her study *Friendships Through The Life Course* (1986).

THE SELF IN BIOGRAPHICAL APPROACHES

As implied earlier, the biographical approach takes from interactionism its concern with subjectively defined reality – or how the individual who is being interviewed, assessed, or receiving therapy interprets the world. This interpretive 'self' is central to our conception of the biographical approach. It derives from the founding father of interactionism, George Herbert Mead:

> The self is something which has a development: it is not here at birth but arises in the context of social experience and activity, that is, develops in the given individual as a result of his relations to that process as a whole and to other individuals within that process. (Mead, G.H. 1934b, in Thompson and Tunstall, 1971: 144)

This constantly developing self is the product of any individual's biography at a given point in time, what we might more usually refer to as her identity. It is also the self which, from the vantage point of the present, enables the subject to reconstruct her biography in the context of the biographical interview or reminiscence session. Writing within the interactionist tradition, Anselm Strauss and others have suggested ways in which we might view identity in adult life and old age (see Strauss, 1962; Deutscher, 1962; Cavan, 1962).

Our own preferred approach is based on our view that the biographical interview is a discursive process in which the subject is enabled to reconstruct his or her past life. This allows concepts such as 'self', and 'identity' to be used in interpretation and analysis, and for their 'continuity/discontinuity' in later life to be studied. The following 'case example' is intended to illustrate this process. It is an extract from the analysis of an interview with one man from a biographical research study in which one of us (BG) participated (see Cornwell and Gearing, 1989). It draws on the concepts identified earlier to analyse occupational retirement and other significant life changes – both before and after retirement – in terms of the continuities with earlier stages in the life, the sense of self/identity which seemed to characterise his way of looking at himself, and the most important experiences or motivations in his life. Because this biographical study focused on explanations of the health beliefs of older people, connections are suggested in the analysis between these categories and how the subject views dependency and ill health.

Case example – Mr Groves

Mr Groves is 71, the son of a self-employed cab driver whom he admired for his size and strength. His mother was also a strong person, making sure that the three children were well fed and looked respectable, and encouraging them all to be self-reliant.

After joining Morris Motors in the early 1930s, Mr Groves progressed to a job at Pressed Steel as Inspector on the Standard car production line, where he worked for the next 41 years. His job was to inspect the quality of the car panels as they came off the line and before they went into the paint shop. At that time Pressed Steel were introducing into their factory the new American method of producing car bodies quickly in the form of large panels. The men on the production line were on piece-work rates as an incentive to produce as many car bodies as possible. Mr Groves had been recruited as 'a body in white' to stand at the end of the line and be responsible to management for the quality of the panels he passed.

Situated between the men and management, the Inspector's job was a lonely and difficult one, with great potential for conflict with either side. In this passage Mr Groves describes his relationship with the other people in the factory.

> Being Inspector you're against everybody see. Once you've passed that car you're responsible. The Production Foreman, they're responsible for getting the stuff out the door, they got the schedule to get. The schedule was printed every week and they must get that. Alright, I passed it if it was

good enough. I think I was hard . . . . I might have been tight, but I was fair, try and keep the same standard all the time, not up and down . . . . The standard required of the car . . . and of course, I was up against the Foreman, the Senior Foreman, the Superintendent. They weren't my bosses. I used to have terrific rows. I've been threatened physically by men because I wouldn't pass their job, but nobody ever hit me.

At a time of industrial slump and few employment opportunities elsewhere, it was a well-paid job, so he decided to stay, although work was a personal battle which was beginning to get him down. He had to find a way of coping or go under. He describes the solution:

> You get so you sort of harden yourself . . . . Soon after I went there I had eight men to look after. And they were right bastards . . . . Threatened me. I was stretched so far that I used to hate to go in on a Monday morning; but in the end I got toughened up. I mean I'm talking about 1938, and I realised that it was either them or me. My job or theirs. And after that [they] didn't intimidate me. I got really hardened. People might say I'm a bit hard now.

Mr Groves thinks that the job changed him, made him a different person altogether to the one he might have been. He takes pride in what he sees as the strength of character he acquired in order to survive in that hostile environment where he could trust nobody but himself. He identifies himself as someone who is both morally and physically strong and self-reliant; someone other people will rely on. He compares himself favourably to other men in the factory who couldn't do their own fighting, and had to rely on their bosses to resolve conflicts. Mr Groves' conception of himself in relation to others seems to be crucial, not just in understanding how he coped in the early difficult years at Pressed Steel, but how he makes sense of his life and his relationships now as a retired person.

Mr Groves' successful struggle to survive at Pressed Steel seems to have left him with a marked sense of personal superiority to men who couldn't cope with similar pressures. And his own identity rests on ideas about strength of character and self-reliance developed at that time. In his mind this seems to set him apart from other men. Though he is retired he continually compares what *he* can do with what others can't, and he still feels he cannot really trust other people. His retirement is characterised by a commitment to self-reliance. He sees himself as helping others who are always described as less strong or competent than himself. He does many practical things for friends and relatives – like mending their cars or running them to the hospital or some small building jobs. They all rely on him, but they are not really grateful and take him for granted. Even his best friend George, who has a heart condition, and is always telling Mr Groves how much he relies on him, really takes him for granted.

Just as he learned not to trust or rely on other people in the factory, he would hate to have to rely on others as he grows older. He would hope other people would do the same for him as he does for them but says:

> I'm sure I would hope they would do the same for me. I hope I never have to depend on them, because I don't really think I could rely on them. I've only asked that bloke George a couple of times to do things for me and he's found some bloody excuse. Two lots of things I've just asked him. I wouldn't like to rely on anybody to do anything . . . . I never have to rely on anybody . . .
> I hope I'm never in that position; I'll look after myself. I hope to Christ I never. If I go out it's going to be quick . . .

He thinks that if it came to it he would rather go into an institution than be looked after by anybody he knows. *He* would rather look after somebody else, though he adds that with what he's done for his family they should really look after him:

> I'd rather go into a hospital I think. I wouldn't want anyone to look after me. My son-in-law, when I get old I shall probably have to look after him. He's a bullshitter. He's a nice chap. If you talk to him for an hour, you'd think what a charming chap he was, but after a time it would soon wear off. He's a bit insincere. Very very nice chap. Interested in the same sort of things that I am, very well read, but he says things, he wouldn't argue with you, he says things to please you.

In the case of Mr Groves, a very particular identity emerged through the biographical interview that coalesced around his sense of superiority to others, particularly men. Allied to this is his independence; he not only values his own self-reliance, it is a feature of his identity that separates him from other people. This has continued into his retirement and affects how he copes with his present life and relationships and his view of any possible future period of ill health involving dependency on others.

THE USES OF THE BIOGRAPHICAL APPROACH

As we wrote earlier, the biographical approach can serve a number of approaches. The biographical interview – and certain principles about eliciting biographical information – may apply in all three main approaches therefore: reminiscence, assessment and research.

We will discuss all three, referring to recent published work or work that is currently in progress. Our main concern is the last of these – research – and we have deferred consideration of the biographical interview method, as such, to this discussion.

Reminiscence

In reaction to a tendency to see reminiscence as a 'bad thing', as 'living in the past', there is a current trend towards encouraging reminiscence as a normal and sometimes satisfying practice in old age.

Social workers, care assistants and occupational therapists run reminiscence groups that encourage old people, with the aid of photographs and interested questions, to talk about their past.

We noted earlier that the biographical approach has relevance to professional practice as well as to social research. More than 20 years ago, the American gerontologist and psychologist, Robert Butler (1963), had commended the life review as a positive method of working with older people, one which could enhance the quality of later life. This therapeutic use of the life history of the individual has gained further momentum in the 1980s in Britain. Mary Marshall (1983) advocated biographical listening by social workers as part of communication with older clients. Members of the Oral History Society (see Wright, 1984, 1986; Adams, 1984 and Bornat, 1985) have explored its uses within health and social work settings. Perhaps most importantly, Peter Coleman (1986) has assessed the therapeutic functions of reminiscence through a longitudinal study of a group of old people in sheltered housing. Coleman considered a number of issues surrounding reminiscence and assessed its value in terms of the psychological state of old people.

He was interested both in Butler's theory of 'life review' as a component of normal ageing, and of 'identity maintenance' as a way of boosting morale in old age in the face of deprivation and loss (Coleman, 1986: 14, 34). Coleman found that while reminiscence is something that some people do naturally and find of value, others just do not do it or they may consciously avoid it. The important point here is that, for some, reminiscence can provide a disagreeable experience and this can also affect assessment for social care, and research, if they use a biographical approach. Moreover, both Coleman's research and our own experience in setting up biographical interviews indicate that people's willingness to reminisce will inevitably affect their willingness to be research subjects.

Assessment

The second use we have mentioned is that of assessment. Here the purpose of the interview is different. In the pure reminiscence interview, the interviewee is assumed to be gaining from the (therapeutic) experience. Where the interview is for the purposes of assessment, however, the benefit is more indirect, through the provision of an appropriate service – though they may of course enjoy the conversation and gain from the experience of reminiscence. Johnson (1976) argued for the importance of the biographical approach as an assessment tool; and in a current action research project based in Gloucester, 'Care for Elderly People at Home', concerned with finding new ways of helping older people to avoid institutional care, an approach is being explored to develop a method for assessing the health and social needs of elderly people which is based on an understanding of their biographies. (This is reported in detail in Johnson and Gearing, 1989). Here, as with reminiscence, it does not suit everybody: some people know what their needs are and do not want to tell their life story before these needs can be met! However, at a very minimum, the biographical approach can help to establish rapport between an old person and someone who has suddenly come into their life to 'assess' them (for domiciliary services, for example). The worker can develop an understanding of the person's needs in the context of under-standing the whole person. It then becomes possible for the old person to say to the worker, 'You know what I want', which has happened from time to time in the Gloucester study.

In the Gloucester project, the research team started by distilling from life history and biographical research some principles which seemed relevant to the assessment of older people's needs in the context of health and social care (Johnson et al., 1988). These were:

- Those who listen to the life stories of older people whom they wish to help, gain markedly different pictures of the person and their needs, from those who administer traditional assessment techni-ques.
- Self-esteem can be greatly enhanced by skilful encouragement of reminiscence.
- The way people cope with the multiple losses associated with later life is directly dependent on earlier life experiences and on the remaining core of valued relationships, statuses and activities.

The research task has been to develop an approach to assessment which reflects these principles and, moreover, is demonstrably effec-tive and efficient in the context of the everyday practice of health care professionals. It has to work within that specific context if it is to meet its aim of eliciting a view of the older person's needs which will *also* lead to more appropriate and acceptable forms of assistance.

The approach the worker (who is a Gloucester Health Authority employee) adopts in the assessment interview starts with the building of a relationship of trust through which the worker can begin to get to know the elderly person. Rather than asking a set of questions about the person's functional ability and current circumstances, the worker encourages the elderly person to offer up a life history and to describe their present circumstances in that context. The life history has a structure based on major stages in most lives (childhood up-bringing, school, work, married life, retirement/life as a pensioner, widowhood and so on), 'life-events' (births, marriages, deaths, major events) and 'orientations' (values, beliefs). The approach does not depend on a set of pre-planned questions in a rigid sequence of events. Structure is given to the life history by the worker's understanding of the issues to be covered and by the post-interview recording done with the aid of biographical record and analysis sheets (see appendices in Johnson et al., 1988). The biographical approach can yield information about the older person's ability to cope with changing circumstances and about their relatives and friends and the role that relationships play in the life of the person. As with reminiscence, different individuals respond differently to the biographical assessment interview. Some are keen to tell their life story in one go at the first meeting. Others prefer to get to know the workers slowly and tell their story over a number of meetings. As this suggests, the approach requires time to be spent while stories are told and circumstances discussed but the rewards for this can be in avoiding inappropriate offers of help and establishing a rapport which will form a solid basis for work with that person. The latter is realised through a 'contract' between the worker and the older person in which the former explicitly shares an assessment of need which is subject to the latter's agreement, as is the other part of the contract, the plan of action (or 'package of care') to meet agreed needs.

This biographical approach to assessment is still being developed and refined. So far the areas where the approach has been particularly useful include:

- eliciting older people's attitudes (for example in relation to residential care);
- understanding family relationships;
- finding out about relationships between carers and the older person;
- discovering kinds of help which would be unacceptable;
- relating to and understanding people labelled 'difficult';
- learning how people coped with past difficulties and hardship;
- assessing how people might react and be helped effectively in some future crisis.

Research

Johnson's 1976 paper contains no more than implicit prescriptions for conducting biographical research, but since its publication a number of gerontological studies have been carried out which use a biographical or life history method. Among these have been Johnson's own study, with di Gregorio and Harrison, which took life histories from recipients of meals on wheels to establish older people's nutritional preferences (1980), Coleman's longitudinal study (1986) of older people's attitudes towards reminiscence, di Gregorio's doctoral study based on the life histories of a group of older people in Leeds and her analyses of the strategies adopted for 'managing' old age (1986a, 1986b, 1987), Sidell's life-history-based study of confusion in old age (1986) and a biographical study by Cornwell and Gearing (1989) aimed at establishing the health beliefs of a group of older people living in Oxford.

Whilst all of these studies attempted to elicit information about interviewees' past lives to understand better their current perceptions, there were significant differences between these studies in their methods, and in particular over how full a life history each attempted to take from its interview subjects. This supports our view that the particular biographical research method employed (interview method, length and number of interviews, how many areas of the life are included) must vary with the particular purpose or focus of the research enquiry.

The biographical interview

What then is the essence of the biographical research method? Following Levinson (1978) we would suggest that it is the biographical interview itself. Levinson and colleagues studied male adult development through biographical interviews with 40 subjects aged 35 to 40. The following passage captures well the process of biographical interviewing, including its similarities with and differences from other exchanges between people:

> A biographical interview combines aspects of a research interview, a clinical interview and a conversation between friends. It is like a structured research interview in that certain topics must be covered, and the main purpose is research. As in a clinical interview, the interviewer is sensitive to the feelings expressed, and follows the threads of meanings as they lead through diverse topics. Finally, as in a conversation between friends, the relationship is equal and the interviewer is free to respond in terms of his own experiences. Yet each party has a defined role in a substantial task, which imposes its own constraints. (Levinson et al., 1978: 15)

The last sentence introduces a necessary qualification. There is a tension in the biographical interview between, on the one hand, the need of the interviewer to establish and maintain a rapport and a trusting relationship in which the interviewee will disclose significant personal information and, on the other, the practical demands and constraints of any research enquiry. In the event, what transpires is inevitably something of a balancing act. But as Levinson goes on to indicate, there are satisfactions to be gained by both parties to the transaction:

> What is involved is not simply an interviewing technique or procedure, but a relationship of some intimacy, intensity and duration. Significant work is involved in forming, maintaining and terminating the relationship. The recruiting of participants, the negotiation of a research contract, and the course of the interviewing relationship are phases within a single, complex process. Understanding and managing this process is a crucial part of our research method. Managed with sensitivity and discretion, it is a valuable learning experience for the participant as well as the researcher. Although therapy was not a primary aim, the interviews may have had some therapeutic effects. Virtually all of the men, we believe, found this a worthwhile undertaking. (Levinson et al., 1978: 15)

The process of the biographical interview is not then simply one of someone telling their life story. The story is a reconstruction of the life with the help of the interviewer. It is particular to the situation and will vary, at least in some aspects, with a different interviewer on a different occasion. What emerges is the product of a particular time and place and a particular interaction between interviewer and interviewee. For example, a large factor in affecting what happens is the interest of the interviewer and how well the interviewer and subject get on with each other.

It is worth pointing out that the characteristics of the biographical interview have roots in everyday experience – it is an ordinary way of people getting to know one another. The first meetings of people who are interested in each other and wish to do things together involve a certain measure of biography taking. Think of the meetings of people who are attracted to each other, couples on holiday seeking companionship, people whose acquaintance is turning into friendship. The biographical approach is also characteristic in more formal settings: the job interview, the medical history, the social work assessment.

However, these uses of a biographical approach are related to a particular personal or functional interest in the other person. The biographical interview conducted for research purposes is concerned with the search for meaning or explanation which illuminates either an aspect or, more rarely, the whole of the person's life. This information can in turn be related to research questions which focus the interview and provide the basis for analysis. There is no single correct way to conduct the biographical research interview. The following description of the approach and the methods used in the biographical study of health beliefs referred to earlier involving one of the present authors (Cornwell and Gearing, 1989), is included here to bring the reader closer to how such research may be conducted in practice.

Example of a biographical study (derived from Cornwell and Gearing, 1989)

This biographical study of the beliefs about health and illness of 40 older people involved multiple tape-recorded interviews, of between 1 and 3 hours length each with the same person. Behind the approach lay the assumption that the beliefs and ideas people have about health and illness would be connected to their own lived experience and that the researchers' understanding of their views would be enhanced by knowing something about the context from which these had emerged.

In the first interview, the interviewer aimed to establish an overall picture of the person's biography, beginning with the circumstances of their childhood and education and working forwards through the history of their adult life at work, in marriage, and bringing up children, to the point at which they left work, to their lives as pensioners. A schedule of topics was available for the interviewer to refer to during the interview to remind him or her of the areas to be covered. However, no attempt was made to impose the order in which topics appeared on the schedule on the interview, nor was there any standard way of asking questions. Instead, the older people interviewed were encouraged to recall events and to talk about their past in the way that best suited them. An attempt was made to ensure that all the topics on the schedule and every possible area of the person's life had an airing so that if something was not talked about it was not because it had been forgotten.

Having sensitised themselves through the first interview to areas of the life which might be significant and require further exploration, the researchers focused the second and any subsequent interviews more directly on the aims of the enquiry. It was decided to obtain a health history and to ask the older people what their experience had been of the health care system, their ideas about ageing and health in old age, the causes of illness and the possibilities of prevention. The researchers' aim was to use the biographical account obtained earlier to evoke these views in the context of concrete lived experience and to understand why the subject held these beliefs. To do this involved two quite different processes. First, it often became necessary to seek further clarification, elaboration or discussion of the ideas raised by the subject's statements. How and when to do this in a way which does not disrupt the flow of the subject's recollections is essentially a matter of interviewer judgement. It involves, to quote an apt phrase, using 'the right type of probe at the right time' (Plummer, 1983: 97).

The second problematic issue was in discovering, in a more general sense than is often explicitly stated by the subject, how aspects of the life had contributed to their sense of identity. The researchers were concerned to know whether the interviewee had, like Mr Groves, any overarching way of viewing and coping with their world as it was felt that this would have implications for their views about health and illness. This sometimes involved a degree of interpretation which the interviewer tried to validate, where diplomatically possible, by checking it with the subject.

Biographically based interviews like these can more closely resemble a conversation than an interview. If they are to 'work' they require the subject to talk at length, in detail, and with a considerable degree of personal disclosure to a virtual stranger. That many people are willing to do so perhaps testifies to the point made earlier about potential therapeutic or other benefits for some interviewees, however intangible these may appear. They also depend on interviewer sensitivity and a degree of rapport being established between interviewer and subject. It should also be remembered, however, that interviewer skills and sensitivity notwithstanding, some biographical interviews will fail either because, as in everyday life, the people involved simply did not take to each other, or because the older person sees no point in reminiscing about past events.

Analysing biographical research interviews

In-depth interviews with people are a rich source of data on a wide range of topics – biographical interviews share this quality. The drawback with all types of unstructured interview is twofold. Firstly, the unstructured nature of the interview means that it is difficult to organise the data in such a way as to make comparison between one interview and another on the same basis. Doing so destroys much of the richness of the data – with biographical interviews the thread of a person's story would be lost. The second drawback is related to the first. The larger the sample that is used, the greater the difficulty of establishing a systematic basis for comparison. Because of the difficulty of organising data for comparative analysis, the sample size is usually small, which makes a poor basis for generalisation. With a survey approach these problems are obviated by structuring the data *before* it is gathered, using pre-planned questionnaires and often multiple-choice responses.

The aim then of unstructured interviews is not usually to make generalisations that are reliable for a given population, but to explore ideas and find out about processes. The value of the biographical approach, like other qualitative methods of research, lies in the kind of data it is capable of generating: concrete, highly differentiated, richly detailed, and accessible to meanings and interpretations (Fischer, 1983). As such it can contribute to the development of gerontological theory. But there are problems – in particular the sheer volume of data produced which can involve many hours of tape-recorded material and a vagueness about methods of analysis.

Of course, the feature of biographical interviews which marks them out from other unstructured interviews is that there is an apparent structure: the story of someone's life. Johnson (1976) lays emphasis on the notion of 'career', derived from interactionist sociology, in which the continuity in a person's biography is expressed through career strands that add up to make someone's 'life career'. Such an approach is in danger of obscuring particular features of the processes involved. Firstly, in the search for the continuities that constitute a career, discontinuities may be overlooked that may have played a significant part in that life. Secondly, the gathering of the biography in an interview is an interactive process in which the biography is constructed by the respondent with the help of the interviewer. Its structure may be more a quality of telling a story, or of being interviewed, than of the life as lived.

Our own experience suggests that there is no neat and clear-cut temporal division between the processes of data collection (interviewing) and the analysis of the material. In the study in which Mr Groves was interviewed, sufficient data had been collected after the first few interviews for the researchers to form provisional ideas which were compared with material emerging from subsequent interviews and modified, developed or discarded, partly as a result of reading interview transcripts and listening to interview recordings. Glaser and Strauss (1967) describe systematically a process known as the 'constant comparative method' of qualitative analysis through which formal categories are established as a result of continuous comparison and cross-checking of interview material. More recently Anselm Strauss (1988) has written a handbook which attempts to show how qualitative analysis is actually done and uses many examples from the author's own research and that of his students.

The story of an individual's life may have many versions and have episodes with varying significance in terms of the individual's development. Psychoanalysis attends to the biography of an individual, focusing on specific features of development and events that are remembered. Events reported in the biography are used to interpret other events and all are linked to an underlying theory of the process of individual development to 'normal' maturity. Sources of biographical material appropriate to psychoanalytic interpretation include not only conscious accounts but also dreams and odd events in everyday life. (See, for an interesting and lucid discussion of psychobiography and life history, Runyan, 1984).

The biographical method we are considering can be distinguished from psychoanalysis on two counts; it is not a therapy intended to reveal the nature of an individual's true being to herself and it is not based on a given theory of normal development. However, there are some features of the psychoanalytical method which are present in the biographical method. For example, both are interpretive and move from normative ideas to personal experience and back, using one to understand and modify the other. Both are interested in the accounts by individuals of their lives and in relating those accounts to their identity and development. Whereas psychoanalysis is derived from a theory which is applied in therapy, the biographical method in gerontology is intended to generate theory and explore general issues.

The biographical method takes into account the dimensions of time and individuality. This enables the consideration of changes over time that may be related to the ageing process. In the interview with Mr Groves referred to earlier, the focus was on health beliefs and ageing. It can be seen, even from the few quotes presented, that some of his attitudes to health and strength were applied to different situations at different stages of his life – to work and to how he would be cared for when old and frail.

Gerontology is largely concerned with issues that surround the changes occurring for individuals through the passage of time. The biographical method is therefore an appropriate way of addressing such issues as 'disengagement' or 'activity' theory, the role of reminiscence as life review or identity maintenance, the effects of major life events or specific historical events on the life course, and the study of attitudes and their origins, including attitudes to ageing. We would not argue that research questions on these areas can be finally answered by research study based on the biographical approach but that such research can illuminate the topics and expand the database which informs discussion.

The biographical method is a way of gathering and beginning to make sense of data. Like all other research strategies it needs to be guided by research questions that focus the study. Research questions will determine what sorts of topic the interviewer will cover and in what depth and the questions will also begin to provide a basis for analysis – the research questions frame the normative ideas which are then used to make sense of the responses of individuals.

Analysing the interview: an example

It is easiest to illustrate this process by reference to an example. In some biographical interviews undertaken by the authors, the role of 'home' in the life of people was one of a number of research questions that focused the interviews. It is a topic that has been the subject of some analysis of the interviews (Dant, 1988). Here are some extracts that show the significance of 'home' to a particular couple at different stages in their life put into context by drawing from other material from the interview.

Mr and Mrs Harkness each left their parents' home to marry – 58 years ago. They remember moving from a small town in Kent to the outskirts of London to get a flat when they were 25 years old.

> Mr H: We had a flat, couldn't afford a house.

They had one son and though they were poor, buying a house was very important. They bought a house in a pleasant London suburb after they had been married for 27 years.

> Mrs H: But we were able to do it by 1957 . . . I got a part-time job in Hammersmith and I saved almost every penny of that and with the savings certificates that he had we went to, was it Abbey National?
> Mr H: Abbey National.
> Mrs H: And see if they could give us, you know, allow us a mortgage. Because we were getting on and we hadn't got a lot of money to put down, but houses were cheaper.

Mr Harkness worked overtime to pay their mortgage and if they had stayed put they would have been 77 by the time it was paid off. When they retired they sold the house, paid off the mortgage and were able to buy their present home, a bungalow, outright. They moved to be near their son and his family, to a small village in Gloucestershire.

They've lived in the bungalow for 18 years, dependent on public transport and neighbours to help them get to the shops and facilities of town. Mr Harkness had had driving lessons once:

Mr H: But I decided at the late hour that I wouldn't carry on with that.
Mrs H: Having our own front door was the main thing.
Mr H: Yes.
Mrs H: Because we couldn't afford both.

While it is not possible to offer rules for proceeding with analysis, there are a number of points that can be made about beginning to unravel the data from biographical interviews.

First, the data can be organised into patterns. This may involve, as in the example with Mr and Mrs Harkness, a broad making sense of themes that make up the content of the interview. Such an approach may be contrasted to interpretation in everyday life which is likely to be based on what has just been said. Patterns may become apparent within one biography, or analysis may reveal a pattern that occurs across a number of different interviews. Patterns in biographical material, especially when being utilised in gerontological research, are likely to be across time. Such patterns may be indicated by continuities or discontinuities. For the Harknesses, the jointly possessed home has been a continuous feature of their life together that was bounded by the discontinuity of leaving their parents' homes. Their tenure, eventually ownership, has clearly been of great significance to them, dominating their income and other aspects of their lives (work, freedom to travel).

Second, the data is in the form of language. The words that Mr and Mrs Harkness use to tell their story, the way they put phrases together, the way they jointly construct their story, interrupting and adding to each other's contributions may be crucial in communicating its meaning. Linguistic data could be reduced to numbers through a content analysis but this would be to lose its richness and its quality as a 'story' that spans time. It could alternatively be treated to a detailed linguistic analysis, taking account of the way the participants use language to express themselves and how the conversational exchange is managed by the participants (Boden and Bielby, 1983, 1986).

Third, the analysis is interpretive. The utterances of human beings are a mode of communicating meaning. The meaning of utterances is not simple; words do not simply stand for meanings. In normal conversation the process of utterance and interpretation is continuous and unquestioned. To subject a text to *analysis* is to render problematic the issue of what was meant. It is not clear for example whether 'having their own front door' always was the main thing for the Harknesses or whether it is a *post hoc* rationalisation of how their lives ran.

Fourth, the interview is an interactive process. The interviewer interprets what is said at the time and that will affect her/his response. If there are other people present then they will also be participants who are contributing on the basis of their understanding of what has been said to them. It is Mrs Harkness who interprets the meaning of Mr Harkness' account of having given up his driving lessons. The interpretive process is then continuous; the person offering a biographical account will interpret their own life, the interviewer will interpret the account that is offered, the analyst will continue the interpretation at some remove in time and with the ability to move backwards and forwards through the account. The analyst will also interpret in the light of other similar interviews. (Many of the issues relating to the status and analysis of interview and other qualitative data are discussed in detail by Silverman, 1985.)

CONCLUSION

What we have tried to do in this chapter is to raise some issues about the biographical approach and suggest some strategies that might be appropriate to using the approach in gerontological study and practice. We have not been able to consider all of the practicalities of the process (such as how to deal with stories that have been more or less intentionally 'made up' or the differences between interviewing individuals and couples). Nor have we dealt with the issues of the validity of material which relies on human memory to cover the past. (This important issue is discussed in Plummer, 1983.) In our discussion of the analysis of biographical data we have only been able to indicate a general approach and its sources in the literature. What we have done is to outline the origins and main features of the biographical approach and we have discussed its uses in the three areas of reminiscence, assessment and research. We have identified the central importance of the biographical interview in all three areas and discussed its main characteristics. Finally, we have indicated an approach to the analysis of biographical research interviews.

The use of biographical and life story data in gerontology is comparatively recent and much remains to be done in developing methods of interview and analysis. However, the further refinement of methods will only serve gerontology well if it is carried through without losing what is most valuable and distinctive about the biographical approach: its concern with the rich variability of the lives of individual older people.

PART THREE

ISSUES

Introduction

The final part of this book presents three chapters which look at some of the most fundamental issues concerning research in social gerontology: ethics, funding and dissemination. In the first of these Alan Butler considers ethical issues in research with old people. He begins by posing the question 'do old people require special ethical consideration?' and answers his question with a resounding 'no', suggesting that all social research should be conducted according to a strict ethical code which if adhered to should prevent old people from becoming a 'special case'. Such an ethical code must take on board the issues of informed consent; protection of privacy and avoidance of harm – all areas where old people may be particularly vulnerable to abuse. The author discusses each of these areas in detail and draws upon examples of research where the rights of older people have been abused due to mental frailty, their status as recipients of a service and the ageist and/or sexist attitudes prevailing amongst those undertaking the research. He concludes with a timely reminder that 'because as a society we still evidence many ageist attitudes there exists a danger that, when working with older people, ethical corners will be cut and respect for persons eroded'.

In a detailed discussion of the funding of research Margot Jefferys draws upon her years of experience as a researcher and teacher to chart developments in social gerontology from the perspectives of both funders and researchers. She considers in detail the funding practices of non-governmental agencies, government departments and the research councils, and then relates trends in funding to the supply of academic social researchers throughout the 1960s and 1970s and to the growth of research units and institutes. She considers the strengths and weaknesses which researchers in the field of social gerontology, who are drawn from a wide range of social sciences, bring to their work. Her chapter provides a realistic account of funding issues at the present time and the author acknowledges that 'appeals for support for fundamental or "pure" research on issues of ageing, in the present climate, are likely to fall on deaf ears'. She calls for researchers to be 'flexible and innovative' and to use their initiative in finding ways of addressing their own agendas and interests within the confines of contracted research.

Innovation and initiative are skills which feature prominently in Averil Osborn and Dianne Willcocks' paper on the dissemination of research, where their main concern is what happens to the product of research. In 'Making Research Useful and Usable', the authors start from the premiss that 'researchers need to be sensitive to the impact of research work upon the older people they study' and that 'social gerontology research can be used to enable older people to participate in social change'. The dissemination of research is *the* activity within the research process most closely linked to social change, and the authors consider how research material can be put to good use. They ask: what are the barriers to effective dissemination?, and what skills do researchers need to disseminate effectively? They debate the issues of responsibility surrounding dissemination and challenge the accusation that researchers are 'going native' when they move into policy and action, a position which some authors feel is detrimental to the status of research (see Smith, 1989). In this chapter dissemination is not just seen as an optional extra at the end of the 'real work'; it is a fundamental part of the research, which needs to be thought out at an early stage and which demands commitment, energy and skill. The authors end by offering a good practice guide to dissemination, outlining areas which enable and inhibit the dissemination process.

11

Research Ethics and Older People

ALAN BUTLER

INTRODUCTION

Do older people require special ethical consideration as research subjects? At various times particular groups of research subjects, for example young children, prisoners and the mentally handicapped, have been accorded special status and thereby greater protection. To suggest that older people come into a similar category is to fall into the trap of ageism and adopt a paternalistic attitude. The term 'older people' may be taken to refer to anybody aged between 60 and 105. It would be difficult to find a more heterogeneous group of citizens. Some of them will be infirm, lonely, isolated and confused – and our research may lead us to such people – but we must be wary of assuming that everybody in a particular age category shares the characteristics of the most infirm members of that group.

Older people do not then need different ethical consideration from the rest of the population when they are being considered as research subjects. All social research should be conducted in the light of a strict ethical code. The Social Research Association has published a useful set of guidelines (SRA, 1983). If this is adhered to then nobody would need to be treated as a special case. However, we live in a less than perfect world and particular groups in our society are vulnerable to certain types of abuse when the subjects of research. In such cases we must be meticulous in applying the ethical canons of social research.

The proper ethical standards of research should of course be applied whenever a project is being planned on whatever type of population. However, in practice sometimes only lip service is paid to some of them and, in the pressure to complete a project, corners are cut. I would suggest that when considering work with older people, close adherence to the letter and the spirit of ethical standards is a requirement. In addition researchers should be aware that there are a number of areas where older people, because of their particular circumstances or state of health, may be vulnerable to abuse. These may include their status as recipients of services as well as basic characteristics such as age, sex, race and the state of their mental health.

Mental frailty

A number of the subjects may share some of the characteristics evidenced by the special groups of citizens already referred to. For example, some older people will be suffering from Alzheimer's disease and, therefore, rather confused. In the case of somebody suffering from a dementia, responsibility may be so diminished that they are unable to give realistic consent. This poses problems parallel to those posed when seeking to use young children as research subjects. The SRA (1983) guidelines suggest two forms of approach. One would be to utilise observational techniques in the study ensuring that 'private space' is not invaded. The other is to use a proxy to answer questions on behalf of the subject. The use of a proxy raises a number of issues. Care should be taken not to disturb the relationship between subject and proxy; information should not be sought which the subject might object to and finally once again 'private space' should not be invaded (see Chapter 9 by Mike Bury and Anthea Holme for a discussion of the use of proxies).

Institutional care

A great deal of research upon older people has been among those who live in institutions. In that respect they may share some of the dilemmas faced by those in prison – what right then have they to refuse to cooperate; how far is cooperation seen as a requirement by those running the institution; will they suffer in some way if they do not agree to the research procedure, and so on? Tim Booth (1983: 32) has graphically described the difficulties in seeking to gather the consumers' view of residential life. He paints a picture of a world in which powerlessness and dependence is engendered: 'The net result is that either residents' views are considered unreliable and treated with suspicion or when asked residents are found to have very little to say.'

In so far as older people are a 'captive' audience for researchers, they deserve special consideration.

Service delivery

Another focus for research with older people concerns the delivery of services to them, such as meals-on-wheels or various forms of home care and assistance. Once again the research subjects may feel that continued delivery of services is dependent upon their apparently willing cooperation in the research enterprise. As Booth (1983: 33) points out, 'It can take a lot of courage to "bite the hand that feeds".'

Ageism and sexism

Potential interviewers of the elderly are likely to share many of the attitudes and views of the wider citizenry. Historically, we have viewed old age as akin to a 'second childhood', and some of these ideas still prevail. Subsequently, fieldworkers may believe that they do not really *need* fully to explain their procedures, ensure that proper consent has been obtained, or insist upon proper safeguards with regard to confidentiality. We know that many older people will be living in impoverished circumstances, and that a demographic fact of life is that the majority are female, thus risking compounding age discrimination with sexism (Eichler, 1988). To be poor, female and old in our society is to carry a heavy burden of disadvantage. A younger researcher, perhaps unaware of their own attitudes may easily talk down to the subject and fail to give due weight to the respondent's own voice. Ann Oakley, in a paper entitled 'Interviewing women: a contradiction in terms' (Oakley, 1981) has questioned the conventional wisdom of interviewer-based research. She advocates a more inter-active two-way process whereby the interview becomes more of a shared dialogue.

Research management

There are a number of factors that should be within the control of the research director. For example, the researchers may conduct their own fieldwork interviews, or recruit – usually younger – research assistants to complete this work. Part of the recruitment and selection procedure should involve some testing for ageist attitudes. After recruitment good supervision of the fieldworkers is necessary. However, on major projects the actual fieldwork may be placed with a large – and rather anonymous – agency which recruits its own interviewers. Then the control may easily slip from the researcher's grasp and corner-cutting and slipshod practices flourish unnoticed. If a large agency is used – and some are much better than others – the research team should maintain a close involvement at all stages of the work. For example, team members should be present at the briefing and debriefing of fieldworkers. They should also conduct spot checks on the collection of the data, accompanying interviewers to the site, and reinterviewing a small number of subjects in order to ensure that no corner-cutting takes place and that ethical standards are maintained. An executive of a large agency, when being pressed on the issue of confidentiality for institutionalised subjects, typified this problem with the remark 'Oh, don't worry, old people never complain about anything anyway.'

These, then, are just some of the areas where researchers must be aware of the potential for abuse. For a number of reasons, which I intend to explore, older people have in the past been exposed to some particularly shoddy research practices. In order to outline the case for the meticulous application of ethical rules to research with older people, I have divided the remainder of this chapter into the following sections: Informed Consent; The Protection of Privacy; and The Avoidance of Harm. (See Chapter 6 by David Challis and Robin Darton for discussion of informed consent and protection of privacy within experimental research designs.)

INFORMED CONSENT

Definition

Informed consent has been defined as 'a voluntary, uncoerced decision, made by a sufficiently competent or autonomous person on the basis of adequate information and deliberation, to accept rather than reject some proposed course of action that will affect him or her' (Gillon, 1985). The concept of consent rests upon the moral principle of respect for an individual's autonomy (Kant, 1964; Faden and Beauchamp, 1986).

Criteria

In order to exercise consent certain criteria may have to be fulfilled for or by the subject. The research subject should have the capacity or competence to give their consent. This may need to be established by the researcher if, for example, the subject is physically ill or confused for some reason. Next, the subject should be given sufficient information about the project upon which to make a considered judgement. This does not mean that they have to be swamped with minutiae about every aspect of a project, merely that they have a clear understanding of the project's aims and how the research procedure (interview and so on) will affect them. Finally, they need to be free from any constraints when making their decision. As the SRA (1983) guidelines point out, research subjects 'should be aware of their entitlement to refuse at any stage for whatever reason and to withdraw data just supplied'.

Consent and the service provider

Berkowitz (1978) makes the point that service users may feel that they have to participate in a particular study in order to maintain what they currently receive. An added problem is the difficulty that some people have in disentangling the researcher from the staff of the agency that provides the service. Strain and Chappell (1982) have addressed this issue empirically. They found that subject compliance was greater among a study population that was receiving a particular welfare service than among the control group that was not. This suggests that those in receipt of the service felt that in some way a failure to go along with a requested interview would jeopardise continued delivery.

Subjects should have it made clear to them that they have the right to decline to participate, may refuse to answer part or all of any planned interview, and that this in no way compromises their rights to future health or welfare services.

The problem of subtle enforced compliance is arguably greater when the study population is living within some form of institution. This is an issue which has long been considered when it comes to research upon prisoners. In 1976 a US National Commission commented that: 'When persons seem regularly to engage in activities which, were they stronger or in better circumstances, they would avoid, respect dictates that they be protected against those forces that appear to compel their choices.'

The analogy between a prisoner and an elderly person living in residential care may appear rather strained but similar pressures to conform and to go along with a suggested research procedure may exist. As Booth (1983: 33) indicates, residents in institutional care may become very quiescent: 'Their powerlessness and overall dependence on staff fosters both a fear of retribution if they should press a complaint too forcefully and, possibly, a feeling of indebtedness which makes honest criticism seem more like ingratitude.'

Practical steps

In order to counter these problems, various simple practical steps should be undertaken by the researcher. The SRA (1983) guidelines provide a useful check list. First, consideration should be given to providing easily readable and assimilable consent forms. The subjects should be given sufficient time to consider their position and make an informed decision. Some attempt should be made to test out their competency and, if this is compromised, other family members may have to be involved. For example, a relative may make a rather better job of explaining a project to an elderly subject than the researcher. The SRA (1983) document notes that on occasions a 'gatekeeper' may block the researchers' access to their subjects. This is a particular problem when approaching older subjects since so many people, particularly residential care staff, feel the need to intercede and 'protect' the older person. The guidelines warn against inadvertently disturbing the relationship between subject and gatekeeper but stress that researchers should 'adhere to the principle of obtaining informed consent directly from subjects once they have gained access to them'.

Pressure on the researcher

Researchers are often placed under considerable pressure to complete a project on time. They will also strive to obtain a high compliance rate since this increases the validity of the study and represents an economical use of time and resources. Indeed, a project leader may regard the fact that some research subjects have refused to answer some or all of the interviewer's questions as reflecting poor interview technique on the part of the fieldworker. The need to be seen to be good at one's job becomes extremely important when, as is frequently the case, those at the sharp end of research are on temporary contracts. In the drive to complete a piece of research on time and with a large sample, the fragile concept of consent may easily be overlooked, or overridden.

THE PROTECTION OF PRIVACY

Sissela Bok in *Secrets: on the Ethics of Concealment and Revelation* (1986), defines privacy as 'the condition of being protected from unwanted access by others – either physical access, personal information, or attention. Claims to privacy are claims to control access to what one takes – however grandiosely – to be one's personal domain.'

Research frequently involves us in trying to obtain information that is considered to be confidential by our research subjects (Barnes, 1979). We have a duty to ensure that such information is either rendered anonymous, so that it may not subsequently be linked with a particular individual, or held securely in such a way that it is not accessible to other people. This means that the researcher must ensure safe storage of the data; refuse to discuss it with other people; and, whenever possible, by means of coding and so on, render it meaningless to a casual onlooker.

Control of data

Maintaining these standards is not always easy. Research may be conducted in the field and control over data thereby rendered difficult. We may inhabit offices without lockable doors and filing cabinets. As an aside, I am often amazed, when visiting researcher colleagues, at just what is left lying around on their desk tops!

Furthermore, we may come under pressure to reveal certain information to an agency which is facilitating our fieldwork. A hospital consultant, in permitting us to interview his or her patients, may assume the right of access to the material. Similarly, a housing manager may assume that some informal information about his or her customers' views on the service is in order. Work in residential settings may be particularly taxing in this regard. By the very enclosed nature of the establishment, information about residents too easily 'leaks' out of files. Anonymity in such circumstances may not be sufficient. The SRA (1983) document points out that 'a particular configuration of attributes can, like a finger print, frequently identify its owner beyond reasonable doubt'. In order to counter this the social researcher may have to regroup data so as to disguise identities or utilise other techniques that are described by Flaherty (1979).

Researchers have an obligation to make clear to those who facilitate their research just what information they are prepared to share with them. The limits and boundaries of shared information should also be made clear to the research subjects when their consent is being sought.

Because our society is still infused with ageist attitudes it is too easy to ignore the rights to privacy amongst our oldest citizens. The right to control the boundary around what is known about us in the outside world should not be diminished by age.

THE AVOIDANCE OF HARM

The subjects of research

Social research, unlike biological or medical research, does not usually expose the subject to any direct risk of harm. Nonetheless, even though the risks of harm may be low they should not be ignored. When planning any project careful consideration should be given to the potential harm (or 'costs') involved for the respondents. Any anticipated harm should be minimised, and always carefully weighed against the anticipated benefits.

Usually the type of harm engendered by social research with older people involves the provocation of anxiety, embarrassment or some other form of mental anguish. In seeking 'the truth' we must think very carefully about the types of question that we pose and the manner in which we present them. Cassell (1982) has argued that people may feel wronged without being harmed by research. This may happen if they are left with the feeling that they are being treated simply as an object of measurement without due account being given to their individual values and sense of privacy. The SRA (1983) guidelines point out that one of the most frequent causes of complaint is not invasion of privacy but the overburdening of subjects by the collection of 'too much' information.

The problems of responding

Because some older people may have plenty of time available to them, interviews may become protracted. Indeed, in seeking to understand an individual's view of the world, it may be necessary to listen patiently as they reconstruct their past life. A lengthy session with an apparently understanding and sympathetic interviewer may, however, arouse in the subject quite false expectations. It is all too easy to engender the idea that some change in the respondent's personal circumstances will occur as a direct result of the interview, or indeed that this is about to become a regular part of their life.

For the interviewer a difficulty may be posed when they uncover a problem of service need which may be quite unrelated to the project in hand. Yordi et al. (1982) discuss this dilemma and attempt to develop a typology of need which is then related to the appropriate interviewer response. The conclusion reached is that only 'emergency service needs' should prompt the interviewer to step out of role and contact the appropriate medical or welfare agency on behalf of the respondent.

Butler (1975) has commented that research involving the aged, 'has concentrated primarily on studies of the 5% of elderly who are in institutions'. He points out that this captive audience is easily subject to exploitation and suffers a diminution of freedom and of voluntariness. Booth (1983) makes the same point when, in talking about residents, he states that 'following admission they are identified as people who are not fully capable of managing their own lives, and hence whose competence cannot be trusted'. Particular care should be taken when working in such a setting. With the subjects' autonomy and privacy already compromised, it is too easy for the researcher to fall prey to the view that 'no harm can be done'.

The researcher

Thus far I have considered the potential harm to the respondents in the research enterprise. However, there is another side to this. All fieldwork, whether it involves observation or conversation, is time-consuming and demanding. In many ways the difficulties are compounded when working with older people. Some of the subjects will be infirm or even in the process of dying. They are likely to have many unmet service needs and their frailty may make the interview process extremely taxing.

Many older people will have suffered sometimes multiple bereavements in their recent past, and a typical young researcher may find that this fact infuses the interview. In such circumstances it is all too easy to be drawn into a lengthy and emotionally demanding session when the role of researcher is abandoned in favour of concerned listener.

All fieldwork interviewers should be offered some framework of support which enables them to talk over and reflect upon the work that they are doing. This may be of particular importance when the research subjects are the frail elderly. It is unfair to expect a young

research assistant to carry the burden of disclosures. They should have
the facility to talk to a supervisor, not only about the empirical content
of the material that they have collected but also to allow them some
space to reflect upon the emotional context (see Eileen Fairhurst's
account of ethical issues raised in carrying out observation on a
geriatric ward, in Chapter 7).

If we fail to provide this, a heavily burdened interviewer will become
blunted in responsiveness, and inattentive in subsequent interviews.
The imprecation to 'do no harm' applies to staff as well as to
respondents.

CONCLUSION

As the number and proportion of older individuals has increased, so
research activity in this field has grown. As I have pointed out, older
people do not constitute an homogeneous group and we should be
wary of treating them as if they do.

They deserve to be treated with the equal respect that all other
citizens should command. This means that when we come to undertake social research with older people we should observe the normal
ethical codes which have developed over the years to govern such
work. The Social Research Association ethical guidelines that I have
already alluded to (SRA, 1983) provide a good introduction.

However, because as a society we still evidence many ageist
attitudes, there exists the danger that, when working with older
people, ethical corners will be cut and respect for persons eroded. The
danger is compounded by the fact that the majority of older people are
female, and thereby subject to sexist discrimination, and that some of
their number will be frail and/or in poverty, thereby reinforcing the
view, held by some at least, that they are rather marginal citizens with
views that do not carry much weight. For example, Helen Evers (1981)
has commented upon the depersonalisation of elderly women patients
that occurs on geriatric wards.

Particular ethical issues may be created when working with particular sections of the older population, as I have indicated. The
confused elderly are one obvious example. Another example would be
those older people living in institutions of some kind. As a captive
audience they may already be subject to invasion of their privacy, and
an undermining of their autonomy.

In the relentless pressure to find out more about the world around
us, we must ensure that the questions that we pose really are important enough to outweigh the, albeit usually minor, harm that we may
cause to our research subjects.

12

The Funding of Social Gerontological Research

MARGOT JEFFERYS

Some of the issues relating to the funding of social gerontological research in Britain in these last decades of the twentieth century are similar to those facing social science research in general and, in particular, that which seeks primarily to develop explanatory propositions rather than accumulate empirically based description. Other issues are either specific to gerontological research or are likely to assume greater significance in it than in most other fields of enquiry or scholarly concept development.

In this chapter, I begin by setting out the definition of social gerontology I propose to use. Then, adopting the 'economese' which characterises the language in which our political masters now compel us to consider research as well as welfare questions, I consider first some issues affecting the 'client' or demand side of the 'market' for social science research, following this with a review of 'contractor' or supply side issues. I conclude with some highly speculative comments about future trends.

For the purposes of this chapter only, I propose to define social gerontological research as consisting mainly of systematic, non-routine enquiry concerning the lives of men and women of statutory pensionable age and of their multifold relationships with others. Studies which deal with preparation for or early retirement, as well as those which compare the functional capacity or performance of people of different ages in different social settings, however, are not excluded. Nor is research designed to elucidate societal responses to older people whether these responses are behavioural or attitudinal, and whether they relate to individuals, groups or institutions.

RESEARCH FUNDING – THE MARKET

There are various agencies, most of them governmental or voluntary rather than commercial, which are willing to buy the output of researchers concerned with social gerontological issues. In recent years, following the 1972 Rothschild proposals on the way in which the government should support research and development, the agencies buying research have come to be called clients (HMSO, 1972). Most commonly they pay for the research not by buying the already completed product but by contracting with the researchers to pay the labour costs and consumables involved in carrying out and reporting on the research undertaken and giving the conclusions which the researchers consider flow from it. There may also be a tacit assumption that the researchers point to the policy or practice implications of the findings for their clients or other agencies. There is also a convention, hitherto widely respected, that the researchers are free to make their results available to general or specific publics by publishing them in book form or in journals, and through broadcasting and meetings. (I discuss later a disquieting change in the research contracts now being drawn up by the Department of Health which appears to renege on this convention.)

It is these agencies which constitute the 'demand' for social gerontological research as defined in this chapter. Researchers themselves, the 'supply' side, were slow to come to terms with the new terminology and to recognise the new climate which its introduction symbolises. They still tend to think of these agencies as their potential 'suppliers' of resources, their patrons or sponsors, rather than as 'clients' for their products. They see themselves as engaged in a learned activity – adding to the storehouse of human knowledge – undertaken primarily for its intrinsic professional rewards rather than for profit, and not involved in market activities. In so far as they have recognised that they have a 'client', academic researchers like to think of it as the general public and particularly those members of it who are most likely to benefit from their work. Given too that social researchers – and those in gerontological research are no exception – frequently hold dear such values as social justice and equity, they may see their activities as designed primarily on behalf of those who are generally agreed to be socially disadvantaged, rather than those who provide the financial resources for the research.

It was only gradually in the post-Second World War years that research began seriously to be considered as a potential guide to policy-making on major societal issues, including the care of needy older people. The large, charitable foundations were the first to recognise the potential value of the results of careful systematic enquiry in the process of policy formation and/or practice development. It was they who constituted the first clients for independent research.

Non-governmental research funds

One of the bigger, if not the biggest, clients among non-governmental bodies for research on the care of elderly people has been the Nuffield Foundation.[1] Its commitment to this field began in the 1940s and has continued ever since. During the first two post-Second World War decades it made direct grants to a number of researchers with interests in various socio-biological aspects of ageing including the relationship between chronological age and cognitive capacity.[2] It has also been a major source of research funding for studies of problems affecting the well-being of old people through its continuing core support for the National Corporation for the Care of Old People (NCCOP) which, particularly since 1980 when it was renamed the Centre for Policy on Ageing (CPA), has become a research organisation in its own right rather than a dispenser of research funds to others.[3]

The Joseph Rowntree Memorial Trust (JRMT) has also been a major source of funding for social welfare research and experiment. Over the years, its programme has included many projects concerned with the welfare of old people.[4] Since the late 1970s, a number of seasoned researchers have advised the Trust on the worth of the research and development projects submitted to it, and have served on the advisory committees to the projects which it became its standard practice to set up once a grant was given.

The JRMT also played a significant part in the establishment of two organisations which have also contributed to ageing research in Britain, and it continues to give them financial support. The first is the National Institute of Social Work which has a research unit now funded mainly by the DoH.[5] The second is the Policy Studies Institute (PSI), formed by the amalgamation in the late 1970s of two independent research bodies, Political and Economic Planning (PEP) and the Centre for Studies in Social Policy (CSP).[6]

The British Foundation for Age Research, established in 1976, raises funds mainly from industrial concerns.[7] Its review committee, composed in the main of medical doctors and bioscientists, considers applications for research, and its grants, usually for one-off inexpensive projects, go mainly to medical institutions for clinical or laboratory research.

The contribution to old age research of other charitable bodies, such as the City Parochial Foundation whose bailiwick is London,[8] and, by contrast, Help the Aged,[9] the Carnegie[10] and Rockefeller Foundations,[11] whose oysters are the world, have been less sustained than those of the Nuffield Foundation and the JRMT, but significant from time to time.

During the 1980s, the voluntary charitable foundations have not been able to increase their overall contributions to social research, not because they do not wish to, but because their income has not increased as much as has the cost of professionally conducted research. They have tightened up their scrutiny of requests for funding in an effort to improve the quality of the work which they decide to fund.

Given the prevailing social and economic climate they, in common with direct and indirect government agencies which provide research funds, have proved more likely to favour research which makes many observations and uses increasingly sophisticated statistical methods to draw conclusions. Like government departments, they are also likely to give priority to research the results of which may have short- or medium-term applications, rather than research which is frankly exploratory and cannot promise such pay-offs.

Finally, where non-governmental funds for research are concerned, there are commercial enterprises. They have not been a major source of finance for social gerontology, but some multinational drug companies, like Sandoz,[12] for their own good purposes, sponsor a good deal of research by medical doctors and bioscientists which is relevant to ageing or old people. They usually require the research to have the respectability of a medical impress, but they sometimes support conferences where social gerontologists alongside other scientists have reported their studies, for example, the European Ageing Well International Congress at Brighton in 1987. Presumably, investment of this kind helps to improve the public image of a company as a 'caring concern'.

Government departments as clients for old age research

In 1968, under a Labour government, the newly formed Department of Health and Social Security (DHSS) established a research management division, distinct from the statistics division, and began to fund research by members of university departments and some independent research institutes into the health and social welfare needs of particular groups of the population, including old people, and the way in which services were meeting them (HMSO, 1969). Probably at no time since has there been such relatively great enthusiasm in both the political and executive branch of government for social science research as a tool of government. The new department (comprising the erstwhile Ministry of Health, the Ministry of Pensions and National Insurance and the National Assistance Board) also set up its own Social Science Research Unit.

In the early 1970s, after the return of the Conservative government under Mr Heath, Lord Rothschild, the government's Chief Scientist, was invited to review the evolving research arrangements of the central government departments. His report was broadly accepted and the proposals of a government White Paper (HMSO, 1972), based on his proposals, implemented (HMSO, 1973). From then on the central government departments regarded themselves as 'clients' for research and those who undertook it as 'contractors'. Rothschild suggested that these departments should look for research which had short- or medium-term applicability and that 'basic' or fundamental research should be the responsibility of the quasi-independent Research Councils whose finance came from the Department of Education and

Science. The government also decided that the DHSS should recruit a recognised medical scientist as its Chief Scientist both to advise the department's client sections on the research which might benefit them most and to help them select the contractors best able to provide it.

In implementing the Rothschild principles the DHSS established a Chief Scientist's division headed by a medical 'elder statesman'.[13] It was staffed by administrative and professional civil servants, the latter, among other duties, acting as chairpeople of research liaison groups (RLGs) formed to consider specific areas of the Department's responsibility, one such being the care of the elderly, another physical handicap, a third, mental illness and handicap and a fourth, local authority social services. The members of the RLGs included representatives of the relevant client sections and academic and other research or professional workers who were called Scientific Advisers. These RLGs met, mostly irregularly, both to review proposals made to them for funding by researchers and to establish research priorities in line with government policy. Since 1979, the part they have played in the DHSS research programme planning and management has diminished through a process of slow erosion rather than as a result of any firm policy statement indicating the intention to phase them out.

At the time of writing, the DHSS's* professional staff attached to the Chief Scientist's Office, itself attached to the Research Management division, act as liaison officers to DHSS-sponsored research units based in universities and elsewhere. These units are given broad or specific terms of reference and the assumption is that, provided their work is considered scientifically respectable by a visiting party of scientists and others, their six-year contracts will be rolled on at regular intervals. These contracts enable the units to employ 'core' research, technical and administrative staff with some expectation of security of tenure. One of these units was founded in 1978 specifically to research issues associated with the care of the elderly.[14] Others with less specific terms of reference have also been active in this area (see p. 182).

During the 1970s, an increasing proportion of the department's research contracts went to these units and a smaller proportion to other researchers. The concentration of DHSS resources on their own sponsored units was, not unnaturally, welcomed on the whole by the unit directors who saw the opportunity to establish some research career posts in which individuals could pursue specialised research interests at a time when the universities were unable or unwilling to do so. It was deplored, again not surprisingly, by those outside the units who were finding it more and more difficult to find research funding from public sources. By the end of the decade, the relatively expansive research funding of the earlier part of the decade had given

* In 1988 the DHSS was replaced by two departments: the Department of Health and the Department of Social Security – see 'Future Prospects', p. 183.

way to parsimony. Economy in all forms of public expenditure became the order of the day, and, on the return of a Conservative government in 1979, this trend was accentuated and has continued.

In the early Rothschild days, many of the contracts given were for research suggested by the contractors themselves. In the last few years, however, the DHSS itself and subsequently, the two new departments – of Health and Social Security – have set out their priorities and have not been likely to fund research which does not rate high on their lists. In other words, the research policy of the government has been to become more proactive, less reactive. Not unnaturally, the main priorities were and remain research intended to help guide policy-makers on problems concerning immediate service provision, especially in areas where those in power feel most vulnerable to criticism from the official opposition or influential pressure groups, professional and lay. The emphasis is on the factors likely to influence the level of need for domiciliary services which, were it to be met, could reduce the demand for both hospital beds and residential places for old people. Some consideration was also given to the methods employed by service providers to assess and estimate needs and by fieldworkers to meet them. Given the expansion in the number of old people, it is not surprising to find that research relating to their needs has usually figured – with varying degrees of prominence – on successive priority lists. From time to time, however, other issues, affecting far fewer people but capturing the public's concern – for example AIDS – have been the flavour of the month.

Other government departments also were and are concerned directly or indirectly with older people. For example, the Department of the Environment has responsibilities for housing, and its Housing Research Department takes an active part in sponsoring and then closely monitoring research by outside bodies as well as undertaking in-house research of its own on such matters as sheltered housing accommodation and the effect of owner-occupation housing tenure on elderly, increasingly disabled people.[15]

Some government-sponsored research has been incidentally, rather than centrally, concerned with older people. For example, in the light of the widespread belief that old people were increasingly the victims of crime against the person, the Crime Survey undertaken in the early 1980s by the Home Office's Research Unit paid particular attention to the age and gender distribution of the victims of crime and the circumstances in which crimes against the person were most likely to occur.[16]

Alongside government attempts in the 1980s to achieve general economies in the public purse has gone greater scrutiny of the output of the research units as well as of their scientific standards. The adjective 'scientific' tends to be defined in such a way as to emphasise the value of research designed to produce quantitative results rather than new concepts, hypotheses or theories concerning human motivations and decision-making by exploring in some depth the attitudes and behaviours of 'actors' in everyday situations. Research which employs ethnographic and/or other essentially social anthropological methods and paradigms has to that extent been disadvantaged in the competition for funds, the disposition of which is largely in the hands of those whose scientific standards have been established on a biological, or at least epidemiological, model which makes extensive use of statistical methods.

Indirect government funding

There are two government-financed Research Councils which have funded research relevant to ageing. Both are independent bodies but come under the general aegis of the Department of Education and Science.

The Medical Research Council (MRC), established during the First World War, has had a long history of funding research concerned with the effect of age on cognitive capacity and on work or task performance.[17] It provides funds both in the reactive mode (that is, for projects and programmes suggested by individual researchers) and, from time to time, in the proactive mode by inviting its established units to undertake work which it believes requires to be done. Most of the work which the MRC has commissioned on ageing – other than that concerning broadly the physiology of ageing – has been done in their own units in Applied Psychology Units in Cambridge, Liverpool and Sheffield. It is fair to say that, in general, the psychologists working on issues of ageing have been more interested in the psychophysiological than in the psychosocial aspects of human potential or performance.

The Social Science Research Council (SSRC) was established in 1965. In 1984 its name was changed to the Economic and Social Research Council (ESRC).[18] Its methods of soliciting research proposals and determining priorities have varied over the 23 years of its existence. In the main, it has acted in the reactive mode with peer review as an essential element in its selective process. That is to say, one of the Council's committees composed of seasoned academic researchers, guided by reports from referees, has considered for funding the proposals spontaneously submitted by researchers. This system has applied to research proposals concerned with older people.

Until 1982, the SSRC committees taking decisions on research applications were primarily single-discipline committees. In 1982–3, the Council reorganised itself, abolishing the discipline committees and substituting for them six multidiscipline committees each with a general topic area remit. One of these new committees, the Social Affairs Committee, decided to allocate a proportion of the sum made available to it to research on ageing. It appointed a consultant to review the field of age-related research and advise it on how best it could distribute its limited resource to elucidating issues in the field.

In the event, the total sum available for this research initiative (under £300,000) was too small to allow investment in either large-scale cross-sectional surveys or longitudinal cohort research for which it had at first recognised the need. For the most part, therefore, the short-term projects it funded required only limited resources. A volume of papers, dealing mainly with the research done under this initiative, was published in 1989 (Jefferys, 1989). Another SSRC (ESRC) committee – the Education and Human Development Commit-tee – supported in part a substantial research programme now based in Manchester, which included a longitudinal study of cognitive capacity in older people in three English areas.[19]

Between 1983 and 1987, the government reduced the resources available to all the Research Councils, thus requiring them to reduce both their research and research training programmes.[20] In addition, the decade has seen a particular onslaught on the SSRC on ideological grounds. It was reliably rumoured that Sir Keith Joseph, when Secretary of State for Education and Science, made a sustained attempt to abolish the SSRC altogether. In response to public concern, he summoned Lord Rothschild, the architect of the government's research funding administrative strategy, to investigate the affairs of the SSRC. Lord Rothschild did not condone the proposal which apparently had Sir Keith's approval to abolish the Council (HMSO, 1982); but it was required to change its name to meet Sir Keith's view that there were no such things as the social sciences.

Since 1987, another Council reorganisation has replaced the six multidisciplinary topic-based committees with three groups responsi-ble respectively for initiatives and development programmes in (1) human behaviour and development, (2) industry, the economy and the environment, and (3) society and politics. Spontaneous requests for funding are now submitted to and considered by a single research board.

The Human Behaviour and Development group in January 1989 announced that it proposed to undertake a new major research initiative on ageing. In the proactive mode it invited applications for project and programme grants incorporating research on:

- the relationship between the economy, an ageing work force, the substitution of older for younger workers, work organisation, pay structure and the educability and flexibility of older workers at different skill and status levels, intergenerational transfers of income and wealth, flexible retirement, part-time work and the trends in the distribution of income and wealth;
- historical research on collective support systems, on the changing

characteristics and performances of age groups over time, on the
persistence of stereotypes and the selective development and
maintenance of images;
- the daily activities, relationships, expectations and quality of life of
  age groups and social categories between 50 and 100 years and their
  relationship to attitudinal and structural constraints;
- differential ageing between social sub-groups and between successive cohorts in cognitive and functional abilities, social skills and
  performances, the quality of life, health status and life expectancy –
  with a special emphasis on the factors sustaining and developing
  human potential in a cost-effective manner.

The ESRC statement made clear too that it expected the research it
proposed to fund to entail a wide variety of different types of
methodology and perspectives. It ended by stating that it anticipated
'that a new longitudinal cohort study may prove of particular value in
the field of the research on Ageing' (ESRC, 1989).

This is certainly the most encouraging indication so far from official
'clients' that the last decade of the twentieth century will see a
substantial input of resources into gerontological research.

To conclude on the 'demand' for social gerontological research, the
restriction on money for social research by government departments,
research councils and voluntary organisations has not affected every
field equally. The inexorable increase in the numbers of very old
people makes greater demands on health and personal social services
and on the national exchequer for pensions and other forms of financial support. Because the state in Britain, through the NHS and local
government, is a major supplier of services, and has the major role to
play in meeting the costs of such service use, it continues to need
information to enable it to meet its commitments to older people with
a more economical and/or more effective use of resources. The Department of Health still lists such research among its priorities, and the
ESRC, as evidenced in its 1989 Initiative, as well as the MRC have also
made clear their continuing intention to finance research on various
aspects of age and ageing.

'SUPPLY' SIDE FUNDING ISSUES

As with the 'demand' side, issues of particular interest to gerontological researchers must be seen within the context of those affecting
social research in general. Broadly, the researchers who meet the
'demand' can be found in one of two types of institutional setting. The
first is the university department and the second the research institute
or unit which may or may not be attached to a university or
polytechnic.

The university department as a supplier of gerontological research

With the implementation of the recommendations of the Robbins Report, the decade of the 1960s saw a great expansion of university education, including postgraduate research training. The numbers studying one or other of the social sciences, and sociology in particular, expanded at both undergraduate and graduate level. The small departments which existed in a few universities expanded to meet this influx. Universities which hitherto had no departments of sociology or social policy hastened to establish them, as did new universities. Polytechnics, now able to award degrees under CNAA jurisdiction, followed suit.[21] In 1965, the recently established SSRC was given responsibility for financing the training and maintenance costs of postgraduate research students. In these ways, the scene was set for the emergence of a body of aspiring social researchers.

In quantitative terms, much of the social science research undertaken since the 1970s in the universities, including that which would fall under the rubric of social gerontology, has been carried out by students still being trained for research rather than by fully-fledged researchers. The value of such work, which if it is successfully completed earns the student the degree of MSc, MA, M.Phil or PhD, is thus inevitably variable. Despite the continuing requirement that a PhD thesis should add to the body of knowledge in a particular area, it is not to be expected, perhaps, that more than a small number of scholars will make an original and valuable addition to the storehouse of human wisdom. Moreover, it is clear that some of the factors influencing the learning process and the quality of the research achieved reside not in the capacity of the individual student but in the extent of other demands made on supervisors of postgraduate students, not to speak of their varying research competence and conscientiousness.

One feature of the social climate in the universities and polytechnics of the early 1970s which affected the choice of research field of entrants was the surge of feminist consciousness and the growth of the women's movement. For the first time, many of those aspiring to research careers were women. Until then, teaching, nursing and various branches of social work had soaked up most women with any further education. Stimulated by the new concern to improve women's life prospects, increasing numbers now saw themselves as contributing to this cause by research into the condition of contemporary women. Since they were young themselves, it was not unnatural for them to think in terms of the issues affecting *young* women. Research relating to the inculcation of sexist attitudes or assumptions in the young of both sexes abounded in theses produced in the 1970s and early 1980s, and, in so far as women were drawn into research on other contemporary issues, they were not likely to ignore the gender issues.

In this intellectual climate, it was understandable that few students evinced interest in research on questions relating to an ageing society and old people. Work with or on behalf of old people was not, after all, the first choice of many practitioners in health and social welfare services. There was – perhaps still is – a subliminal widespread ageism from which researchers as well as caring professionals were not immune. In the late 1970s, however, it was becoming clear that the clients for social policy relevant research, both governmental and voluntary, were giving priority to the subject of old age. Gradually, attention began to be paid in undergraduate academic courses to issues related to ageing and/or the care of older people, and would-be social researchers with qualifications in sociology, anthropology, psychology, geography, demography and epidemiology began to iden- tify topics which they wanted to explore. Happily many of them discovered that the field was neither as intellectually arid nor as depressing as they had thought.

Something needs to be said too about the social atmosphere in which the students were acquiring their research skills and above all their theoretical and ideological orientation in the 1960s and 1970s. It was one marked by iconoclasm and, particularly in the social sciences, attacks on the 'positivistic' empirical, atheoretical social survey methods which had been the hallmark of what had passed for social research in the previous decades. Indeed, survey research based on large numbers of observations was not possible for the average post- graduate student who wished to work independently, and it was not surprising therefore to find that she/he was attracted to projects based on small intensive studies which were intended to develop 'theory' and apply conceptual propositions to limited data rather than describe or count. Such projects did not necessarily provide students with the apprenticeship in research methods which the research 'clients' wanted to see employed by those to whom they were prepared to give contracts. The latter's expectations of research was that to be effective (as operational research had been judged to be during the Second World War) it had to be oriented to answering questions which were on their order of the day – their agenda – not necessarily those which intrigued the academic researcher anxious to advance the discipline by adding to its theoretical sophistication. Such a mismatch between those wanting a research 'product' and those purporting to provide it has been a factor in restricting the growth of social research in the last decade.

Nevertheless, in the atmosphere of the 1960s and early 1970s, the assumption that university staff and students should be free from political or ideological interference meant that a good deal of research was undertaken by social scientists in the universities which did not conform to the normative assumptions of the established research funders. In particular, by virtue of their decisions, the peer review bodies of the SSRC allowed individuals to explore the practices, underlying assumptions and values of individuals and welfare organisations through projects entailing detailed on-the-spot observations and in-depth non-standardised questioning where the pay-off might be, but not necessarily was, providing significant sections of the public and/or decision-makers with a new way of seeing their social world which might make them more capable of controlling it. And, while the findings of much of the research may not have proved comfortable reading for the more conservative, they may well have partially succeeded in jerking welfare agencies, including those of the state, into rethinking the roles of their practitioners and planners.

Research units and institutes

At present, all the organisations engaged in social gerontological research are charitable, non-profit-making bodies. For the Centre for Policy on Ageing (CPA) (see p. 173) policy-oriented research, as its name implies, is central. By reviews of the present state of knowledge, it has opened up for general debate issues concerned with the quality of life of those in their sixth and later decades. In this way it has dealt with access to and use of transport, educational, cultural and leisure pursuits, public and private income support in retirement, involvement in the political and judicial (jury) process, care of very mentally frail elderly people, the rights and risks allowed older dependent people and the additional jeopardies in old age of members of ethnic minorities living in Britain. It is one of the most fortunate 'contractors' for gerontological research in that it receives continuing financial support from the Nuffield Foundation, from its own not-insubstantial investment portfolio, from the Department of Health and a number of commercial firms.

Age Concern (England) was the new name given in 1971 to the National Old People's Welfare Council. In 1976, it began to conduct its own research under the guidance of Mark Abrams, on his retirement as director of a professional social survey agency.[22] From then to 1986 a steady stream of informative surveys dealing with various aspects of the lives of older people, including their involvement in the political, social and economic affairs of the community, emanated from the in-house research unit. In 1986, Age Concern negotiated the setting up of an Institute of Gerontology bearing its name at King's College, University of London. It has a small core research staff and in 1989 launched a part-time master's degree taught course aimed particularly at planners and practitioners concerned with services for older people.[23]

Mention has already been made of the units which the Department of Health and MRC support and whose terms of reference permit studies of varying aspects of ageing. One for whom research on age was central was the Cardiff-based unit Research Team for the Care of Elderly People. Despite an impeccable record of published research concerned with such vital issues as the interface of domiciliary and hospital health services, and not without protest from many fellow academic research workers in the field of gerontology, the unit's contract with the Department of Health and Welsh Office was terminated in 1989. There was no machinery to allow the director of the unit to appeal against the decision.

Some universities and polytechnics, however, sensing that the greying of the population poses many questions of both immediate and more long-term import, have supported initiatives on the part of their staff to establish institutes or units to engage in research and research training in the burgeoning field. Among the developments in the 1980s were the formation of the Centre for Environmental and Social Studies in Ageing (CESSA) at the Polytechnic of North London;[24] the Institute of Human Ageing at the University of Liverpool;[25] the Centre for Social Gerontology at the University of Keele;[26] the Centre for Applied Gerontology, University of Birmingham;[27] and the Research Group on Ageing in the Department of Health and Social Welfare at the Open University.[28] Many of these new foundations are also at the forefront of educational developments in gerontology and provide postgraduate degree or diploma courses. How far these various ventures will become or remain financially viable in the long run is not clear. Some of them have been able to employ research staff on short-term contracts as a result of the contracts they have won from funding bodies. Others have obtained some minimal back-up technical support from unallocated university or polytechnic funding. Their future can be regarded as precarious and very dependent on the drive and energy of their directors and the goodwill of their parent institution.

The ESRC has also continued to provide some core-funding to the Cambridge Group for the History of Population and Social Structure in the University of Cambridge.[29] The Group, which has done major historical demographic research, has taken a particular interest in the position of older people in the social structure of Britain from the seventeenth to the twentieth centuries. Its research fellows are also undertaking studies and acting as consultants to demographers and gerontologists in other countries including China. It has recently secured some financial support from business enterprises such as Rank Xerox.

FUTURE PROSPECTS

What are the future prospects for the funding of gerontological research in Britain? Many commercial entrepreneurs have found it necessary to stimulate the demand for their product rather than wait for it to grow spontaneously. Will this rule apply also in this field?

The crystal ball, at this moment, is not at its clearest. The government continues to profess its commitment to research as well as to the improvement of services for the increasing number of very old people in the community. However, the two government departments – of Health and of Social Security – which in 1988 replaced the DHSS do not yet appear to have taken the measures necessary to release substantial resources to researchers. For example, the Research Liaison Committee on the Elderly while not formally abandoned has not met for several years. The erstwhile DHSS also abolished a Small Grants Committee which processed requests for modest research resources. The division of the Department into two also raises questions about how research in future is to be managed as well as financed by government clients.

The MRC still maintains the responsibility for allocating resources for applied health services research on behalf of the Department of Health. In the recent past it tended to interpret its brief in limited rather than broad terms. There is no reason at present to think that it might have a change of heart. On the contrary, the emphasis which the present government is giving to efficiency in the operation of the NHS is not likely to encourage research on anything material to the health care of older people, other than its cost to the community.

The ESRC underwent in 1988 yet another reorganisation of its internal bureaucracy and, to boot, moved its headquarters from London to Swindon. Whatever the long-term merits of this move, it is not likely to foster great endeavours on the part of the Council to improve its relationships with potential researchers and the social research community in general. On the other hand, it appears that the societal problems envisaged as arising from the presence of increasing numbers of old people have made the Council aware that its own credibility depends, at least to some extent, on ensuring that social and behavioural scientists are enabled to undertake the empirical and theoretical work needed to clarify future policy and practice options. Hence the initiative launched in 1989 and described above.

Gerontological researchers may still be able to call on funds from the major voluntary foundations, whose commitment to welfare is not in question. In keeping with the spirit of the times, too, they may be able to tap the resources of commercial enterprises at either local or national level.

Another problem appears to be rearing its head for researchers who accept contracts for research from government departments, including the Department of Health. New contracts state that the Department's permission to publish results is required and no time limit is placed on the Department to reach its decision. This condition replaces one which only obliged the researcher to submit the report of findings to the Department for comment which had to be forthcoming within 28 days. Members of research units are not happy with the bland verbal assurance that consent to publish will not be unreasonably withheld, and that the measure is being taken only to safeguard the liability of the Secretary of State to be taken to court by anyone who believes that the research is libellous or defamatory or convenes the confidentiality accorded to individuals who provide data.

The uncertainties on the demand side and the absence of established institution-funded departments of gerontology which would provide basic academic training in the subject in its own right (as having a distinct knowledge base) have meant that many (probably most) of the young researchers who join units or projects engaged in gerontological research have to leave them after a short induction period to pursue careers, either in academic departments of their original discipline (where gerontology if present at all is merely a minor consideration), or in entirely different occupations with no intrinsic concern with gerontology. This problem of wasted expertise is by no means confined to gerontology, but is probably as, if not more, severe in this field as it is in other fields of enquiry. It does not look likely to be satisfactorily resolved in the near future.

The British Society of Gerontology is certainly aware of the problems of obtaining funding which face its growing number of members. The publication in book form of the major papers presented at its annual scientific meetings, together with its active participation on the editorial board of *Ageing and Society*, form part of its strategy to promote the discipline and provide public and private support for those engaged in research.

There is little doubt that the message to would-be researchers in the field is to be flexible and innovative. Appeals for support for fundamental or 'pure' research on issues of ageing, in the present climate, are likely to fall on deaf ears. Research which can help provide answers to questions which policy-makers, planners and practitioners are asking is the most likely to succeed in attracting funding. Ingenuity will be required to build questions into such research which the researchers themselves want answered but which are not on the agenda of the funding organisations.

There is little point in simply sitting back and deploring a gloomy prospect. Researchers must develop the same kind of devotion to achievement in their chosen sphere as the current generation of yuppies have done in theirs!

NOTES

1. Nuffield Foundation: annual reports published from 1947 to date by Oxford University Press. In the early years, the reports contained a section on the Foundation's work for the care of the aged (or elderly), including research it had funded.

2. Amongst others the Foundation's Annual Reports record grants to F.C. Bartlett at Cambridge in 1946; S.B. Rowntree in 1947 for a survey of Problems of Ageing and the Care of Old People; J.H. Sheldon in 1948 for work on his *Social Medicine of Old Age*; Alex

Comfort in Manchester and London, 1951 and 1953; A. Welford in Cambridge, 1951; L.Z. Cosin in Oxford, 1954; Drew in Bristol, 1954; Franklin at Barts, 1955; F. Le Gros Clark in London, 1955; D.A. Hall in Leeds, 1955; Peter Townsend in London, 1957; Utting and Cole in Cambridge, 1958.

3. The National Corporation for the Care of Old People published annual reports from 1947 to 1979. In 1980 it changed its name to the Centre for Policy on Ageing, and its annual reports continue to give a brief account of the work it has undertaken during the year in question as well as grants it has made to others – including research.

4. The Joseph Rowntree Memorial Trust produces triennial reports which review the research and other projects which have been financed since the previous report.

5. The National Institute for Social Work Training was established in 1963 and within a year had appointed a research director. The social welfare needs of old people and how to meet them became one of the Institute's abiding interests. In 1979 it changed its name to the National Institute for Social Work.

6. The Policy Studies Institute was formed in 1977 by the amalgamation of the Centre for Studies in Social Policy, which the JRMT had founded and supported for the previous six years, with a longer-established research organisation, Political and Economic Planning.

7. The British Foundation for Age Research was set up in 1976 and dropped the 'British' from its title in 1988.

8. The City Parochial Foundation was established in 1883 to bring together the monies bequeathed by individuals to various City of London parishes over the previous centuries.

9. Help the Aged was founded in 1961 with the intention of raising funds by public appeals to help the aged poor in a variety of ways. Until the recent past it did not devote much of its substantial resources to financing research on ageing or elderly people.

10. The Carnegie (UK) Foundation was founded in 1913.

11. The Rockefeller Foundation is based in the USA. It is one of the wealthiest of charitable funds, and has had from the start an interest in promoting both research and education.

12. Sandoz is a Swiss-based drug company which has set up an Institute for Health and Socio-economic Studies. One of its major interests is in issues associated with an ageing population.

13. Stuart S. Blume's 'The commissioning of social research by government departments', prepared as an SSRC paper in 1982, gives a good account of the way in which decisions have been reached by the DHSS and other central government departments.

14. The Unit was directed by Dr Norman Vetter, an epidemiologist. It was first called Care of the Elderly, but by 1985 had added 'People' to its title to keep in line with the general effort not to allow an adjective to become a noun.

15. See Blume's report for an account of the methods used by the Housing Research Unit of the Department of the Environment to manage research contracts.

16. See the *British Crime Survey* published in 1983 and 1984 by the Home Office Research and Planning Unit.

17. The Medical Research Council was given a Royal Charter in 1920 and came under the aegis of the Privy Council until it became the responsibility of the Department of Education and Science. It publishes annual reports. In 1981 it entered into a concordat with the DHSS to commission and manage health service research on behalf of the DHSS with funds from the latter's research budget.

18. A short history of the early years of the SSRC and comments on it from various protagonists are contained in the SSRC *Newsletter*, 19 November 1975.

19. The Research Centre for Age and Cognitive Performance at Manchester University headed by Professor Patrick Rabbitt has had programme grants for its two area studies (Manchester and Newcastle-upon-Tyne) from the SSRC/ESRC since 1982.

20. DHSS funding for all forms of health and social services research declined from £13.842 million in 1981–2 to £11.051 million in 1984–5. Since then it has increased but

in 1986–7 at £14.614 million was still worth less in real terms than it had been at the beginning of the decade (*DHSS Handbook of Research and Development*, annually, HMSO).

21. The Council for National Academic Awards was established in 1964 as part of the government's response to the Robbins Report's recommendation for an expansion in the proportion of population going on to higher education.

22. Age Concern changed in the mid-1970s from an exclusive service orientation to one which encompassed research as well.

23. The Age Concern Institute of Gerontology at King's College, University of London, has been established on a multidiscipline basis.

24. The Centre for Environmental and Social Studies in Ageing has sustained a substantial research programme mainly concerned with the lives and care of older people in residential accommodation. It has received grants from both statutory and voluntary funding agencies.

25. The Institute of Human Ageing is multidisciplinary, but the moving spirits in its formation were a psychiatrist, Professor Copeland, and a psychologist, Professor Bromley. Most of its research projects to date have concerned themselves either with mental illness in old age or the cognitive and emotional aspects of ageing.

26. The University of Keele has had a continuing interest in ageing, and has recently extended its commitment by establishing a Chair in Social Gerontology. The current holder, Professor Chris Phillipson, is one of the pioneers of social gerontology in this country.

27. The Birmingham Centre is led by the Department of Geriatrics, whose head, Professor Bernard Isaacs, is a geriatric specialist who is fully aware of the social influences on health and illness in old age.

28. The Chair in the Department of Health and Welfare at the Open University is financed by the JRMT. Its occupant, Professor Malcolm Johnson, has had a longstanding interest in gerontology and a good deal of emphasis in its current research and course-work development lies in this field.

29. The Group owes much to one of its co-founders, Dr Peter Laslett, who is still active in the historical demography of old age.

13

Making Research Useful and Usable

AVERIL OSBORN AND DIANNE WILLCOCKS

INTRODUCTION

Defining what we mean by dissemination is not an easy task. Illustrating certain activities which may be clustered under the umbrella heading of 'dissemination' offers a more helpful starting point. So this chapter begins with examples of dissemination – as both practice and process – in relation to work in which the authors have been active disseminators.

Example one: a survey of old people's homes in England[1]

During 1980–1, researchers at the Centre for Environmental and Social Studies in Ageing (CESSA) carried out a major investigation of residential settings. This involved interviews with 400 staff members and 1000 residents; and it produced substantial material for the sponsors, DHSS Works Division, on design, lifestyle and consumer aspirations with regard to institutional arrangements. For nearly a decade this material has been used to inform policy and practice in residential settings as the messages contained within the data are taken up by different groups of 'interested parties'.

The social policy research community achieved initial access to the data through a voluminous research report (Willcocks et al., 1982a, 1982b). Subsequently, in 1982, government policy-makers sponsored a more elegant and succinct guide to the data, illustrated by photographs and diagrams, which would be attractive to architects, social services managers and other professionals at the local departmental level (Peace et al., 1982). The following year, CESSA negotiated with a voluntary agency, BASE (British Association for Service to the Elderly) to produce a collaborative consumer guide to residential care for older people. This additional work was sponsored by the National Consumer Council. Content was predicated on the kind of questions an elderly person might ask about residential lifestyles, about institutional rules and regulations and about the kind of people who move into care settings (Kellaher et al., 1985).

The next issue to arise was a concern that residential carers should have access to training time and space in order to review contemporary residential care issues in the light of changes they were experiencing on the ground. Accordingly, the Polytechnic of North

London supported the production of a research-based interactive training pack (CESSA, 1986) which was published in association with Age Concern England. Meanwhile an energetic round of conference papers, book chapters and articles was taking the data directly into new arenas: to residential workers; to field-based social workers; to architects and designers; to private home-owners; to pensioner groups; to health and social work students; to academics; to voluntary organisations. More recently, a textbook (Willcocks et al., 1987) was written which incorporates reflections and feedback over the intervening period and which taps into the accumulated wisdom of all those participating in the crucial debate about residential futures. Additional material for the text derived from secondary analysis, which in turn was supported by an ESRC grant.

What this chronology reveals is the potential durability of valid and reliable data, together with its flexibility and relevance to a wide range of different users. Importantly, it raises the possibility that 'end-users': residential clients and residential carers, can be empowered where they have access to proper information. Our second example continues to explore this topic – also in relation to institutional care.

Example two: a survey of old people's homes in Scotland

In 1985 an academic researcher, Rosemary Bland, conducted a major interview survey of older people living in residential care in Scotland. The outcome was a well documented commentary of the views of older people about their circumstances from a researcher with extensive first-hand experience and insight into the feelings and situations of older people (Bland and Bland, 1985). The question she then posed was how might this data become useful and usable?

Such information is of the greatest value to that group of older people who might be considering entry into residential care; and to those with power and influence over them, that is, relatives, social workers and GPs. It is of less utility to people once they are admitted. The points arising in discussion with older people ranged from 'Do I have to share my bedroom?' to 'Can I bring my cat?'. Rosemary Bland then teamed up with Age Concern Scotland, and subsequently HMSO, to produce a handbook for older people entitled *Residential Care: Is It For Me?* (Bland, 1987).

The design and layout were crucial factors in the success of this glossy booklet. It was organised in question and comment format on the left; with summaries of key points on the right. Cartoons were used to highlight these. Older people commented on the material, including the cartoons (which others thought might offend older readers). HMSO produced a high-quality publication quickly and couldn't have been more helpful. The book has been promoted widely and every effort made to get it reviewed and publicised. Subsequently, the Scottish

Consumer Council adapted the headings to form a check list for assessing the adequacy of local home brochures as providers of proper information to potential clients.

The context for disseminating this material is not untypical. No resources were available other than the goodwill and time of the researcher; editorial help came from Age Concern Scotland who converted a rigorous research report into a short, easily read booklet; a cartoonist, Donald Gunn, was generous with his time and talent; older people piloted the material and gave unequivocal support to the controversial cartoons and the unusual layout. The book is selling well.

This second example highlights the process of collaboration and consultation which enables research to be translated so that it crosses the divide from professional purity to practical populism without sacrificing either standards or rigour.

It is against this backcloth that we now explore dissemination. Essentially, this chapter interweaves political and professional perspectives on the role of dissemination in the research process; and it offers a practical guide to all those who seek to maximise the impact of their research work.

DISSEMINATION FOR SOCIAL CHANGE

Debate about objectivity in social science research has created a consensus that research questions cannot be constructed and pursued in ways that are entirely value free. Some argue that central values must be explicit; moreover, that researchers should address the question 'Whose side are we on?'.[2] Adopting this theme, in a keynote address to the 1989 British Society of Gerontology Annual Conference, Margaret Simey likened the relationship between gerontologists and older people to 'them and us' and urged researchers to be sensitive to the impact of research work upon the older people they study. This view argues that, at best, social gerontology research can be used to enable older people to participate in social change: in other words, quality research can underpin the voice of the older 'consumer', giving it force and credibility. Access to relevant research evidence can empower older people to secure the maximum benefit from the changes around them; and access to relevant research can help older people to become actively involved in social change, rather than adopting the residual role of bystander or social victim.

Not everyone agrees with this view of research. Importantly, the particular view that is held will shape perceptions of the place of research in everyday life. It is our view that research operates in the real political world and that it can be a powerful force for social change or stasis. Research 'dissemination' or 'utilisation' refers to that part of the social research process which is linked most directly with social change. Dissemination can enable those who are otherwise less well placed to participate in improving life chances for themselves and for others. This is not an inevitable result of dissemination activity: the dissemination measures taken and the types and form of the information that are made available to different audiences provide differential access to research work for a number of potential users who might benefit.

Dissemination activity can open a crucial channel through which feedback can be received by interested parties. In its most open form it may challenge traditional views about the 'ownership' of knowledge and what this implies, and thereby ensure that research is a two-way process.

In this chapter we look at putting research to good use; at the opportunities and barriers to effective dissemination; at the skills and means at the researcher's disposal; and at utilisation throughout the various stages of the research process. We argue that dissemination is not just an optional extra at the end of the 'real' work.

DISSEMINATION AND THE RESEARCH PROCESS

Logically, what happens during the research process can influence the nature of the dissemination at the end of the study. Initially, the researcher might influence the research agenda, teasing out the crucial questions and involving end-users, thus permeating the world of social action. An early assessment might be made of the potential for change; of the targets for dissemination activity; and about the forms of information exchange that may be feasible and effective. Indeed, if dissemination is to be costed and legitimised as an appropriate activity it will be necessary to make a 'best guess' at what might be involved even before the project starts, and agreement secured with the sponsor/funder that this is a key stage in the research process which must be supported.

Doing research can itself have an impact upon the research subjects, the sponsors and others connected with the work. The researcher may actively use development skills to involve people in new ideas, to change attitudes, or to gain insights. He or she may also be actively gearing up the work and its potential users with a view to effective dissemination later. This sometimes happens coincidentally. The researcher may, on the other hand, strive to reduce any such impact. Much depends on the research issues and the chosen research method, as well as the nature, style and motivation of the individual researcher.

Intentionally or otherwise, directly or indirectly, research will impinge upon the group being studied. The research should not raise unrealistic expectations. The rights of participants and the researcher's responsibilities to participants, as well as the sponsor, need to be clarified and negotiated. This will include an explanation of the project and its relevance to the research subjects; access to results; the use to be made of the work and so on. In other words, part of this negotiation will be about dissemination and use.

This suggests that real dissemination begins prior to the conventional moment associated with the conclusion of a project, when findings are described; implications explored; and research-based materials prepared. The potential of this processual activity must not be overlooked.

WHAT ABOUT DIFFERENT STYLES OF RESEARCH?

Social gerontology research, like research in other disciplinary areas, may be characterised as pure or applied research; basic or problem-oriented research. Dissemination could be aspired to by those engaged in both fundamental and policy-oriented research. For example, there is an increasing interest among gerontologists in structural aspects of old age. It is being recognised that old people, like other groups, vary in terms of social class, gender, ethnicity, health and disability; age itself, that is, old age, can span four decades. This material on the structure of ageing can challenge popular myths and misconceptions about the homogeneity of older people.

Social enquiry into these aspects of the ageing process can attract widely differing audiences. For example, it will not be the social scientist alone who is interested in evidence to show that old age is not a socio-economic leveller – for example that the retired steel worker and the retired architect do not enjoy the same life chances at the age of 65 – and that the life chances of older women are influenced by much the same factors that create disadvantage in earlier life.

We would argue that it is not sufficient to report to the sponsor, possibly the ESRC, for structural work of this kind; nor just to produce a textbook for future academics. Whatever the project, a broad view needs to be taken of utilisation, of potential users; and of the means of communicating outcomes. The need to disseminate, then, is one which should be addressed by researchers working in all modes of research practice.

A range of factors affects the opportunities and the ability of a researcher to disseminate research effectively. The process and practice is rarely easy and many barriers may be encountered.

Some of these, consciously or unconsciously, will actually be put up by the researcher. Some barriers will be there to be overcome whilst others may be accepted as immovable. Likewise, there will be dissemination opportunities to be seized upon, missed or created. Each researcher is unique in his or her own situation and time.

However, the ability to disseminate research successfully will be influenced not only by the researcher's skills, but by organisational factors, practical issues, user resistance, the pre-existing level of interest in the field, professional conventions and expectations and by the researcher's own personal goals and values.

'GOING NATIVE'

The accusation of 'going native' is sometimes made when researchers move into policy and action: that is, it may be argued in some cases that the 'conversion' of the researcher to the value system and lifestyle of the group being studied deprives the researcher of his or her objective stance. However, an empathy for the subjects of research need not imply 'going native'. Indeed, this latter would involve a conflict with research integrity, since going native means taking on the bias and blind spots of a particular group and deserting the prior commitment of a professional researcher to investigate rigorously, interpret honestly and report fairly.

It is also possible that attempts will be made to tar the innocent and rigorous researcher with the brush of bias in an attempt to discredit or reject powerful research work that does not suit the arguments of one interest group or another. Inevitably, dissemination activity in the area of social policy may lead the researcher to tangle legitimately as a researcher with those controlling the political agenda. Uncomfortable though this may be, such contributions represent an important input from the research community.

WHO DISSEMINATES?

Where does responsibility for dissemination lie, who actually performs this function effectively and how is it resourced? Clearly a primary responsibility for dissemination lies in the contract between the commissioning body and the researcher, and primary dissemination will vary in scope and penetration, depending on the links established with a range of end-users during the research process. Following on from this, the researcher may contemplate secondary dissemination where findings are tailored to different audience needs. In the course of this, the researcher may well become involved with others who may assist with or take responsibility for publicising the work. The researcher will also use the available research networks and publications, from which base additional activities to support dissemination naturally spring.

In terms of the responsibility arising through contract, issues of ownership and of resources emerge. For some sponsors, the need to distribute information coming from research will be a priority. For example, if a housing association invests in a study of sheltered housing it probably wishes to make the results widely available to providers and end-users in that field. Alternatively, if a government department is contracting for research it might require that the work remain the property of the sponsoring department who may choose to use it or ignore it. And whereas the housing association may have a sophisticated publicity machine and may be familiar with the preparation of high-quality, easily read documents, the government department may well regard limp-covered research reports of a technical or specialist nature as an adequate medium; or they may be prepared to address the complexities of publication through HMSO. In most circumstances, the incentive to publicise and use the work is likely to be influenced by the perceived benefits or problems such exposure will generate for the sponsor. Even the aforementioned Housing Association might be a little ambivalent if a particular study unexpectedly raised serious doubts about the value or viability of their service.

Dissemination should be part of the plan of action which is developed when drawing up the research contract. The researcher must incorporate initial publication costs within the research agreement, and specify a period at the end of the agreed timetable when the major activity will be to produce and promote accessible material for different users, otherwise he or she will have to convince the sponsor later that this is a worthwhile exercise. Unanticipated demands for dissemination can and do arise. These can be a substantial burden if contingency plans have not been made. Here, contract researchers are disadvantaged compared with in-house researchers, since the latter may be able to renegotiate their work programmes to absorb the demands of dissemination activity. One final word on funding dissemination: it should be noted that publications – written or audio-visual – can represent income-generating activity if appropriately packaged and marketed.

Some researchers may see their role as that of a technician, absolving themselves of responsibility for the dissemination part of the research process. Others may expect end-users to explicitly seek them out, thus obviating the need for targeted action. Many researchers may claim that they do not possess dissemination skills or that dissemination is inappropriate since research does not always 'pull answers out of the hat'. Instead, the research may raise key questions; may expose uncertainties; may elaborate on key issues; or may challenge previously held assumptions. Responsibility to dissemination is not attenuated by the degree of uncertainty generated by the research insights and outcomes. However, the researcher does need some notion of significance and relevance in order to target the message and tailor the medium for ease of use.

If researchers value recognition as serious contributors to the policy process and the improvement of care practices then dissemination must be seriously addressed. Arguably, it is not sufficient to accept a research commission, complete the study itself and then close the file; there remains an obligation over and above the one specifically written into the contract to make sure that any material which is not strictly confidential can be used by different groups.

WHO USES RESEARCH?

For research to be useful and usable the research process must extend beyond merely organising research questions and findings to actually making them *readily available* and understandable to those to whom they are of use. The target users therefore need to be identified. Certainly, the research sponsors are one target group but there will be others in a position to utilise the work and/or to whom the work is significant.

If the researcher has a commitment to making an impact with the research findings then the research must be communicated to different levels of society. As a general rule, prime targets for gerontological research must be the people who make policies; the people who provide services; the people who influence attitudes. Prior consideration for dissemination must be given to the people who are old themselves and those who care for them and about them – the 'consumers' or the 'customers'.

In the field of health and social welfare, for example, there is a wide range of professional and lay interests. The audience for any piece of gerontological research might comprise people with a background in geriatric medicine, district nursing, general practice medicine, occupational therapy, physiotherapy, field social work, residential care, psychiatric nursing, housing management and many more.

Other groups such as carers' movements, the churches and pensioner forums may also wish to be engaged. Equally, people with different disciplinary and interest group backgrounds will be active in different service settings – employed by either a health authority or a local authority, in voluntary groups or, increasingly, in the private care sector or involved as citizens or volunteers. A consideration of their related but sometimes differing needs should lead the researcher to discover that different parts of the research findings might be highlighted for different parts of the audience. Appreciation of audience needs is a prerequisite for adequate dissemination.

It is also important to address the framework within which these groups interact – where their knowledge comes from; what kind of legitimacy it carries; and how the knowledge is transmitted between different groups. This wider audience inevitably involves the different arms of the media who have the power to set the scene for common understandings or misunderstandings on a range of social and cultural issues; the trainers of managers and of health and social workers who inculcate professional values alongside substantive areas of knowledge; and other researchers, who may integrate findings from different sources, taking an incremental approach to knowledge building and information exchange.

The following hypothetical example illustrates the variety of prime targets for research and their differing preoccupations. A local study on the home care service may interest policy-makers where it explores territorial justice – are people in some areas more favoured simply by their geographical location? They will also be interested in the level of service required to keep people independent and in their own homes for as long as they wish to remain there. A local service manager will probably only be interested in geographical inequality if the area stands to gain resources from redistribution, and may be as interested in the pressures resulting from increased number of highly dependent clients as in the evidence of positive achievement in community care. Those representing the consumers may seek evidence on the tendency for clients to have their individual home help changed without notice or consultation or information about the match between the felt needs of clients and carers and the practical supports which may be offered; that is, the focus is on qualitative aspects of the service. The accountants' concern is the cost of assessing charges in relation to income generated; whilst the service manager will need to know whether potential clients refused services or whether they resisted means-testing. Local politicians may be wary of evidence that could bring criticism, particularly in the run-up to local elections; or they may be seeking evidence in support of a bid to committee for more resources. A wider audience may seek involvement in policy discussions on the philosophy of home care services and on the practical interface with community nursing.

Even where the research can satisfy a range of interests and different users, it is unreasonable to expect that the researcher can produce one single piece of written work that would reach and satisfy the needs of the variety of interested parties. Differences in focus and emphasis will be necessary; differences in language; differences in the form of presentation. An imaginative and tailored presentation enables different parts of the potential audience to become 'research literate'. In other words, research dissemination has to be 'user friendly'. This will increase the chances of the research work making an impact. Research methods and research instruments are carefully piloted to ensure that they work as planned. It is perhaps rare for dissemination methods and materials to be carefully tried and tested but arguably this stage might also benefit from piloting in order to ensure that it too is effective.

WHAT ARE THE VEHICLES FOR DISSEMINATION?

Information exchange can occur between many different parties in many different settings. Any strategy for effective dissemination must look at all possibilities and – in relation to the substance and issues around a particular enquiry – assess priorities in terms of key messages and target audiences. The question is to decide which forms and combinations of dissemination vehicles should be used to link the messages with different parts of the target audience. The following vehicles lend themselves to this task; the list is not exhaustive.

The research report: any project generally produces a report for the sponsor. This must be clearly written, properly referenced, produced in sufficient quantities and made available to others beyond the sponsor.
Articles: the researcher can report his or her work through scholarly journals; professional journals or populist magazines (and could be encouraged to attempt all of these).
Chapters: locating the project in an edited book can extend the range of impact.
Books: publishing a book for scholarly, professional or populist audiences reinforces (and sometimes reinterprets) the message from the original research report – often at some later period and in the light of intellectual reflection and the unfolding of subsequent events.
Policy briefing: a distillation of research insights and findings in a short paper highlighting key issues and tailored to policy-makers' needs sharpens the message.
Training materials: research has the ability to generate lively and vivid accounts of social process that can be adapted to produce simple training materials. Based on experience, it will have a veracity which can win the confidence of the trainers and the students/trainees.
Audio-visual material: increasingly the different parts of the audience for research work look for a more imaginative packaging of issues and/or findings and a tape–slide presentation or a video-recording might be considered.
Face-to-face encounters: the researcher can attend conferences and seminars; meet with professional bodies, policy-makers, service providers, groups of older people, pressure groups and other researchers as a way of achieving direct feedback from the research. This may be one-to-one, in small or in large groups.
Media penetration: it is becoming increasingly important to convince the world of press, radio and television at national, regional or local level that the outcomes of research must be taken seriously in order to achieve impact on the mode and content of discourse (particularly about ageing) among members of the general public. The media may also be a more dramatic and effective vehicle for bringing work to the attention of policy-makers or politicians.
Special conferences and other events: this means taking the initiative to bring target audiences together to explore the work. Events may be tightly controlled or have a degree of freedom for agenda setting, workshop discussion, feedback, action plans or policy statements.
Consultancy: a researcher can often convince public, private or voluntary agencies of the unique contribution to be made to policy development – as a spin-off from the research. Consultancy links can also increase the potential for dissemination.

Using the library and information services: this involves recognising the professional specialism associated with information storage, manipulation and information retrieval. Getting your material into appropriate public or specialist library and information service networks will make it much more widely available, especially where agencies operate a current awareness service, produce accessions lists, provide abstracting services and offer a collection that is indexed and classified. Information scientists can also help researchers to identify relevant dissemination networks.

Networking: this means ensuring work is entered in relevant journal listings/directories; communicating with relevant professional bodies; together with an energetic commitment to the conference circuit.

The data archive: depositing well documented research materials in a data archive, such as the ESRC Archive at Essex University, will allow for subsequent utilisation of your work through secondary analysis by other interested parties in the future.

WHAT SKILLS ARE NEEDED?

Successful dissemination is best achieved through a combination of competencies, charisma and stamina. The researcher who is fired by enthusiasm and commitment to make the research of practical value is orientated towards dissemination. At the same time, *motivation* must be matched by a range of practical skills, particularly communication skills. And we should not ignore the role of *opportunism* and *serendipity*; this enables unexpected chances to be seized or unexpected connections to be made. There is no blueprint for dissemination. An essential characteristic of good disseminatory practice is that boundaries are there to be broken; hence the need to use initiative, drawing on appropriate skills.

As is evident from earlier discussion the ability to *identify and reach target users* is fundamental to effective dissemination and is by no means straightforward. Moreover, research generates a wealth of ideas, descriptions and findings. The task of *identifying the key messages* emerging from the work has to dovetail with the targeting of users and an awareness of their interests.

Political sensitivity to the interests, political environment and vulnerable areas of the sponsor and the prime audience helps to avoid pitfalls. Disseminating material in a way that generates hostility is unlikely to win support or move the research into the practice domain.

For example, a study of the use of hypnotics in old people's homes would not be taken seriously by managers if the researcher's first statement was that these drugs were primarily used as a means of social control. It may well be that a more balanced report could lead managers into a consideration of this potentially sensitive issue along with other aspects of the findings. Researchers also need to resist the temptation wilfully to cause dissent (leaving behind them unfinished business) by the introduction of 'naive' questions guaranteed to cause upset.

Skill at reporting and recording is a basic requirement to achieve full documentation of the work. In order to preserve a full and fair research record investigators must satisfy standards of good referencing, provide a clear description of research method, an adequate account of sampling and fieldwork and a fair assessment of the strengths and limitations of the particular project. Moreover, this means avoiding grandiose claims, and it means checking for errors and omissions in reporting. The professional researcher disseminates a clear and honest message.

Skill in communication – verbal, written and presentational – must complement the skill in identifying the crucial information and ideas that the audience is seeking. This will be pertinent when using any of the means described as 'vehicles for dissemination'. It is important to accept that inaudibly muttered pearls of wisdom in the conference setting will be lost irretrievably, whilst patronising or mystifying your audience with jargon will irritate or bemuse. Crammed and unreadable overheads or slides only give eyestrain. And there is little point in trying to impress someone with your expertise if they fail to understand your message.

Practical skills of packaging your product means tailoring your medium and message so that the target audience can extract maximum gain. This means selecting your vehicles for dissemination, using them well and getting the timing right. Researchers who exist predominantly in the academic world are typically seen as far removed from the world of media-hype, glossy covers, working to deadlines, or even writing succinct two-page reports or generally operating in an entrepreneurial mode. Yet successful dissemination demands a number of these practical and creative skills, which can be developed over time.

Information technology skills: the extent to which researchers master technical production and transmission will vary but most will at least use word processing. It is helpful if all researchers understand the basic production processes used in information dissemination. As we move through the 1990s there will be many new developments of which the research community must be cognizant such as electronic information exchange. Desk-top publishing gives direct access to the printing of materials. It is incumbent on the successful disseminator to achieve an appropriate level of mastery over these new methods.

TOWARDS GOOD PRACTICE

Dissemination of research-based information on matters relating to the older population is the mechanism whereby the activities of one section in society – predominantly those wielding power and

Enabling factors	*Inhibiting factors*
Research work is integrated into a policy or practice setting and 'owned' by the people able to apply it.	The research is isolated from the setting and the people able to apply it.
The researcher and the research agency are close to those with power and influence.	The researcher and research agency are distant from those with power and influence.
The research is not seen as threatening to those in key positions to utilise it.	The research threatens those in key positions to utilise it.
The research, whilst challenging existing policy, practice or attitudes, offers a way forward.	The research challenges existing policy, practice or attitudes but suggests no ways forward.
The research is not condemning and does not make users look silly or 'wrong-footed' even where it exposes areas needing attention, and it handles sensitive situations with tact.	The research is presented in a judgmental or derisory way, alienating or humiliating key users or creating friction between different user groups.
The sponsor and researcher have agreed on full dissemination; time and other resources are built in.	The sponsor has control of the work but has no commitment to research use or actively suppresses it; no time or resources are available.
The research group or the sponsor have ready access to good networks of dissemination.	The research group and the sponsor have no networks to tap into.
The research group already has a high reputation and skill as communicators and disseminators.	The research group has no track record or experience of dissemination.
The research method is highly interactive, developing user understanding, commitment and support.	The research method dictates a minimum of interaction with users or has created antipathy or distance.
The research has been working towards dissemination from the point at which the research agenda was set.	The need for dissemination is a surprise at the end of the project and no groundwork has been done.
The research time scale and funding enable a full dissemination programme.	The research resources leave little scope for dissemination.
The researcher does not see the research as an end in itself but a piece of work justified by its usefulness to others.	The researcher sees the research as only an end in itself or a means to a PhD; an entry on the CV etc.
Confidentiality or commercial issues are overcome or do not arise.	Confidentiality or commercial concerns constrain wider use.
The research is in an area of high interest and the audience is keen for information.	The research is in an unpopular, obscure or low-interest area and the target audience is hard to inspire or difficult to find.
The research is regarded as topical or ahead of its time.	The research area is regarded as 'old hat' or unfashionable.

Enabling factors	*Inhibiting factors*
There are positive or new findings or ideas to communicate.	The research has not broken new ground even though the work is valuable.
The researcher is able to tolerate some exposure and risk in opening the work up for scrutiny.	The researcher fears criticism or misuse of the work.
The researcher is of high standing and has credibility with the key users.	The researcher is unknown or is poorly regarded by key users.
The researcher can identify and communicate the areas of relevance to users.	The researcher has no 'feel' for the areas of significance as perceived by users nor how to engage the users' interest.
The researcher is an effective communicator, tailors material to his/her audience and is enthusiastic.	The researcher communicates poorly, cannot adapt to his/her audience and seems uninspired.
The researcher accords high value to dissemination activity.	The researcher sees dissemination as low status or even as unsuitable 'unprofessional' activity.
The researcher can handle a 'popular' style and approach if necessary.	The researcher is over-academic in dealings with non-academic users.
The researcher is aware of jargon and can use plain English and clear presentations.	The researcher is wedded to jargon even when interacting with users not from his/her discipline, and prefers complex mystifying material.
The researcher is aware that research utilisation means relinquishing a position of total control and ownership of the research whilst trying to ensure it is used and interpreted in reasonable ways.	The researcher believes no one else could or should interpret the work.
The researcher finds feedback from users stimulating and challenging.	The researcher dismisses feedback from non-researchers or is threatened by it.

Figure 13.1 *Good practice guide to dissemination*

distributing resources – can be rendered more accountable to other sections of society who will be subject to social arrangements which are largely determined by those with power. A commitment to disseminate widely implies a rejection of the concept of the autonomous researcher; it asserts the primacy of embedding research activities in their social context in order to ensure their usefulness.

In other words, the aim of dissemination can go beyond that of providing particular answers to particular questions asked by particular people. It can be a way of confronting attitudes and assumptions about older people which may contribute unknowingly to the setting of boundaries on choice and opportunity. One view is that dissemination should be about older people and for older people.

In order to achieve good practice in dissemination and to utilise fully the skills and processes outlined here it will be important to confront the context in which dissemination takes place. A full appreciation of enabling and inhibiting characteristics associated with research work will equip the committed disseminator in his or her task (see Figure 13.1).

What underpins this structure of enabling and inhibiting factors is the commitment to make research useful and usable. Arguably, a project which has been defined in association with older people or their agents and has espoused their world view; is carried out by a research team that is supported by those who command resources and determine policy; is looking at issues with an understanding of the structural differences that constrain life chances for older people; and which is not perceived as 'threatening' to dominant values at a populist level will have the greatest potential for stimulating real change.

Conversely, where these conditions do not hold, a range of barriers to dissemination impose limits which affect the researcher's motivation and capacity to make progress with research findings and to locate them in the arena where they might achieve the greatest impact. The challenge to the researcher is that he or she should have the courage and honesty to acknowledge constraints and should seek to devise strategies for overcoming them – in whatever form they may materialise.

The 'Good Practice Guide to Dissemination', given on pp. 200–1 provides a framework of checks and balances that will enable researchers to make a realistic assessment of the ways in which a given piece of research work can best be routed from the producer of usable information to the end-user, who can then maximise its value in the real world.

NOTES

1. See Chapter 8 for further details/discussion of this study.

2. The classic exposition of this argument is given by H.S. Becker in 'Whose side are we on?':

> To have values or not to have values: the question is always with us. When sociologists undertake to study problems that have relevance to the world we live in, they find themselves caught in crossfire. Some urge them to not take sides, to be neutral and do research that is technically correct and value free. Others tell them their work is shallow and useless if it does not express a deep commitment to a value position. This dilemma, which seems so painful to so many, actually does not exist, for one of its horns is imaginary. For it to exist, one would have to assume, as some presumably do, that it is indeed possible to do research that is uncontaminated by personal and political sympathies. I propose to argue that is not possible and, therefore, that the question is not whether we should take sides, since we inevitably will, but rather whose side are we on? (Becker, 1967: 67).

References

Abel-Smith, B. and Townsend, P. (1965) *The Poor and the Poorest*. London: Bell.

Abrams, M. (1978a) *Beyond Three Score and Ten*. Mitcham, Surrey: Age Concern Research Publications.

Abrams, M. (1978b) *The Elderly: an Overview of Current British Social Research*. London: National Corporation for the Care of Old People and Age Concern.

Abrams, M. (1980) *Beyond Three Score and Ten: A Second Report on a Survey of the Elderly*. Mitcham, Surrey: Age Concern.

Abrams, M. (1988) 'Use of time by the elderly in Great Britain', in K. Altergott (ed.) *Daily Life in Later Life, Comparative Perspectives*. London: Sage. Chapter 2.

Abrams, P. (1978) *Neighbourhood Care and Social Policy*. Berkhamsted, Herts: Volunteer Centre.

Abrams, P. (1980) 'Social change, social networks and neighbourhood care', *Social Work Service*, 22: 12–23.

Abrams, P. (1984) 'Realities of neighbourhood care: the interactions between statutory, voluntary and informal social care', in Martin Bulmer (ed.) *Policy and Politics*, 12(4): 413–29.

Achen, C.H. (1986) *The Statistical Analysis of Quasi-Experiments*. Berkeley and Los Angeles: University of California Press.

Adams, J. (1984) 'Reminiscence in the geriatric ward: an undervalued resource', *Oral History*, 12(2).

Agar, M. (1980) *The Professional Stranger*. London: Academic Press.

Alderson, M. (1975) 'Relationship between month of birth and month of death in the elderly', *British Journal of Preventive and Social Medicine*, 29(3): 151–6.

Alexander, J.R. and Eldon, A. (1979) 'Characteristics of elderly people admitted to hospital. Part III: Homes and sheltered housing', *Epidemiology and Community Health*, 33: 91–5.

Allan, G. (1983) 'Informal networks of care: issues raised by Barclay', *British Journal of Social Work*, 13: 417–33.

Allatt, P., Keil, T., Bryman, A. and Bytheway, B. (eds) (1987) *Women and The Life Cycle*. London: Macmillan.

Allan, G.J.B. and Bytheway, B. (1973) 'The effects of differential fertility on sampling in studies of intergenerational social mobility', *Sociology*, 7: 273–6.

Allen, I. (1982) *Short-stay Residential Care for the Elderly*. London: Policy Studies Institute.

Alloway, R. and Bebbington, P. (1987) 'The buffer theory of social support – a review of the literature', *Psychological Medicine*, 17: 91–108.

Altergott, K. (ed.) (1988) *Daily Life in Later Life, Comparative Perspectives*. London: Sage.

Anderson, M. (1971) *Family Structure in Nineteenth Century Lancashire*. Cambridge: Cambridge University Press.

Andersson, L. (1988) 'Elderly people in Nordic time-use studies', in K. Altergott (ed.) *Daily Life in Later Life, Comparative Perspectives*. London: Sage. Chapter 5.

Antonucci, T. (1985) 'Social support: theoretical advances, recent findings and pressing issues', in I. Sarason and B. Sarason (eds) *Social Support: Theory, Research and Application*. Dordrecht, The Netherlands: Nijhoff.

Arber, S. and Gilbert, N. (1989) 'Transitions in caring: gender, life course and the care of the elderly', in B. Bytheway, T. Keil, P. Allat and A. Bryman (eds) *Becoming and Being Old, Sociological Approaches to Later Life*. London: Sage. Chapter 5.

Atkinson, A.B., Maynard, A.K. and Trinder, C.G. (1983) *Parents and Children: Incomes in Two Generations*. London: Heinemann.

Audit Commission (1985) *Managing Social Services for the Elderly More Effectively*. London: HMSO.

Bailey, K. (1987) *Methods of Social Research*, 3rd edn. New York: The Free Press.

Barker, J. (1984) *Black and Asian Old People in Britain*. Mitcham, Surrey: Age Concern Research Unit.

Barnes, J.A. (1979) *Who Should Know What? Social Science, Privacy and Ethics*. London: Penguin.

Barrera, M. (1981) 'Social support in the adjustment of pregnant adolescents: assessment issues', in B. Gottlieb (ed.) *Social Networks and Social Support*. London: Sage.

Barrera, M. (1986) 'Distinctions between social support concepts, measures and models', *American Journal of Community Psychiatry*, 14(4): 413–45.

Barrett, S. and Fudge, C. (eds) (1981) *Policy and Action: Essays on the Implementation of Public Policy*. London: Methuen.

Bateson, N. (1984) *Data Construction in Social Surveys*. London: Allen and Unwin.

Beattie, J. (1964) *Other Cultures*. London: Cohen & West.

Becker, H. (1958) 'Problems of inference and proof in participant observation', *American Sociological Review*, 23: 652–60.

Becker, H. (1967) 'Whose side are we on?', *Social Problems*, 14.

Bell, C. and Newby, H. (eds) (1977) *Doing Sociological Research*. London: Allen and Unwin.

Bengston, V.L., Cutler, N.E., Mangen, D.J. and Marshall, V.W. (1985) 'Generations, cohorts and relations between age groups', in R.H. Binstock and E. Shanas (eds) *Handbook of Aging and the Social Sciences*. New York: Van Nostrand Reinhold.

Berkman, L. (1984) 'Assessing the physical health effects of social networks and social support', *Annual Review of Public Health*, 5: 413–32.

Berkman, L. and Syme, S. (1979) 'Social networks, host resistance and mortality. A nine-year follow up of Alameda County residents', *American Journal of Epidemiology*, 109: 186–204.

Berkowitz, S. (1978) 'Informal consent, research and the elderly', *The Gerontologist*, 18: 237–43.

Bertaux, D. (ed.) (1981) *Biography and Society: The Life History Approach in the Social Sciences*. London: Sage.

Beswick, J. and Zadik, T. (1986) 'Evaluating quality of care: an editorial in introduction', in J. Beswick, T. Zadik and D. Felce (eds) *Evaluating Quality of Care: Proceedings of a Conference held on Friday 4 July 1986*. Conference Series: Midlands Division of the British Institute of Mental Handicap.

Beveridge, W. (1942) *Social Insurance and Allied Services (The Beveridge Report)*. Cmnd. 6404. London: HMSO.

Bhalla, A. and Blakemore, K. (1981) *Elders of the Ethnic Minority Groups*. Birmingham: AFFOR (All Faiths For One Race).

Bigot, A. (1974) 'The relevance of American life satisfaction indices for research on British subjects before and after retirement', *Age and Ageing*, 3: 113–21.

Binstock, R.H. and Shanas, E. (1985) *Handbook on Ageing and the Social Sciences*, 2nd edn. New York: Van Nostrand Reinhold.

Black, J., Bowl, R., Burns, D., Critcher, C., Grant, G. and Stockford, R. (1983) *Social Work in Context: A Comparative Study of Three Social Services Teams*. London: Tavistock.

Blakemore, K. (1985) 'The state, the voluntary sector and new developments in provision for the old of minority racial groups', *Ageing & Society*, 5: 175–90.

Bland, R. (1987) *Residential Care: Is It For Me?* in association with Age Concern. Edinburgh: HMSO.

Bland, R. and Bland, R. (1985) *Client Characteristics and Patterns of Care in Local Authority Old People's Homes*, University of Stirling, mimeo.

Blazer, D. (1982) 'Social support and mortality in an elderly community population', *American Journal of Epidemiology*, 115: 684–94.

Blazer, D. (1983) 'Impact of late-life depression on the social network', *American Journal of Psychiatry*, 140: 162–5.

Blenkner, M. (1969) 'The normal dependencies of ageing', in R. Kalish (ed.) *The Dependencies of Old People*, Occasional Papers in Gerontology No. 6. University of Michigan: Institute of Gerontology.

Blume, S.S. (1982) *The Commissioning of Social Research to Government Departments*. London: SSRC.

Boden, D. and Bielby, D. (1983) 'The past as resource: a conversational analysis of elderly talk', *Human Development*, 26: 308–19.

Boden, D. and Bielby, D. (1986) 'The way it was: topical organisation in elderly conversation', *Language and Communication*, 6(1/2): 73–89.

Bok, S. (1986) *Secrets: on the Ethics of Concealment and Revelation*. Oxford: Oxford University Press.

Bond, J. and Coleman, P. (1990) *Ageing in Society*. London: Sage.

Bond, J., Gregson, B., Atkinson, A. and Hally, M.R. (1989) *Evaluation of Continuing Care Accommodation for Elderly People. Volume 2: The Randomised Controlled Trial of the Experimental NHS Nursing Homes and Conventional Continuing Care Wards in NHS Hospitals*. Report No. 38, Vol. 2. Newcastle upon Tyne: University of Newcastle upon Tyne Health Care Research Unit.

Bond, S. and Bond, J. (1989) *Evaluation of Continuing Care Accommodation for Elderly People. Volume 3: A Multiple Case Study of NHS Hospital Wards and Nursing Homes: Some Aspects of Structure and Outcome*. Report No. 38, Vol. 3. Newcastle upon Tyne: University of Newcastle upon Tyne Health Care Research Unit.

Boneham, M.C. (1989) 'Ageing and ethnicity in Britain: the case of elderly Sikh women in a Midlands town', *New Community*, 15: 447–59.

Bonjean, C., Hill, R. and McLenore, S. (1967) *Sociological Measurement*. San Francisco: Chandler.

Booth, T. (1983) 'Residents' views, rights and institutional care', in M. Fisher (ed.) *Speaking of Clients*. Social Services Monographs: Research in Practice. Community Care and JUSSR University of Sheffield.

Booth, T. (1985) *Home Truths: Old People's Homes and the Outcome of Care*. Aldershot, Hants: Gower.

Booth, T., Barritt, A., Berry, S., Martin, D. and Melotte, C. (1983a) 'Dependency in residential homes for the elderly', *Social Policy and Administration*, 17(1): 46–63.

Booth, T. and Phillips, D., with Barritt, A., Berry, S., Martin, D. and Melotte, C. (1983b) 'A follow-up study of trends on dependency in local authority homes for the elderly (1980–82)', *Research, Policy and Planning*, 1(2): 1–9.

Bornat, J. (1985) 'Reminiscence: the state of the art', *New Age*, Summer.

Bosanquet, N. (1978) *A Future for Old Age*. London: Temple Smith.

Bowling, A., Hoeckel, T. and Leaver, J. (1988) *Health and Social Service Needs for People Aged 85 and Over Living in City & Hackney*. London: Dept of Community Medicine, City and Hackney Health Authority.

Bradburn, N. (1969) *The Structure of Psychological Well-Being*. Chicago: Main Publishing.

British Broadcasting Corporation (1985) *Daily Life in the 1980s*, Vol. 1–4, London: BBC.

Broadhead, W., Kaplan, B., Jaes, S., Wagner, E., Schoenbach, V., Grimson, R., Heyden, S., Tiblin, G. and Gehlbach, S. (1983) 'The epidemiologic evidence for a relationship between social support and health', *American Journal of Epidemiology*, 117(5): 521–37.

Brody, E.M. (1981) 'Women in the middle and family help to older people', *The Gerontologist*, 21(5): 471–9.

Brody, E.M., Johnson, P.T. and Fulcommer, M.C. (1984) 'What should adult children do for elderly parents? Opinions and preferences of three generations of women', *Journal of Gerontology*, 39(6): 736–46.

Brown, G. and Bifulco, A. (1985) 'Social support, life events and depression', in B. Sarason and B. Sarason (eds), *Social Support: Theory, Research and Applications*. Dordrecht, The Netherlands: Nijhoff.

Brown, G. and Harris, T. (1984) 'Establishing causal links: The Bedford College studies of depression', in H. Katschnig (ed.) *Life Events and Psychiatric Disorders*. Cambridge:

Cambridge University Press.

Bruyn, S. (1966) *The Human Perspective in Sociology*. Englewood Cliffs, NJ: Prentice-Hall.

Bryman, A., Bytheway, B., Allatt, P. and Keil, T. (1987) *Rethinking the Life Cycle*. London: Macmillan.

Bucke, M. and Insley, M.L. (1976) 'Centenarians are healthy, but they need mental and emotional care', *Modern Geriatrics*, 6(2): 24–8.

Bull, J. and Poole, L. (1989) *Not Rich: Not Poor, a Study of Housing Options for Elderly People on Middle Incomes*. London and Oxford: SHAC/Anchor Housing Trust.

Bulmer, M. (ed.) (1979) *Censuses, Surveys and Privacy*. London and Basingstoke: Macmillan.

Bulmer, M. (ed.) (1982) *Social Research Ethics*. London and Basingstoke: Macmillan.

Bulmer, M. (1985) 'The rejuvenation of community studies? Neighbours, networks and policy', *The Sociological Review*, 33(3): 430–48.

Bulmer, M. (1986) *Social Science and Social Policy*. London: Allen and Unwin.

Bulmer, M. (1987) *The Social Basis of Community Care*. London: Allen and Unwin.

Burgess, R.G. (ed.) (1982) *Field Research: a Source Book and Field Manual*. London: Allen and Unwin.

Burgess, R.G. (ed.) (1986) *Key Variables in Social Investigation*. London: Routledge and Kegan Paul.

Bury, M.R. (1986) 'Living to be a centenarian', *New Society*, 16 May: 14–15.

Butler, A., Oldman, C. and Greve, J. (1983) *Sheltered Housing for the Elderly: Policy, Practice and the Consumer*. London: Allen and Unwin.

Butler, R.N. (1963) 'The life-review: an interpretation of reminiscence in the aged', *Psychiatry: Journal of The Study of Inter-Personal Processes*, 26: 65–76.

Butler, R.N. (1969) 'Ageism: another form of bigotry', *The Gerontologist*, 9: 243–6.

Butler, R.N. (1975) *Why Survive? Being Old in America*. New York: Harper and Row.

Bytheway, B. (1977) 'Problems of representation in "The Three Generation Family Study"', *Journal of Marriage and the Family*, 39: 243–50.

Bytheway, B. (1987) *The Later Part of Life*, Occasional Paper No. 20. Swansea: School of Social Studies, University College of Swansea.

Bytheway, B., Keil, T., Allatt, P. and Bryman, A. (eds) (1989) *Becoming and Being Old: Sociological Approaches to Later Life*. London: Sage.

Campbell, D.T. and Boruch, R.F. (1975) 'Making the case for randomized assignment to treatments by considering the alternatives: six ways in which quasi-experimental evaluations in compensatory education tend to underestimate effects', in C.A. Bennett and A.A. Lumsdaine (eds) *Evaluation and Experiment: Some Critical Issues in Assessing Social Programs*. New York: Academic Press.

Campbell, D.T. and Fiske, D.W. (1959) 'Convergent and discriminant validity by the multi-trait, multi-method matrix', *Psychological Bulletin*, 56.

Campbell, D.T. and Stanley, J.C. (1966) *Experimental and Quasi-Experimental Designs for Research*. Chicago: Rand McNally.

Cannon, S. (1989) 'Social research in stressful settings: difficulties for the sociologist studying the treatment of breast cancer', *Sociology of Health and Illness*, 11: 62–77.

Cantor, M. (1979) 'Neighbours and friends: an overlooked resource in the informal support system', *Research on Ageing*, 1(4): 434–63.

Caplan, G. (1974) *Social Support and Community Mental Health*. New York: Basic Books.

Cartwright, A. (1986) *Health Surveys in Practice and in Potential: A Critical Review of their Scope and Methods*. London: King Edward's Hospital Fund for London.

Cassel, J.C. (1976) 'The contribution of the social environment to host resistance', *American Journal of Epidemiology*, 104: 107–23.

Cassell, J. (1982) 'Harms, benefits, wrongs and rights in fieldwork', in J.E. Sieber (ed.) *The Ethics of Social Research: Fieldwork, Regulation and Publication*. New York: Springer.

Cavan, R.S. (1962) 'Self and role in adjustment during old age', in A.M. Rose (ed.) *Human Behaviour and Social Processes*. London: Routledge and Kegan Paul.

CESSA (1986) *Images of Residential Life: A Training Game for Staff in Residential Care Homes for Old People.* London: CESSA, Polytechnic of North London.

Challis, D.J. (1981) 'The measurement of outcome in social care of the elderly', *Journal of Social Policy*, 10(2): 179–208.

Challis, D. and Chesterman, J. (1985) 'A system for monitoring social work activity with the frail elderly', *British Journal of Social Work*, 15(2): 115–32.

Challis, D. and Chesterman, J. (1986) 'Devolution to fieldworkers', *Social Services Insight*, 1(24): 15–18.

Challis, D. and Chesterman, J. (1987) 'Feedback to front-line staff from computerised records: some problems and progress', *Computer Applications in Social Work*, 3(3): 12–14.

Challis, D.J. and Darton, R.A. (1990) *Evaluation Research and Experiment in Social Gerontology.* Discussion Paper No. 642. Personal Social Services Research Unit, University of Kent at Canterbury.

Challis, D. and Davies, B. (1980) 'A new approach to community care for the elderly', *British Journal of Social Work*, 10(1): 1–18.

Challis, D. and Davies, B. (1986) *Case Management in Community Care: An Evaluated Experiment in the Home Care of the Elderly.* Aldershot, Hants: Gower.

Challis, D., Chessum, R., Chesterman, J., Luckett, R. and Woods, R. (1988a) 'Community care for the frail elderly: an urban experiment', *British Journal of Social Work*, 18 (Supplement): 13–42.

Challis, D., Knapp, M. and Davies, B. (1988b) 'Cost effectiveness evaluation in social care', in J. Lishman (ed.) *Research Highlights in Social Work 8: Evaluation, 2nd edn.* London: Jessica Kingsley Publishers.

Challis, D., Darton, R., Johnson, L., Stone, M., Traske, K. and Wall, B. (1989) *The Darlington Community Care Project: Supporting Frail Elderly People at Home.* Personal Social Services Research Unit, University of Kent at Canterbury.

Challis, L. and Bartlett, H. (1987) *Old and Ill, Private Nursing Homes for Elderly People.* London: Age Concern, Institute of Gerontology, Research Paper No. 1.

Clark, D. (1987) 'Changing partners: marriage and divorce across the lifecourse', in G. Cohen (ed.) *Social Change and the Life Course.* London: Tavistock.

Clark, M. (1969) 'Cultural values and dependency in later life', in R. Kalish (ed.) *The Dependencies of Old People*, Occasional Papers in Gerontology No. 6, University of Michigan Institute of Gerontology.

Clough, R. (1981) *Old Age Homes.* London: Allen and Unwin.

Cochran, W.G. (1983) *Planning and Analysis of Observational Studies.* New York: Wiley.

Cochrane, A.L. (1972) *Effectiveness and Efficiency. Random Reflections on Health Services.* London: Nuffield Provincial Hospitals Trust.

Cohen, S. and Wills, T.A. (1985) 'Stress, social support, and the buffering hypothesis', *Psychological Bulletin*, 98(2): 310–57.

Cohen, S., Mermelstein, R., Kamarck, R. and Hoberman, H. (1985) 'Measuring the functional components of social support', in I. Sarason and B. Sarason (eds) *Social Support: Theory, Research and Applications.* Dordrecht, The Netherlands: Nijhoff.

Coleman, P. (1986) *The Ageing Process and the Role of Reminiscence.* London: John Wiley.

Collins, A.H. and Pancoast, D.L. (1976) *Natural Helping Networks: A Strategy for Prevention.* Washington, DC: National Association of Social Workers.

Committee of Privy Council for Medical Research (1964) *Report of the Medical Research Council for the Year 1962–1963.* Cmnd 2382. London: HMSO.

Cook, T.D. and Campbell, D.T. (1979) *Quasi-Experimentation: Design and Analysis Issues for Field Settings.* Chicago: Rand McNally.

Cornwell, J. and Gearing, B. (1989) 'Doing biographical reviews with older people', *Oral History*, 17(1): Spring.

Costa, P.T. and McCrae, R.R. (1980) 'Functional age: a conceptual and empirical critique', in S.G. Haynes and M. Feinleib (eds) *Second Conference on the Epidemiology of Aging*, NIH No. 80–969. Washington, DC: US Government Printing Office.

Cowen, E.L. (1982) 'Help is where you find it: four informal helping groups', *American Psychologist*, 37: 386.

Craig, J. (1987) 'Changes in the population composition of England and Wales since 1841', *Population Trends*, 48. London: OPCS, HMSO.

Crossman, R.M.S. (1962) 'Old people', *New Statesman*, 28 December: 930–1.

Cumming, E. and Henry, W.E. (1961) *Growing Old: The Process of Disengagement*. New York: Basic Books.

Dant, T. (1988) 'Home is everything; the significance of home for social policy', paper presented to the annual conference of the British Society of Gerontology, Swansea.

Dant, T., Carley, M., Gearing, B. and Johnson, M. (1989) *Co-ordinating Care. The Final Report of the Care for Elderly People at Home (CEPH) Project, Gloucester*. Department of Health and Social Welfare, The Open University; London: Policy Studies Institute.

Davies, B. (1977) 'Needs and outputs', in H. Heisler (ed.) *Foundations of Social Administration*. London and Basingstoke: Macmillan.

Davies, B. and Challis, D. (1986) *Matching Resources to Needs in Community Care: An Evaluated Demonstration of a Long-term Care Model*. Aldershot, Hants: Gower.

Davies, B. and Knapp, M. (1981) *Old People's Homes and the Production of Welfare*. London: Routledge and Kegan Paul.

Denzin, N.K. (1970) *The Research Act in Sociology*. London: Butterworth.

Depue, R. and Monroe, S. (1985) 'Life stress and human disorder', in I. Sarason and B. Sarason (eds) *Social Support: Theory, Research and Applications*. Dordrecht, The Netherlands: Nijhoff.

Deutscher, I. (1962) 'Socialisation for post-parental life', in A.M. Rose (ed.) *Human Behaviour and Social Processes*. London: Routledge and Kegan Paul.

DHSS (1981) *Growing Older*, Cmnd: 8173. London: HMSO.

DHSS and Welsh Office (1973) *Local Authority Building Note No. 2. Residential Accommodation for Elderly People*. London: HMSO.

di Gregorio, S. (1986a) 'Growing old in twentieth century Leeds: an exploratory study based on the life histories of people aged 75 years and over, with specific reference to their past and present management of everyday living – at home and at work', PhD thesis, London School of Economics.

di Gregorio, S. (1986b) 'Understanding the management of everyday living', in C. Phillipson, M. Bernard and P. Strang (eds) *Dependency and Interdependency in Later Life: Theoretical Perspectives*. London: Croom Helm.

di Gregorio, S. (1987) 'Managing – a concept for contextualising how people live their later lives', in S. di Gregorio (ed.) *Social Gerontology: New Directions*. London: Croom Helm.

diMatteo, M.R. and Hays, R. (1981) 'Social support and serious illness', in B. Gottlieb (ed.) *Social Networks and Social Support*. London: Sage.

Donabedian, A. (1980) *Explorations in Quality Assessment and Monitoring. Volume I. The Definition of Quality and Approaches to its Assessment*. Ann Arbor, MI: Health Administration Press.

Dono, J., Falbe, C., Kail, B., Litwak, E., Sherman, R. and Siegel, D. (1977) 'Primary groups in old age: structure and function', *Research on Ageing*, 1(4): 403–33.

Douglas, J.W.B. (1964) *The Home and the School*. London: MacGibbon and Kee.

Douglas, J.W.B., Ross, J.M. and Simpson, H.R. (1968) *All our Futures*. London: Peter Davies.

Dunnachie, N. (1979) 'Intensive domiciliary care of the elderly in Hove', *Social Work Service*, 21: 1–3.

Edwards, W., Guttentag, M. and Snapper, K. (1975) 'A Decision-theoretic approach to evaluation research', in E.L. Struening and M. Guttentag (eds) *Handbook of Evaluation Research*, Vol. 1. Beverly Hills, CA: Sage.

Eichler, M. (1988) *Non-Sexist. Research Methods: Failure to Identify Gender Differences*. London: Allen and Unwin.

Elder, G.H. (1974) *Children of the Great Depression*. Chicago: University of Chicago Press.

Emmett, I. and Morgan, D.H.J. (1982) 'Max Gluckman and the Manchester shop-floor ethnographies', in R. Frankenberg (ed.) *Custom and Conflict in British Society*. Manchester: Manchester University Press, pp. 140–65.

Erikson, E.H. (1959) 'Identity and the life cycle', *Psychological Issues*, 1: 18–164.

ESRC (1989) *Research Initiative on Ageing*. London: ESRC.

Estes, C. (1979) *The Aging Enterprise*. San Francisco, CA: Jossey-Bass.

Evans, G., Hughes, B. and Wilkin, D. with Jolley, D. (1981) *The Management of Mental and Physical Impairment in Non-Specialist Residential Homes for the Elderly*. Research Report No. 4. University of Manchester Depts of Psychiatry and Community Medicine.

Evers, H. (1981) 'Care or custody? The experiences of women patients in long stay geriatric wards', in B. Hutter and G. Williams (eds) *Controlling Women: The Normal and the Deviant*. London: Croom Helm.

Evers, H. (1982) 'Professional practice and patient care: multi-disciplinary teamwork in geriatric wards', *Age and Ageing*, 2: 57–75.

Evers, H. (1985) 'The frail elderly woman: emergent questions in ageing and women's health', in E. Lewin and V. Olesen (eds) *Women, Health and Healing: Towards a New Perspective*. London: Tavistock.

Faden, R. and Beauchamp, T. (1986) *A History and Theory of Informed Consent*. New York: Oxford University Press.

Fairhurst, E. (1975) 'Rehabilitation in geriatric medicine: first days in the field', paper presented to the annual conference of the British Sociological Association Medical Sociology Group, York, November.

Fairhurst, E. (1979) 'Historical trends in the management of the climacteric', *Mims Magazine*, 15 July: 21–5.

Fairhurst, E. (1980) *A Preliminary Study of the Meaning of the End of the Reproductive Cycle in Women*. Final Report to the SSRC on grant number HR6156.

Fairhurst, E. (1981a) ' "What do you do?" Multiple realities in occupational therapy and rehabilitation', in P. Atkinson and C. Heath (eds) *Medical Work: Realities and Routines*. Aldershot, Hants: Gower.

Fairhurst, E. (1981b) 'A sociological study of the rehabilitation of elderly people in an urban hospital', University of Leeds, PhD thesis.

Fairhurst, E. (1983a) 'Organizational rules and the accomplishment of nursing work on geriatric wards', *Journal of Management Studies*, 22: 315–32.

Fairhurst, E. (1983b) 'The menopause: trauma on the road to serenity?', *Meridan*, 2(1): 4–8.

Fairhurst, E. (1987) 'The empty nest and middle age: who's flying the nest?', paper presented to the Conference on the Future of Adult Life: First International Conference (April) Leuwenhurst Conference Centre, The Netherlands.

Fairhurst, E. (1988) 'Social and cultural concomitants of the menopause', paper presented to the 12th International Congress of Anthropological and Ethnological Sciences (July) Zagreb, Yugoslavia.

Fairhurst, E. and Lightup, R. (1982) 'Are there people after 50? Issues in qualitative research on growing older', in R. Taylor and A. Gilmore (eds) *Current Trends in British Gerontology*. Aldershot, Hants: Gower.

Faragher, T. (1978) *Notes on the Evaluation of Residential Settings*, University of Birmingham: Clearing House L.A.S.S. Research, No. 2: 59–85.

Felce, D. and Jenkins, J. (1978) *Engagement in Activities by Old People in Residential Care*. Health Care Evaluation Research Team, Report No. 150. Winchester: University of Southampton.

Felce, D., Powell, L., Hunt, B., Jenkins, J. and Mensell, J. (1978) *Measuring Activity of Old People in Residential Care: Testing a Handbook for Observers*. Health Care Evaluation Research Team, Research Report No. 149. Winchester: University of Southampton.

Fennell, G. (1986) *Anchor's Older People, What Do They Think?* Oxford: Anchor Housing Association.

Fennell, G. and Way, A. (1989) *Growth and Change in Anchor's Tenant Population*. Oxford: Anchor Housing Association.

Fennell, G., Phillipson, C. and Evers, H. (1988) *The Sociology of Old Age*. Milton Keynes, Bucks: Open University Press.

Field, J. (1985) *Survey of Anchor Housing Association Tenants*, Methodological Report. London: Social and Community Planning Research.

Fielding, N. and Fielding, J. (1986) *Linking Data*. Qualitative Research Methods Series 4. London: Sage.

Fillenbaum, G.G. (1984) *The Well-being of the Elderly: Approaches to Multi-dimensional Assessment*. Geneva: World Health Organisation.

Finch, J. (1986) 'Age', in R.G. Burgess (ed.) *Key Variables in Social Investigation*. London: Routledge and Kegan Paul.

Finch, J. and Groves, D. (eds) (1983) *A Labour of Love: Women, Work and Caring*. London: Routledge and Kegan Paul.

Fischer, L.R. (1983) 'Sociology and life history: methodological incongruence?', *International Journal of History*, 4(1) Feb.: 29–40.

Fisher, R.A. (1966) *The Design of Experiments*, 8th edn. Edinburgh: Oliver and Boyd.

Flaherty, D.H. (1979) *Privacy and Access to Government Data Banks: An International Perspective*. London: Mansell.

Foote Whyte, W. (1984) *Learning from the Field*. London: Sage.

Frost, W.H. (1939) 'The age calculation of mortality from tuberculosis in successive decades', *American Journal of Hygiene*, 30: 91–6.

Galtung, J. (1967) *Theory and Methods of Social Research*. London: Allen and Unwin.

George, L.K. and Bearon, L.B. (1980) *Quality of Life in Older Persons: Meaning and Measurement*. New York: Human Sciences Press.

Gilbert, J.P., Light, R.J. and Mosteller, F. (1975) 'Assessing social innovations: an empirical base for policy', in C.A. Bennett and A.A. Lumsdaine (eds) *Evaluation and Experiment: Some Critical Issues in Assessing Social Programs*. New York: Academic Press.

Gilbert, J.P., McPeek, B. and Mosteller, F. (1977) 'Statistics and ethics in surgery and anesthesia', *Science*, 198(4318): 684–9.

Gilhooly, M.L.M. (1986) 'Ethical and legal issues in therapy with the elderly', in I. Hanley and N.L.M. Gilhooly (eds) *Psychological Therapies for the Elderly*. London: Croom Helm.

Gillon, R. (1985) 'Consent', *British Medical Journal*, 291: 1700–1.

Gittus, E. (ed.) (1972) *Key Variables in Social Research*. London: Heinemann.

Glaser, B. and Strauss, A. (1967) *The Discovery of Grounded Theory: Strategies for Qualitative Research*. New York: Aldine.

Glendenning, F. (ed.) (1979) *The Elders in Ethnic Minorities: A Report of a Seminar*. Stoke-on-Trent: University of Keele, Beth Johnson Foundation Publications.

Godlove, C., Richard, L. and Rodwell, G. (1982) *Time for Action. An Observation Study of Elderly People in Four Different Care Environments*. Sheffield: Joint Unit for Social Services Research, University of Sheffield.

Goffman, E. (1961) *Asylums: Essays on the Social Situation of Mental Patients and Other Inmates*. New York: Doubleday.

Gold, R.L. (1958) 'Roles in sociological field observations', *Social Forces*, 36: 217–23.

Goldberg, E.M. (1981) 'Monitoring in the social services', in E.M. Goldberg and N. Connelly (eds) *Evaluative Research in Social Care*. London: Heinemann Educational.

Goldberg, E.M. (1984) 'Evaluation studies: past experience and possible future directions', *Research, Policy and Planning*, 2(1): 1–6.

Goldberg, E.M. and Connelly, N. (1982) *The Effectiveness of Social Care for the Elderly. An Overview of Recent and Current Evaluative Research*. London: Heinemann Educational.

Goldberg, E.M. and Warburton, R.W. (1979) *Ends and Means in Social Work: The Development and Outcome of a Case Review System for Social Workers*. London: Allen and Unwin.

Goldberg, E.M. with Mortimer, A. and Williams, B.T. (1970) *Helping the Aged: A Field Experiment in Social Work*. London: Allen and Unwin.

Goldfarb, A.I. (1969) 'The psychodynamics of dependency and the search for aid', in R. Kalish (ed.) *The Dependencies of Old People*, Occasional Papers in Gerontology No. 6. University of Michigan Institute of Gerontology.

Gorbach, P. and Sinclair, I. (1989) 'Monitoring the home help service: clues to improving performance from analysing data in a computerised client information system', *Research, Policy and Planning*, 7(1): 24–30.

Gottlieb, B. (1978) 'The development and application of a classification scheme of informal helping behaviours', *Canadian Journal of Behavioural Science*, 10: 105–15.

Gottlieb, B.H. (ed.) (1981) *Social Networks and Social Support*. London: Sage.

Gottlieb, B.H. (1985a) 'Assessing and strengthening the impact of social support on mental health', *Social Work*, July–Aug.: 293–300.

Gottlieb, B.H. (1985b) 'Social networks and social support: an overview of research, practice and policy implications', *Health Education Quarterly*, 12(1): 5–22.

Granovetter, M. (1973) 'The strength of weak ties', *American Journal of Sociology*, 78: 1360–80.

Gubrium, J.F. (ed.) (1974) *Late Life*. Springfield, IL: Charles Thomas.

Gubrium, J.F. (1975) *Living and Dying in Murray Manor*. New York: St Martin's Press.

Gubrium, J.F. (1980) 'Patient exclusion in geriatric settings', *Sociological Quarterly*, 21: 335–47.

Gubrium, J. and Silverman, D. (eds) (1989) *The Politics of Field Research*. London: Sage.

Gupta, H. and Marston, N. (1979) 'Can we de-institutionalise an institution?', Parts I and II, *Concord*, 23: 23–57.

Gurland, B., Copeland, J., Kuriansky, J., Kelleher, M., Sharpe, L. and Dean, L.L. (1983) *The Mind and Mood of Aging. Mental Health Problems of the Community Elderly in New York and London*. London and Canberra: Croom Helm.

Hakim, C. (1979) 'Census confidentiality in Britain', in M. Bulmer (ed.) *Censuses, Surveys and Privacy*. London and Basingstoke: Macmillan.

Halfpenny, P. (1979) 'The analysis of qualitative data', *Sociological Review*, 27: 799–827.

Hammersley, M. and Atkinson, P. (1983) *Ethnography: Principles in Practice*. London: Tavistock.

Harris, A. (1968) *Social Welfare for the Elderly*. London: HMSO.

Harris, C.C. (1987) 'The individual and society: a processual approach', in A. Bryman, B. Bytheway, P. Allatt and T. Keil (eds) *Rethinking the Life Cycle*. London: Macmillan.

Harris, H. and Lipman, A. (1980) 'Social symbolism and space usage in daily life', *Sociological Review*, 28: 415–28.

Harris, H., Lipman, A. and Slater, R. (1977) 'Architectural design: the spatial location and interactions of old people', *Journal of Gerontology*, 23: 390–400.

Havighurst, R.J. (1968) 'Personality and patterns of ageing', *The Gerontologist*, 8: 20–3.

Hazan, H. (1980) *The Limbo People. A Study of the Constitution of the Time Universe among the Aged*. London: Routledge and Kegan Paul.

Hedges, B. (1977) 'Sampling', in G. Hoinville and R. Jowell (eds) *Survey Research Practice*. London: Heinemann.

Henderson, S. (1984) 'Interpreting the evidence on social support', *Social Psychiatry*, 19: 49–52.

Henderson, S., Duncan-Jones, P., Byrne, D.G. and Scott, R. (1980) 'Measuring social relationships: the interview schedule for social interaction', *Psychiatric Medicine*, 10: 723–34.

Hendriksen, C., Lund, E. and Stromgard, E. (1984) 'Consequences of assessment and intervention among elderly people: a three year randomised controlled trial', *British Medical Journal*, 289 (6457): 1522–4.

Henretta, J.C. and Campbell, R.T. (1978) 'Net worth as an aspect of status', *American Journal of Sociology*, 83: 1204–22.

Hill, A. Bradford (1971) *Principles of Medical Statistics*, 9th edn. London: The Lancet.

Hirsch, B.J. (1981) 'Social networks and the coping process', in B. Gottlieb (ed.) *Social Networks and Social Support*. London: Sage.

HMSO (1969) *Annual Report of the DHSS for the Year 1968*, Cmnd 4100. London: HMSO.

HMSO (1972) *Framework for Government Research and Development*, Cmnd 5046. London: HMSO.

HMSO (1973) *Annual Report of the DHSS for the Year 1973*, Cmnd 5700. London: HMSO.

HMSO (1982) *An Enquiry into the Social Science Research Council by Lord Rothschild*, Cmnd 8554 (May). London: HMSO.

HMSO (1989a) *Social Trends, 1988*. London: HMSO.

HMSO (1989b) *Caring for People: Community Care in the Next Decade and Beyond*, Cmnd 849. London: HMSO.

Hochschild, A.R. (1973) *The Unexpected Community*. Englewood Cliffs, NJ: Prentice-Hall.

Hogg, J., Moss, S. and Cooke, D. (1988) *Ageing and Mental Handicap*. London: Croom Helm.

Hoinville, G., Jowell, R. and Associates (1978) *Survey Research Practice*. London: Heinemann Educational.

Home Office, Research and Planning Unit (1983) *British Crime Survey*, London.

Hooyman, N. (1983) 'Social support networks in services to the elderly', in J. Whittaker and J. Garbarino (eds) *Social Support Networks*. New York: Aldine.

Hughes, B. and Wilkin, D. (1987) 'Physical care and quality of life in residential homes', *Ageing and Society*, 7: 399–425.

Hunt, A. (1978) *The Elderly at Home, A Study of People Aged Sixty-Five and Over Living in the Community in England in 1976*. London: HMSO.

Illsley, R. (1980) *Professional or Public Health? Sociology in Health and Medicine*. London: Nuffield Provincial Hospitals Trust.

Isaacs, B., Livingstone, M. and Neville, Y. (1972) *Survival of the Unfittest, a Study of Geriatric Patients in Glasgow*. London: Routledge and Kegan Paul.

Jefferys, M. (1989) *Growing Old in the Twentieth Century*. London: Routledge.

Jerrome, D. (1981) 'The significance of friendship for women in later life', *Ageing and Society*, 1: 175–98.

Jerrome, D. (1986) 'Me Darby, you Joan', in C. Phillipson, M. Bernard and P. Strang (eds) *Dependency and Interdependency in Old Age*. London: Croom Helm.

Johnson, J.M. (1978) *Doing Field Research*. New York: The Free Press.

Johnson, M.L. (1976) 'That was your life: a biographical approach to later life', in J.M.A. Munnichs and W.J.A. Van Den Heuval *Dependency and Interdependency in Old Age*. The Hague: Nijhoff.

Johnson, M.L. (1983) 'Independence and old age: the contribution of the voluntary sector', *Research, Policy and Planning*, 1(1): 12–15.

Johnson, M.L. and Gearing, B. (1989) 'A biographically based health and social diagnostic technique: a research report', in *Ageing Well in Ageing Nations*. London: Oxford University Press.

Johnson, M.L., di Gregorio, S. and Harrison, B. (1980) *Ageing, Needs and Nutrition*. Leeds: University of Leeds, Centre for Health Service Studies.

Johnson, M.L., Gearing, B., Carley, M. and Dant, T. (1988) 'A biographically based health and social diagnostic technique: a research report', Project Paper No. 4, obtainable from Department of Health and Social Welfare, The Open University, Walton Hall, Milton Keynes, MK7 6AA.

Johnson, S.K. (1971) *Idle Haven, Community Building Among the Working-Class Retired*. Berkeley, CA: University of California Press.

Jowell, R. and Airey, C. (eds) (1984) *British Social Attitudes, the 1984 Report*. Aldershot, Hants: Gower.

Jowell, R., Witherspoon, S. and Brook, L. (eds) (1987) *British Social Attitudes, the 1987 Report*. Aldershot, Hants: Gower.

Junker, B.H. (1960) *Field Work, an Introduction to the Social Sciences*. Chicago: University of Chicago Press.

Kane, R.A. and Kane, R.L. (1981) *Assessing the Elderly: A Practical Guide to Measurement*. Lexington, MA: Lexington Books.

Kant, I. (1964) *Groundwork of the Metaphysics of Morals*, trans. H.J. Paton. New York: Harper and Row.

Katz, S., Ford, A.B., Moskowitz, R.W., Jackson, B.A. and Jaffe, M.W. (1963) 'The Index of ADL: a standardized measure of biological and psychosocial function', *Journal of the American Medical Association*, 185(12): 914–19.

Kellaher, L.A., Peace, S.M. and Willcocks, D.M. (1985) *Living in Homes: A Consumer View of Old People's Homes*. London: Centre for Environmental and Social Studies in Ageing, Polytechnic of North London and British Association of Service to the Elderly.

Kessler, R., McLeod, J. and Wethington, E. (1985) 'The costs of caring: a perspective on the relationship between sex and psychological distress', in I. Sarason and B. Sarason (eds) *Social Support: Theory, Research and Applications*. Dordrecht, The Netherlands: Nijhoff.

Kish, L. (1987) *Statistical Design for Research*. New York: Wiley.

Knapp, M.R.J. (1984) *The Economics of Social Care*. Basingstoke and London: Macmillan.

Kohli, M. (1978) 'Expectations towards a sociology of the life course', in M. Kohli (ed.) *Sociologie des Lebenlaufs*. Darmstadt: Luchterland.

Laing, W. (1988) 'Living environments for the elderly: the mixed economy in long-term care', in N. Wells and C. Freer (eds) *The Ageing Population*. London: Macmillan.

Latto, S. (1982) *The Coventry Home Help Project*. Coventry: Social Services Department, Coventry City Council.

Lawton, M.P. (1975) 'The Philadelphia Geriatric Center morale scale – a revision', *Journal of Gerontology*, 30(1): 85–9.

Lawton, M.P. (1977) 'The impact of the environment on ageing and behaviour', in J.E. Birren and K.W. Schaie (eds) *Handbook of the Psychology of Ageing*. New York: Van Nostrand Reinhold. pp. 276–301.

Lawton, M.P. (1980) *Environment and Ageing*. Monterey, CA: Brooks/Cole.

Lawton, M.P. (1983) 'Environment and other determinants of well-being in older people', *The Gerontologist*, 23(4): 349–57.

Levinson, D.J. with Darrow, C.N., Klein, E.B., Levinson, M.H. and McKee, B. (1978) *The Seasons of a Man's Life*. New York: Ballantine Books.

Lipman, A. (1967) 'Chairs as territory', *New Society*, 20 April: 564–6.

Lipman, A. and Slater, R. (1977) 'Homes for old people: towards a positive environment', *The Gerontologist*, 17(2): 146–56.

Litwak, E. (1985) *Helping the Elderly: The Complementary Roles of Informal Networks and Formal Systems*. New York: Guilford Press.

Litwak, E. and Szelenyi, I. (1969) 'Primary group structures and their functions: kin, neighbours and friends', *American Sociological Review*, 34: 465–81.

Lord, F.M. (1963) 'Elementary models for measuring change', in C.W. Harris (ed.) *Problems in Measuring Change*. Madison: University of Wisconsin Press.

Lowenthal, M. and Haven, C. (1968) 'Interaction and adaptation: intimacy as a critical variable', *American Sociological Review*, 33: 20–30.

Lupton, T. (1963) *On The Shop Floor*. Oxford: Pergamon.

Mack, J.H. and Lansley, S. (1985) *Poor Britain*. London: Allen and Unwin.

Marshall, M. (1983) *Social Work with Old People*. London: Macmillan.

Marshall, V.W. (ed.) (1986) *Later Life: the Social Psychology of Ageing*. London: Sage.

Matthews, S.H. (1986) *Friendships Through the Life Course, Oral Biographies in Old Age*. London: Sage.

McCall, C. and Simmons, J.L. (1969) *Issues in Participant Observation*. Chicago: Addison-Wesley.

McDowell, I. and Newell, C. (1987) *Measuring Health: A Guide to Rating Scales and Questionnaires*. New York: Oxford University Press.

McIntyre, S. (1977) 'Old age as a social problem: historical notes on the English experience', in R. Dingwall et al. (eds) *Health Care and Knowledge*. London: Croom Helm.

Meacher, M. (1972) *Taken for a Ride*. London: Longman.

Mead, G.H. (1934a) 'Mind, self and society', reprinted in Anselm L. Strauss (ed.) (1956) *The Social Psychiatry of George Herbert Mead*. Chicago: University of Chicago Press.

Mead, G.H. (1934b) 'Mind, self and society', reprinted in K. Thompson and J. Tunstall (1971) *Sociological Perspectives*. Harmondsworth, Middlesex: Penguin Books in association with the Open University Press.

Milne, J.S. (1985) *Clinical Effects of Ageing, a Longitudinal Study*. London: Croom Helm.

Moos, R. (1980) 'Specialised living environments for older people: a conceptual framework for evaluation', *Journal of Social Issues*, 36(2): 75–94.

Moos, R.H. and Igra, A. (1980) 'Determinants of the social environments of sheltered care settings', *Journal of Health and Social Behaviour*, 21: 88–98.

Morris, J.N. and Sherwood, S. (1975) 'A retesting and modification of the Philadelphia Geriatric Center morale scale', *Journal of Gerontology*, 30(1): 77–84.

Morris, L. (1987) 'The life cycle and the labour market in Hartlepool', in A. Bryman, B. Bytheway, P. Allat and T. Kiel (eds) *Rethinking the Life Cycle*. London: Macmillan.

Morton-Williams, J. (1979) *Alternative Patterns of Care for the Elderly*. Methodological Report for a study designed by the Institute for Economics and Social Research, University of York, Social and Community Planning Research.

Moser, C.A. and Kalton, G. (1971) *Survey Methods in Social Investigation*, 2nd edn. London: Heinemann Educational.

Murphy, E. (1982) 'Social origin of depression in old age', *British Journal of Psychiatry*, 14: 135–42.

Myerhoff, B. (1978) *Number Our Days*. New York: Simon and Schuster.

Nachmias, C. and Nachmias, D. (1982) *Research Methods in the Social Sciences, Alternate Second Edition without Statistics*. London: Edward Arnold.

Neill, J., Sinclair, I., Gorbach, P. and Williams, J. (1988) *A Need for Care? Elderly Applicants for Local Authority Homes*. Aldershot, Hants: Avebury.

Neugarten, B.L. (1968) *Middle Age and Aging*. Chicago: University of Chicago Press.

Neugarten, B.L., Havighurst, R.J. and Mobin, S.S. (1961) 'The measurement of life satisfaction', *Journal of Gerontology*, 16: 134–43.

Neugarten, B.L., Moore, J.W. and Lowe, J.C. (1965) 'Age norms, age constraints, and adult socialization', *American Journal of Sociology*, 70: 710–7.

Newson, J. and Newson, E. (1963) *Infant Care in an Urban Community*. London: Allen and Unwin.

Newson, J. and Newson, E. (1968) *Four Years Old in an Urban Community*. London: Allen and Unwin.

Newson, J. and Newson, E. (1976) *Seven Years Old in the Home Environment*. London: Allen and Unwin.

Nydegger, C.N. (1987) 'Cohort', in G.L. Maddox (ed.) *The Encyclopedia of Aging*. New York: Springer.

Oakley, A. (1981) 'Interviewing women: a contradiction in terms', in H. Roberts (ed.) *Doing Feminist Research*. London: Routledge and Kegan Paul.

O'Connor, P. and Brown, C. (1984) 'Supportive relationships: fact or fancy?', *Journal of Social and Personal Relationships*, 1(2): 159–76.

OPCS (1984) *The Proportion of Elderly People in Each Local Authority District of Great Britain, 1981 (Census 1981): Key statistics for local authorities*. London: HMSO.

OPCS (1986) Unpublished population estimates kindly made available by OPCS.

Oppenheim, A.N. (1966) *Questionnaire Design and Attitude Measurement*. London: Heinemann.

O'Reilly, P. (1988) 'Methodological issues in social support and social network research', *Social Science and Medicine*, 26(8): 863–73.

Orth-Gomer, K. and Unden, A. (1987) 'The measurement of social support in population surveys', *Social Science and Medicine*, 24(1): 83–94.

Paillat, P. (1976) 'Criteria of independent (autonomous) life in old age', in J.M.A. Munnichs and W.J.A. Van den Heuvel (eds) *Dependency or Interdependency in Old Age*.

The Hague: Nijhoff.

Palmore, E. (1981) *Social Patterns in Normal Aging, Findings from the Duke Longitudinal Study*. Durham, NC: Duke University Press.

Parker, R. (1981) 'Tending and social policy', in E. Goldberg and S. Hatch (eds) *A New Look at the Personal Social Services*. London: Policy Studies Institute.

Parkes, C.M., Benjamin, B. and Fitzgerald, B.G. (1969) 'A broken heart: a statistical study of increased mortality among widows', *British Medical Journal*, 1: 740–3.

Paterson, E. (1977) 'Care work: the social organization of old people's homes', PhD thesis, Institute of Medical Sociology, University of Aberdeen.

Peace, S.M. (1986) 'The forgotten female: social policy and older women', in C. Phillipson and A. Walker (eds) *Ageing and Social Policy: A Critical Assessment*. Aldershot, Hants: Gower.

Peace, S.M. (1987) 'Can we measure quality of life?' unpublished paper presented at Workshop on Quality Assurance (22 June) Kings Fund College, London.

Peace, S.M., Hall, J.F. and Hamblin, G. (1979) *The Quality of Life of the Elderly in Residential Care, Research Report No. 1*. London: Polytechnic of North London.

Peace, S.M., Kellaher, L.A. and Willcocks, D.M. (1982) *A Balanced Life: A Consumer Study of Life in 100 Local Authority Old People's Homes*. Research Report 13. CESSA, Polytechnic of North London.

Peace, S.M., Kellaher, L.A. and Phillips, D. (1986) *A Model of Residential Care: Secondary Analysis of Data from 100 Old People's Homes*. Final Report to ESRC, No. G00232019.

Phillipson, C. (1978) 'The experience of retirement', PhD thesis, University of Durham, Durham.

Phillipson, C. (1981) 'Women in later life: patterns of control and subordination', in B. Hutter and G. Williams (eds) *Controlling Women: The Normal and the Deviant*. London: Croom Helm.

Phillipson, C. (1982) *Capitalism and the Construction of Old Age*. London: Macmillan.

Phillipson, C. and Walker, A. (eds) (1986) *Ageing and Social Policy: A Critical Assessment*. Aldershot, Hants: Gower.

Phillipson, C. and Walker, A. (1987) 'The case for a critical gerontology', in S. di Gregorio (ed.) *Social Gerontology: New Directions*. London: Croom Helm.

Phillipson, C., Bernard, H. and Strang, P. (eds) (1986) *Dependency and Interdependency in Old Age – Theoretical Perspectives and Policy Alternatives*. London: Croom Helm.

Pilisuk, M. and Parks, S.H. (1985) 'Support networks: the measure of caring', *Academic Psychology Bulletin*, 7: 337–60.

Pincus, A. (1968) 'The definition and measurement of the institutional environment in homes for the aged', *The Gerontologist*, 8(3): 207–10.

Pincus, A. (1970) 'Methodological issues in measuring the environment in institutions for the aged and its impact on residents', *International Journal of Ageing and Human Development*, 1: 117–26.

Plummer, K. (1983) *Documents of Life: An Introduction to the Problems of a Humanistic Method*. London: Allen and Unwin.

Power, M. and Kelly, S. (1981) 'Evaluating domiciliary volunteer care of the very old: possibilities and problems', in E.M. Goldberg and N. Connelly (eds) *Evaluative Research in Social Care*. London: Heinemann Educational.

Power, M., Clough, R., Gibson, P. and Kelly, S. with Kaul, E. (1983) *Helping Lively Minds: Volunteer Support to Very Elderly People Living in Residential Homes*. Bristol: The Social Care Research Team, School of Applied Social Studies, University of Bristol.

Pressat, R. (1970) *Population*. London: Pelican.

Punch, M. (1986) *The Politics and Ethics of Fieldwork*. London: Sage.

Punch, M. (1989) 'Researching police deviancy: a personal encounter with the limitations and liabilities of fieldwork', *British Journal of Sociology*, 40: 177–204.

Purkiss, A. and Hodson, P. (1983) *Housing and Community Care*. London: Bedford Square Press.

Qureshi, H. (1986) 'Responses to dependency: reciprocity affect and power in family relationships', in C. Phillipson, M. Bernard and P. Strang (eds) *Dependency and Interdependency in Old Age – Theoretical and Policy Alternatives*. London: Croom Helm.

Qureshi, H. and Walker, A. (1989) *The Caring Relationship: Elderly People and their Families*. London: Macmillan.

Raynes, N.V., Pratt, M.W. and Roses, S. (1979) *Organisational Structure and The Care of the Mentally Retarded*. London: Croom Helm.

Reid, W.J. and Hanrahan, P. (1981) 'The effectiveness of social work: recent evidence', in E.M. Goldberg and N. Connelly (eds) *Evaluative Research in Social Care*. London: Heinemann Educational.

Ridley, J.C., Bachrach, C.A. and Dawson, D.A. (1979) 'Recall and reliability of interview data from older women', *Journal of Gerontology*, 34(1): 99–105.

Riley, M.W., Johnson, M. and Foner, A. (1972) *Aging and Society, Vol. 3. A Sociology of Age Stratification*. New York: Russell Sage Foundation.

Robb, B. (ed.) (1967) *Sans Everything, a Case to Answer*. London: Nelson.

Roberts, H. (ed.) (1981) *Doing Feminist Research*. London: Routledge and Kegan Paul.

Robertson, A. and Gandy, J. (1983) 'Policy, practice and research: an overview', in J. Gandy, A. Robertson and S. Sinclair (eds) *Improving Social Intervention*. London: Croom Helm.

Rock, P. (1979) *The Making of Symbolic Interactionism*. London: Macmillan.

Roethlisberger, F.J. and Dickson, W.J. with Wright, H.A. (1939) *Management and the Worker: An Account of a Research Program Conducted by the Western Electric Company, Hawthorne Works, Chicago*. Cambridge, MA: Harvard University Press.

Rose, A.M. and Peterson, W.A. (eds) (1965) *Older People and their Social World*. Philadelphia, PA: F.A. Davis.

Rosenmayer, L. (1981) 'Objective and subjective perspectives of life span research', *Ageing and Society*, 1: 29–49.

Rosow, I. (1967) *Social Integration of the Aged*. New York: The Free Press.

Ross, J.K. (1977) *Old People, New Lives: Community Creation in a Retirement Residence*. Chicago: University of Chicago Press.

Rossi, P.H. and Freeman, H.E. (1985) *Evaluation: A Systematic Approach*, 3rd edn. Beverly Hills, CA: Sage.

Roth, J. (1962) '"Management bias" in social science study of medical treatment', *Human Organisation*, 21: 42–50.

Roth, J. (1963) *Timetable: Structuring the Passage of Time in Hospital and Other Careers*, Indianapolis, cited in Johnson (1976) 'That was your life: a biographical approach to later life', in J.M.A. Munnichs and W.J.A. Van Den Heuvel, *Dependency and Interdependency in Old Age*. The Hague: Nijhoff.

Rowles, G.D. (1978) *Prisoners of Space: Exploring the Geographical Experience of Older People*. Boulder, CO: Westview Press.

Runyan, W.M. (1984) *Life Histories and Psychobiography: Explorations in Theory and Method*. New York and Oxford: Oxford University Press.

Ryder, N.B. (1965) 'The cohort as a concept in the study of social change', *American Sociological Review*, 30: 843–61.

Sarason, I. and Sarason, B. (eds) (1985a) *Social Support: Theory, Research and Applications*. Dordrecht, The Netherlands: Nijhoff.

Sarason, I.G., Levine, H.M., Basham, R.B. and Sarason, B.R. (1983) 'Assessing social support: the social support questionnaire', *Journal of Personality and Social Psychology* 44: 127–39.

Schaie, K.W. (1977) 'Toward a stage theory of adult cognitive development', *Aging and Human Development*, 8: 129–38.

Schaie, K.W. (1986) 'Beyond calender definition of age, time and cohort: the general developmental model revisited', *Developmental Review*, 6(3): 252–77.

Schatzman, L. and Strauss, A. (1973) *Field Research: Strategies for a Natural Sociology*. Englewood Cliffs, NJ: Prentice-Hall.

Schwartz, M.S. and Schwartz, C.C. (1955) 'Problems of participant observation', *American Journal of Sociology*, 60: 343–53.

Seeman, T. and Berkman, L. (1988) 'Structural characteristics of social networks and their relationship with social support in the elderly: who provides support?', *Social Science and Medicine*, 26(7): 737–49.

Shanas, E. (1962) *The Health of Older People: Social Survey*. Cambridge, MA: Harvard University Press.

Shanas, E., Townsend, P., Wedderburn, D., Friis, H., Milhoj, P. and Stehouwer, J. (1968) *Old People in Three Industrial Societies*. London: Routledge and Kegan Paul.

Shearer, A. (1987) 'The burdens of old age', *The Guardian*, 15 July, referring to a health centre study of people aged 75 and over for which the 'official lists they started with, supplied by GPs and others, were no less than 50% out'.

Sheldon, B. (1988) 'Group-controlled experiments in the evaluation of social work services', in J. Lishman (ed.) *Research Highlights in Social Work 8: Evaluation*, 2nd edn. London: Jessica Kingsley Publishers.

Sheldon, J.H. (1948) *The Social Medicine of Old Age, Report of an Inquiry in Wolverhampton*. Oxford: Oxford University Press.

Shock, N.W. (1980) 'Physiological and chronological age', in A.A. Dietz (ed.) *Aging – its Chemistry*. Washington, DC: The American Association of Clinical Chemistry.

Shock, N.W. (1987) 'Physiological age', in G.L. Maddox (ed.) *The Encyclopedia of Aging*. New York: Springer.

Sidell, M. (1986) 'Coping with confusion: the experience of sixty elderly people and their informal and formal carers', PhD thesis, University of East Anglia.

Silverman, D. (1985) *Qualitative Methodology and Sociology*. Aldershot, Hants: Gower.

Sinclair, I. and Clarke, R. (1981) 'Cross-institutional designs', in E.M. Goldberg and N. Connelly (eds) *Evaluative Research in Social Care*. London: Heinemann Educational.

Smith, G. (1989) 'Missionary zeal and the scholarly stance: policy and commitment in research in old age', *Ageing and Society*, 9(2): 105–22.

Smith, G. and Cantley, C. (1985) *Assessing Health Care: A Study in Organisational Evaluation*. Milton Keynes, Bucks: Open University Press.

Smith, G. and Cantley, C. (1988) 'Pluralistic evaluation', in J. Lishman (ed.) *Research Highlights in Social Work 8: Evaluation*, 2nd edn. London: Jessica Kingsley Publishers.

Snedecor, G.W. and Cochran, W.G. (1980) *Statistical Methods*, 7th edn. Ames: Iowa State University Press.

Social and Community Planning Research (1979) 'Survey research and privacy. Report of a working party established by Social and Community Planning Research, London' in M. Bulmer (ed.) *Censuses, Surveys and Privacy*. London and Basingstoke: Macmillan.

Social Research Association (1983) *Social Research Association Ethical Guidelines*. London: SRA.

Solomon, R.L. (1949) 'Extension of control group design', *Psychological Bulletin*, 46: 137–50.

Specht, H. (1986) 'Social support, social networks, social exchange, and social work practice', *Social Service Review*, 60(2): 219–40 (University of Chicago, USA).

Stacey, M. (ed.) (1969) *Comparability in Social Research*. London: Heinemann.

Stanley, B., Stanley, M. and Pomara, N. (1985) 'Informed consent and geriatric patients', in B. Stanley (ed.) *Geriatric Psychiatry: Clinical, Ethical and Legal Issues*. Washington, DC: American Psychiatric Press.

Starker, H. (1986) 'Methodological and conceptual issues in research on social support', *Hospital and Community Psychiatry*, 37(5): 485–90.

Stimson, G.V. and Oppenheimer, E. (1982) *Heroin Addiction, Treatment and Control in Britain*. London: Tavistock.

Strain, L.A. and Chappell, N.L. (1982) 'Problems and strategies: ethical concerns in survey research with the elderly', *The Gerontologist*, 22(6): 526–31.

Strauss, A. (1962) 'Transformation of identity', in A.M. Rose (ed.) *Human Behaviour and*

Social Processes. London: Routledge and Kegan Paul. pp. 63–85.

Strauss, A. (1987) *Qualitative Analysis for Social Scientists*. Cambridge: Cambridge University Press.

Strauss, A. (1988) *Qualitative Analysis*. Cambridge: Cambridge University Press.

Streib, G.F. (1983) 'The frail elderly, research dilemmas and research opportunities', *The Gerontologist*, 23: 40–4.

Streib, G.F., Folts, W.E. and La Greca, A.J. (1985) 'Autonomy, power and decision-making in thirty-six retirement communities', *The Gerontologist*, 25: 403–9.

Suchman, E.A. (1967) *Evaluative Research*. New York: Russell Sage Foundation.

Svensson, T. (1984) 'Gerontological research in Sweden', *The Gerontologist*, 24: 427–34.

Tardy, C.H. (1985) 'Social support measurement', *American Journal of Community Psychology*, 13: 187–202.

Taylor, R. and Ford, G. (1981) 'Lifestyle and ageing', *Ageing and Society*, 1: 329–45.

Taylor, R. and Ford, G. (1983) 'Inequalities in old age: an examination of age, sex and class differences in a sample of community elderly', *Ageing and Society*, 3: 183–208.

Thomas, N. (1988) 'Evaluative research and the personal social services', in J. Lishman (ed.) *Research Highlights in Social Work 8: Evaluation*, 2nd edn. London: Jessica Kingsley Publishers.

Thomas, W.I. and Znaniecki, F. (1958) *The Polish Peasant in Europe and America*, 2 vols. New York: Dover Publications. (Original editions 1918–20.)

Thompson, C. (1983) 'The assessment of elderly people in residential care', unpublished dissertation, Department of Sociology, University of Manchester.

Thompson, K. and Tunstall, J. (eds) (1971) *Sociological Perspectives*. Harmondsworth, Middlesex: Penguin Books in association with the Open University Press.

Tinker, A. (1984) *The Elderly in Modern Society*, 2nd edn. London: Longman.

Tobin, S.S. and Lieberman, M.A. (1976) *Last Home for the Aged*. San Francisco, CA: Jossey-Bass.

Townsend, P. (1957) *The Family Life of Old People, An Inquiry in East London*. London: Routledge and Kegan Paul.

Townsend, P. (1962) *The Last Refuge*. London: Routledge and Kegan Paul.

Townsend, P. (1963) *The Family Life of Old People, An Inquiry in East London*. Abridged edn. with new postscript. Harmondsworth, Middlesex: Penguin.

Townsend, P. (1981) 'The structural dependency of old people', *Ageing and Society*, 1(1): 5–28.

Townsend, P. (1986) 'Ageism and social policy', in C. Phillipson and A. Walker (eds) *Ageing and Social Policy: A Critical Assessment*. Aldershot, Hants: Gower.

Tunstall, J. (1966) *Old and Alone: A Sociological Study of Old People*. London: Routledge and Kegan Paul.

Turnbull, C. (1973) *The Mountain People*. London: Cape.

Ungerson, C. (1983) 'Why do women care?' in J. Finch and D. Groves (eds) *A Labour of Love*. London: Routledge and Kegan Paul.

United Nations (1956) *The Ageing of Populations and Its Economic and Social Implications*. *Population Studies*, 26, New York: United Nations.

van den Heuvel, W. (1976) 'The meaning of dependency' in J. Munnichs and W. van den Heuvel (eds) *Dependency or Interdependency in Old Age*. The Hague: Nijhoff.

de Vaus, D.A. (1986) *Surveys in Social Research*. London: Allen and Unwin.

Vaux, A. (1985) 'Variations in social support associated with gender, ethnicity and age', *Journal of Social Issues*, 41(1): 89–110.

Vaux, A., Phillips, J., Holly, L., Thomson, B., Williams, D. and Stewart, D. (1986) 'The social support appraisals (SS-A) scale: studies of reliability and validity', *American Journal of Community Psychology*, 14: 195–219.

Veiel, H.O.F. (1985) 'Dimensions of social support: a conceptual framework for research', *Social Psychiatry*, 20: 156–62.

Vetter, N.J., Jones, D. and Victor, C. (1984) 'Effect of health visitors working with elderly patients in general practice: a randomised controlled trial', *British Medical Journal*, 288(6414): 369–72.

Victor, C. (1987) *Old Age in Modern Society: A Textbook of Social Gerontology*. London: Croom Helm.

Walker, A. (1981) 'Towards a political economy of old age', *Ageing and Society*, 1: 73–94.

Walker, A. (1983) 'Disability and dependency: a challenge for the social services', *Research Policy and Planning*, 1(1): 1–7.

Walker, A. (1986a) 'The politics of ageing in Britain', in C. Phillipson, M. Bernard and P. Strang (eds) *Dependency and Interdependency in Old Age*. London: Croom Helm.

Walker, A. (1986b) 'Pensions and the production of poverty in old age', in C. Phillipson and A. Walker (eds) *Ageing and Social Policy: A Critical Assessment*. Aldershot, Hants: Gower.

Wall, R. (1984) 'Residential isolation of the elderly, a comparison over time', *Ageing and Society*, 4: 483–503.

Warnes, A.M. (1987) *The Ageing of Housing Schemes and Their Residents*, Working Paper 3, Age Concern Institute of Gerontology, Kings College, London.

Wax, R.H. (1972) *Doing Fieldwork: Warnings and Advice*. Chicago: University of Chicago Press.

Way, A. and Fennell, G. (1985) *Anchor Tenants Moving from Sheltered Housing into Residential Care, a Pilot Study*. Oxford: Anchor Housing Association.

Webb, E.J., Campbell, D.T., Schwartz, R.D. and Sechrest, L. (1966) *Unobtrusive Measures: Nonreactive Research in the Social Sciences*. Chicago: Rand McNally.

Weiss, C.H. (1972) *Evaluation Research. Methods for Assessing Program Effectiveness*. Englewood Cliffs, NJ: Prentice-Hall.

Weiss, R. (1974) 'The provisions of social relationships', in Z. Rubin, *Doing Unto Others*. Englewood Cliffs, NJ: Prentice-Hall.

Wellman, B. (1981) 'Applying network analysis to the study of support', in B. Gottlieb (ed.) *Social Networks and Social Support*. London: Sage.

Wellman, B. with Hiscott, R. (1985) 'From social support to social network', in I. Sarason and B. Sarason (eds) *Social Support: Theory, Research and Applications*. Dordrecht, The Netherlands: Nijhoff.

Wenger, G.C. (1984) *The Supportive Network*. London: Allen and Unwin.

Wenger, G.C. (1985) 'What do dependency measures measure? Challenging assumptions', paper presented to British Society of Gerontology Annual Conference.

Whittaker, J. and Garbarino, J. (eds) (1983) *Social Support Networks*. New York: Aldine.

Wilcox, B.J. (1981) 'Social support in adjusting to marital disruption: a network analysis', in B.H. Gottlieb (ed.) *Social Networks and Social Support*. London: Sage. pp. 97–115.

Wilkin, D. (1987) 'Conceptual problems in dependency research', *Social Science and Medicine*, 24(10): 867–73.

Wilkin, D. and Hughes, B. (1987) 'Residential care of elderly people: the consumers' views', *Ageing and Society*, 7: 175–201.

Wilkin, D. and Thompson, C. (1989) *Users' Guide to Measures of Dependency for the Elderly*. Social Services Monographs: Research in Practice. University of Sheffield Joint Unit for Social Services Research.

Willcocks, D.M. (1984) 'Consumer research in old people's homes', *Research, Policy and Planning*, 2(1): 13–18.

Willcocks, D.M., Ring, A.J., Kellaher, L.A. and Peace, S.M. (1982a) *The Residential Life of Old People: A Study of 100 Local Authority Homes*. Vol. 1. Research Report No. 12, Survey Research Unit, Polytechnic of North London.

Willcocks, D.M., Ring, A.J., Kellaher, L.A. and Peace, S.M. (1982b) *The Residential Life of Old People: A Study of 100 Local Authority Homes*. Vol. II. Appendices, Research Report No. 13, Survey Research Unit, Polytechnic of North London.

Willcocks, D.M., Peace, S.M. and Kellaher, L.A. (1987) *Private Lives in Public Places: A Research-based Critique of Residential Life in Local Authority Old People's Homes*. London: Tavistock.

Wing, J.K. and Hailey, A.M. (1972) *Evaluating a Community Psychiatric Service: The Camberwell Register 1964–71*. London: Oxford University Press.

World Health Organisation (1980) *International Classification of Impairments, Disabilities and Handicaps*. Geneva: WHO.

Wright, M. (1984) 'Using the past to help the present', *Community Care*, 533: 20–2.

Wright, M. (1986) 'Priming the past', *Oral History*, 14(1): 60–5.

Yordi, C.L., Chu, A.S., Ross, K.M. and Wong, S.J. (1982) 'Research and the frail elderly: ethical and methodological issues in controlled social experiments', *The Gerontologist*, 22: 72–7.

Index

Lightning Source UK Ltd.
Milton Keynes UK
UKOW03f0733240913

217801UK00001B/21/A